THE UNFINISHED
ELECTION OF 2000

THE
UNFINISHED
ELECTION
OF 2000

JACK N. RAKOVE, EDITOR

Henry Brady • *John Milton Cooper, Jr.* • *Stephen Holmes*
Pamela S. Karlan • *Alexander Keyssar* • *Larry D. Kramer*

BASIC
BOOKS

A Member of the Perseus Books Group

Published by Basic Books,
A Member of the Perseus Books Group

Designed by *Brent Wilcox*

Library of Congress Cataloging-in-Publication Data
The unfinished election of 2000/Jack N. Rakove, editor.
    p. cm.
  Includes bibliographical references and index.
  ISBN 0-465-06837-5

    1. Presidents—United States—Election—2000. 2. Political campaigns—United States—History—20th century. 3. Contested elections United States—History—20th century. 4.United States—Politics and government—1993–2001. I. Rakove, Jack N., 1947– .

JK526 2000n.
324.973'0920–dc21

                  2001043009

01 02 03 04 / 10 9 8 7 6 5 4 3 2 1

To the memory of
Helene Keyssar

CONTENTS

ACKNOWLEDGMENTS

In organizing this book, I had the sage counsel of three of its contributors: my Stanford colleague Pam Karlan, my New York University colleague Larry Kramer, and my old Leverett House colleague, Alex Keyssar. I also received useful advice from several other Stanford colleagues, notably Mo Fiorina, David Kennedy, and Barry Weingast. To Dedi Felman, we owe both bittersweet thanks (and an apology) for helping us conceive the basic idea. At Basic, Vanessa Mobley has been an enthusiastic supporter and editor. I owe special thanks to Andrea Talbott, a favorite student, for making other inquiries on behalf of this project and for providing me with additional editorial distractions.

The preparation of this book took place at the Stanford Humanities Center, amid the bonhomie made possible by its acting director, Peter Stansky, its wonderful staff, and the good company of all its fellows this past year, the last spent in the pleasant surroundings of Mariposa and Rogers houses. I especially enjoyed all the probing questions that Wang Zheng asked me about the arcana of the American political and constitutional system. I hope that none of the "humanites" (as they were called during my last tour here) regret too much the distraction this book provided from my original project or the excessive interest I may have demonstrated in discussing the subject during the memorable fall of 2000.

This book is dedicated to another scholar, in another field, whose career ended, far too soon, not long after the events we have analyzed. May her memory be a blessing to all who knew her, to her family, colleagues, and students, and especially to her brother.

Jack Rakove
Stanford Humanities Center
June 11, 2001

INTRODUCTION:
DANGLING QUESTIONS

JACK N. RAKOVE

It is a rare presidential election indeed when the two leading candidates both wage losing campaigns, but so it was in 2000. George W. Bush, the eventual winner, led in virtually every national poll conducted between the first televised debates in October and election eve. His staff was so confident of victory that in the closing days of the campaign they sent their candidate to California and New Jersey, states he had little chance to carry (or if he did carry, would not need because he would almost certainly be doing so well everywhere else). Yet Bush awoke on the morning after the election to discover that he was trailing in the national popular vote and clinging to a razor-thin margin in the decisive state of Florida. As recounts proceeded across the country and absentee ballots were tallied, Bush's initial national deficit of roughly a quarter million votes grew to more than half a million. Prior to the election, some Bush aides worried that the popular plurality they expected might not produce a majority in the electoral college; afterward, they had to remind Americans that the constitutional majority of electors was not the same thing as a popular majority of the electorate.

On November 8, Vice President Al Gore faced other sources of discomfiture. The edge he enjoyed in the national vote may have steeled his determination to pursue the legal challenges in Florida, but it did not spare him the unpleasant truth that the election had been widely regarded as his to lose—and lose it he was now poised to do. How could the heir apparent of the incumbent administration, running in a time of profound peace and prosperity, have found himself playing catch-up against a candidate like George W. Bush, often lampooned as an intellectual lightweight with an unsteady grasp of his native language and world geography? Why had Gore taken so long to fashion a coherent campaign strategy or establish who he really was or wanted the public to believe him to be, as he shifted back and forth in his multiple personalities as didactic policy wonk, alpha male, loving and faithful husband, and earth-toned Tennessean (despite his upbringing as a privileged princeling born and reared in Washington, D.C.)? And why, Democrats wondered, had his estrangement from Bill Clinton prevented Gore from allowing the outgoing (in both senses) president to campaign in two states, Arkansas and West Virginia, where his intervention could have provided the handful of electors Gore needed?

So neither candidate ran a campaign to be emulated; both came close to plucking defeat from victory; and each found his political fate hinging on the tao of the chad, the design of the butterfly ballot, and ultimately on an unprecedented judicial intervention into presidential politics. All of these events and circumstances—all the what-ifs and might-have-beens of election 2000—should produce a bumper crop of the campaign books that routinely appear after every presidential election. That literary genre was virtually invented by the late Theodore White, who opened his great book, *The Making of the President 1960*, with a wonderful account of John Kennedy, his advisors, and family on another election night when the country was similarly poised to swing either way.[1] Although none of the countless election books written since has quite matched White's original creation, the turbulent five-week aftermath of the election of 2000, ending only with the Supreme Court's controversial ruling in *Bush v. Gore*, may help to revive a genre of political writing that many observers now find unoriginal and tiresome.[2]

The contributors to this volume believe that the election of 2000 deserves a different treatment. What is needed, we believe, is not another dramatic retelling of campaign anecdotes and vignettes: the thinking behind Bush's visit to Bob Jones University, or the passion in Al and Tipper's famous convention smooch, or any of a number of other good tales that journalists and pols will swap for years to come. As much as these stories reveal about the real stuff of politics and the urgent trivia of campaigns, they do not allow us to perceive what was truly distinct and significant about this presidential election, or to set the extraordinary events in Florida in their proper context.

The Unfinished Election of 2000 is a proper title for our effort, for several reasons, but not the one that many readers might suspect we had in mind. Although all of the contributors to this book believe that the Supreme Court erred grievously in halting the Florida recount and suspect that Gore probably did command a plurality of the citizens who entered that state's polling places on November 7, it is not our purpose to suggest that the outcome of the election somehow remains unresolved. We recognize that some uncertainty will always persist as to which candidate, Bush or Gore, "really" won Florida. Democrats alive today will go to their graves believing that a slim but solid plurality of all the voters who went to the polls in Florida November 7 really did intend to vote for Al Gore. In this view, the election was not lost when *Bush v. Gore* came down on the fateful evening of December 12, but rather when the election officials of Palm Beach County had their butterfly-ballot brainstorm. Republicans will always counterclaim that any revised results produced by a manual recount of either the entire state or select counties would have been no more accurate than the original recounts completed within days of the election. Skeptics of both parties, in calmer times, might freely concede that, with an electorate as closely divided as Florida's was that day, any recount, conducted under any standard of ascertaining a voter's intent, was destined to produce statistically insignificant results that would always fall within any reasonable margin of error.

But if the election is over, it nonetheless raises a host of intriguing and disturbing questions about both our political and constitutional systems. These questions transcend the relatively mundane issues on which the campaign was waged, as well as the appeal and merits of the candidates. In our view, the election of 2000 remains an *unfinished* one, not because of its inherent importance but rather for what it revealed about our politics, institutions, and perhaps even the Constitution itself.

First, any election in which a voting population of 100 million citizens divides into two nearly equal halves raises interesting questions about the political forces that have split American society so evenly. The narrow gap separating the major candidates nationally was replicated not only in Florida but in five other states (New Hampshire, Iowa, Wisconsin, Oregon, and New Mexico), where a swing of a few thousand or even a few hundred votes would have shifted the electoral prize from one candidate's column to another. Neither party proved capable of converting advantages it thought it had gained in the mid-1990s into a decisive victory in 2000. Democrats thought that Bill Clinton's success in making their party again competitive for the presidency should have been transferable to his vice president; Republicans hoped their capture of Congress in 1994 had laid the foundation for the new national majority that had been beckoning since the 1980s. Both parties were disappointed, and both presidential candidates found themselves maneuvering around an elusive center of undecided voters, at the risk of alienating partisans who wondered where their standard-bearers' hearts really lay.

How the parties and the electorate reached this state is the subject of the first two chapters of this book. In different ways, both essays challenge the conventional view that allegiance to the parties within the electorate is waning, a view that the conduct of close elections might seem to confirm by the amount of attention that candidates have to pay to undecided voters in narrowly divided states. As the historian John Milton Cooper, Jr., suggests in the first essay, election 2000 was in reality a "battle of the bases" between the parties, which remain alive and well and highly competitive. The very closeness of the outcome, Cooper suggests, should be seen not as an anomaly but rather as a reflection of the underlying political forces that have prevented either party from securing the dramatic and winning realignments of the electorate that Republicans gained in 1896 and Democrats secured after 1932. In the second essay, Henry Brady also reflects on the remarkable inversion in the American political map that has taken place over the last century, before examining in closer detail the underlying clusters of attitudes on moral and economic issues that distinguish the voting blocs the parties mobilize. Both Cooper and Brady concur in reflecting on the curious way in which the new electoral map of presidential politics replicates (by inversion) an older pattern of regional alignments.

For most Americans, the closeness of the election was a curiosity, but what proved far more shocking was the revelation of the dirty little secret of the ballot booth. When they cast their ballots on November 7, Americans assumed that their votes would be duly counted and accurately recorded. The idea that significant numbers of votes would be wasted, through the technical deficiencies of punch-card or optical-scan systems, or because ballots were improperly or even illegally designed, would never have occurred to them. The ballot wars in Florida shattered that illusion. All too soon, Americans acquired a new technical vocabulary of voting (chads, dimples, and butterflies, undervotes and overvotes) and got used to the strangely hypnotic image of Florida election officials rotating punch-cards in the search for voters' intent. It now turned out that election officials and a handful of technical and academic experts had known all along that the machinery of voting sorely needed improvement. Here was a scandal of the kind Americans relished, a corruption of the fundamental ritual of democracy, re-flecting a familiar pattern of under-investment in the public sector, but also one that should be amenable to the national genius for effi-ciency, can-do engineering, and innovative technology.

But to treat these revelations as a mere problem of the design and upkeep of voting machines obscures a more fundamental question. Charges that faulty voting systems or inadequately staffed polling places were more likely to be found in districts with large minority populations recalled a more ominous chapter in the nation's politi-cal history, when the one-party South, then dominated by Demo-crats, developed a whole array of techniques to strip African-Americans of the suffrage granted by Reconstruction and the Fifteenth Amendment. As Alexander Keyssar explains in his con-tribution to this volume, issues of access to the ballot and the right to have one's vote truly counted involve more than the mechanics of voting. The deeper history of suffrage in the United States is not a simple story of the progressive widening of the democratic "we the people." It is rather a history of agitation and reaction, of efforts to restrict as well as broaden the people's access to the ballot. Seen in this light, the controversy in Florida no longer appears as an aberration in a happy democratic story; it is, instead, only the most recent chapter in a more complicated and ongoing struggle over the real meaning of the right to vote.

Time will tell whether the revelations of 2000 will produce wholesale improvement in the modes of voting, whether Congress will enact legislation mandating or encouraging reform (as it can do either under its constitutional authority over the conduct of congressional elections or through the carrot and stick of its appro-priation power), or whether individual states will decide whether their systems need change. Only time can tell, too, whether the sin-gle most controversial aspect of the election drama—the Supreme Court's decision in *Bush v. Gore*, effectively terminating the legal struggle over the Florida recount—will have lasting implications for the institutional stature of the Court, the already tortured process of judicial appointments, or the substantive law of voting rights and equal protection.

The Court's intervention was stunning in a number of respects. Most legal observers were surprised when the Court agreed to hear the Bush campaign's initial appeal of the Florida Supreme Court's decision allowing the recount to continue even after Secretary of State Katherine Harris certified a Bush slate of electors. Under long-established doctrine, interpretation of state election law fell squarely to state courts, which is why the federal Court of Appeals for the Eleventh Circuit declined to take jurisdiction over the Bush challenge. Moreover, when challenges arise to the results of a presidential election, both the Constitution and the relevant federal statute (dating to 1887) strongly appear to delegate responsibility for resolving those disputes to Congress, not the Court. And further still, once the justices chose to intervene in so momentous and politically charged a matter as a presidential election, many observers thought that concern for the reputation and legitimacy of the Court would have required them to reach a strong measure of consensus, even unanimity, before issuing any substantive decision.

The Court's proceedings and decision in *Bush v. Gore* violated all of these expectations, and in doing so fueled suspicions that the five-member majority were driven far more by their political preferences and even private desires than by existing doctrine or compelling legal argument.[3] Whether these were the true motives of the majority will never be definitively known. So, too, we cannot yet know whether the Court's decision will come to be regarded as another "self-inflicted wound" (the phrase customarily applied to its infamous decision in *Dred Scott v. Sandford*); whether it will further poison the already tortuous process of Supreme Court appointments; or whether *Bush v. Gore* simply marks another assertion of the current majority's confidence in the competence of the Court to resolve any problem it chooses to address, even one as sensitive as the outcome of a presidential election.

In the meantime, however, we can assess the Court's intervention and its final decision in the light of its own recent jurisprudence. Here, two fundamental criticisms already seem paramount. First, the decision to accept the Bush appeal not only contradicted the established rule that disputes involving state election laws are for state courts to resolve but also reversed the general commitment to the revival of federalism and the autonomy of the states that the majority had so frequently avowed in recent years. Second, the reliance that the Court placed on the Equal Protection Clause of the Fourteenth Amendment in *Bush v. Gore* struck its critics as a doubtful, even hypocritical application of a provision that the five-member majority had previously revealed little interest in applying or expanding in other areas.

Because *Bush v. Gore* remains so controversial a ruling, we have devoted two essays to assessing the logic and rationale of the Court's actions. In the first of these essays, Larry Kramer patiently describes the nexus of legal and constitutional issues that the supreme courts of Florida and the United States had to consider as the key cases bounced back and forth between Tallahassee and Washington. While critically examining the arguments of both parties and the decisions and opinions of both courts, Kramer levels his strongest objections against the underlying disdain for democratic politics that he finds manifest in the five-member majority of the federal Court. The logic and merits of their decision in *Bush v. Gore* are the subject of Pamela Karlan's essay. Karlan locates the unlikely reliance the five-justice majority ultimately placed on the Equal Protection Clause in the broader context of the Court's use of the same clause in its landmark reapportionment decisions of the 1960s. Like Kramer, Karlan concludes that *Bush v. Gore* represents a dangerous exercise of political clout on behalf of a Court that has displayed little confidence in the judgment and wisdom of other branches of government.

In constitutional terms, *Bush v. Gore* was certainly the most dramatic aspect of the election of 2000. But the nation's absorption in the legal wrangling leading to that decision also diverted attention from another constitutional consequence of the election: the realization that our state-based system of electing presidents had indeed allowed one candidate to lose the national popular vote yet still carry the electoral majority constitutionally required for victory. The electoral college—an "accident waiting to happen"—had misfired at last (or again). For the Bush victory was a function not only of the Court's willingness to protect his minuscule plurality in Florida. Its political arithmetic also depended on the significant advantage that Bush gained by carrying more states—and especially more small states—than did Gore, thereby capitalizing on the advantage that the constitutional rule for allocating electors gives to the least populous members of the Union. Even had Gore managed to emulate his whopping New York majority in populous states like Pennsylvania, Michigan, and Illinois, and thereby increased his popular plurality to an actual majority, it would have left the electoral result unchanged.

In both its origins and its operations, the electoral college is probably the least understood institution in the entire constitutional system, and because the smallest states have such a stake in its perpetuation, the chances of reforming it through the daunting route all constitutional amendments must take are between slim and nil. Even so, the election exposed the persisting contradiction between the anachronism of the electoral college—which never operated as the Framers of the Constitution either intended or expected—and the modern democratic principle of one person, one vote. In my own contribution to this volume, I accordingly trace the origins and rapid early evolution of this curious institution, then critically examine the leading arguments made in favor of its retention.

All of these essays strive, we hope, to speak about the election with relative dispassion, although our personal opinions and political convictions are certainly evident. In his afterword, Stephen Holmes addresses the meaning and outcome of the election in more direct terms. Like many realists, Holmes recognizes that law is often an extension of politics by other means. Who would ever imagine, Holmes observes, that the five-justice majority in *Bush v.*

Gore would have rendered the same holding, or deployed the same reasoning, had the position and stakes of the two candidates been reversed? The common-sense answer to that question leads to an equally telling assessment of the true role that the Supreme Court has generally played in American politics, a role that bears little resemblance to the heroic image of the Court favored by liberals who cannot recognize that the heyday of the Warren Court was the exception that proves the rule.

In framing *The Unfinished Election of 2000* in this way, we are aware that we have manifestly not attempted to represent or replicate the divisions in the electorate or to provide ideological or political balance. Instead we have sought a different kind of balance, by bringing together scholars from history, law, and political science and asking them to examine the election from the distinctive perspectives of their disciplines. It is our hope that even those readers who disagree with our perspective or conclusions will appreciate our effort to situate this extraordinary set of events—arguably the strangest election in our history—in a variety of contexts, ranging from the origins of the Constitution and the sectional dynamics of American politics to the recent jurisprudence of the Supreme Court and the gender gap in the last three elections. Not all of the contributors are historians, but these essays, taken together, represent a first attempt to set the political events of 2000 in a context that transcends the frenzy of an election campaign or, in this case, the turmoil of its aftermath.

NOTES

1. In one especially memorable scene, Bobby Kennedy places a call to Richard J. Daley, the Democratic mayor of Chicago, and receives the reassuring reply that everything will be all right in Illinois: He knows

which of his precincts are still out, which of the Republicans'. One wonders whether Jeb Bush was equally confident on November 7. Anyone who knows anything about Illinois politics will doubt that whatever political tomfoolery took place in Illinois in the 1960 election was confined to the Democratic precincts of Cook County.

2. Thus Garry Wills opened a review disparaging the first set of books on the election with the caustic remark that, "The campaign book deserves to die, and it is doing its duty." Wills, "The Making of the President, 2000," *New York Times Book Review*, April 1, 2001.

3. *Newsweek* opened its report of the final decision by reporting that on election night Justice Sandra Day O'Connor had been heard to exclaim "This is terrible" when the networks first posted Florida in the Gore column. Her husband explained that they hoped to retire soon to Arizona, but that Justice O'Connor would only do so if a Republican president appointed her replacement. Evan Thomas and Michael Isikoff, "The Truth Behind the Pillars," *Newsweek*, December 25, 2000, 46.

PART ONE

The Politics of
a Presidential Election

1

"THE LEAVING IT"

The Election of 2000 at the Bar of History

JOHN MILTON COOPER, JR.

TWO OF SHAKESPEARE'S MOST OFTEN-QUOTED LINES come early in *Macbeth*, to describe the death of the traitorous Thane of Cawdor: "Nothing in his life/Became him like the leaving it." Those lines apply equally well to the election of 2000. Not the contest itself, but its ending, made it memorable, exciting, and revealing. Those qualities arose out of its outcome and the postmortem disputes over how people actually voted and who really won. Otherwise, this election could easily have gone down in the historical record as yet one more unremarkable and forgettable contest.

Issues and perceptions of differences between the two major candidates and parties actually played a greater role in deciding the election than some observers had predicted. Throughout the campaign, however, it became commonplace to complain that the stakes seemed small and that few differences of policy and principle appeared to separate the main contenders. Great crusades, domestic or foreign, were on the agenda of neither Democrats nor Republicans, and neither party's candidate promised any sweeping remedy to current problems. Instead, incrementalism and piecemeal approaches were the order of the day. Some liberal commentators quipped that, as a centrist "New Democrat," Vice President Al Gore was making the election a race between "two Republican parties separated by the abortion issue." Across the partisan fence, the Republicans' hunger for victory and the appearance of unity largely spared them comparable complaints from their own right wing, as they preached "compassionate conservatism" and projected gauzy images of harmony and inclusiveness. Television viewers could be forgiven for thinking that the Republican party had become a model coalition of multiracial, multiethnic, and multidenominational constituencies.

The two main candidates likewise failed to infuse the contest with color or excitement. Gore's wooden personality and bumbling as a campaigner never ceased to attract criticism, especially in contrast to the seeming political "genius" of his party's incumbent president, Bill Clinton. Gore's apparent failings loomed large in the second-guessing about the outcome of the election that resembled Monday morning arguments in sports. The widely held belief that peace and prosperity should have swept Gore to victory reinforced the belief that personal shortcomings were a major factor in his defeat. Governor George W. Bush also proved a disappointment on the campaign trail, but less so than his opponent because his managers skillfully played the game of lowering expectations about him. Even so, a number of top Republican operatives complained that his inexperience and poor political judgment made the outcome much closer than it should have been. Otherwise, Bush could have spared himself the double embarrassment of trailing Gore in the popular vote and winning the electoral college by the slender margin of four votes.[1]

Finally, this presidential race produced few surprises in its state-by-state results. Each candidate carried virtually all of the states that knowledgeable observers had predicted he would carry. Each suffered disappointments. Gore lost not only his home state of Tennessee, where he and his father had served as senators, but also the congressional district that he and his father had represented. Winning Tennessee (or any other state) would have given him a majority in the electoral college, regardless of the result in Florida. Almost as painful for Gore were losses in such erstwhile Democratic bastions as West Virginia and Arkansas, Clinton's home state. Either of those states would also have given him an electoral majority without Florida. For Bush the outcome in Florida was almost equally galling. Not only was his brother its governor, but Florida had gone Republican in all but two elections since 1948. Losing other states with strong Republican governors, such as Michigan and Wisconsin, furnished additional disappointments to Bush. Winning those two states would have given him a majority in the electoral college regardless of the result in Florida.

Even the closeness of the result should have raised few eyebrows. As the distinguished historian William E. Leuchtenburg has observed, the place to look for explanations for the outcome of a close election like this one is not so much the "what-ifs" of the contest as its larger context. Leuchtenburg has compared this election with the cliffhanger of 1884, which he maintains can be understood only as one in a series of comparably tight races in the late nineteenth century. As he and others have also observed, those close contests produced the other two elections in which the popular vote winner lost the electoral college, the elections of 1876 and 1888. It should also be noted that between Ulysses S. Grant's reelection in 1872 and William McKinley's victory in 1896, no winning candidate carried a popular majority. In 1880, 1884, and 1892, the winners also gained only pluralities, and 1892 was the only election during that time in which a third party siphoned off an appreciable number of votes from the two major parties. The five elections of that era consistently produced minority presidents.[2]

Historians of the election of 2000 do not yet enjoy the advantage of comparing it with later contests. But they can draw some advantages by examining its immediate predecessors. In 1992 and again in 1996, Bill Clinton racked up comfortable majorities in the electoral college, but he won only pluralities in the popular vote and failed to gain a national majority. The first time, he carried exactly 43 percent, and four years later he garnered just over 49 percent. The circumstances surrounding those results differed in one significant respect. In 1992, running as the nominee of the Reform Party, Ross Perot won almost 19 percent of the popular vote. That was the best showing by a third-party candidate since Theodore Roosevelt's Progressive (or "Bull Moose") candidacy in 1912. In 1996, Perot's share shrank to about 8.5 percent. Yet even with that shrinkage, Clinton still did not win a popular majority. It should have come as no surprise, therefore, that in 2000 neither Bush nor Gore attracted a majority of the popular vote, even though the progressive spoiler Ralph Nader proved to be no Perot.

What, then, should historians make of this election? Does it deserve to be brushed off with those other oft-quoted lines from *Macbeth*: "full of sound and fury,/Signifying nothing"? Of course not. Any presidential election, no matter how unremarkable or forgettable, has consequences. Who wins and loses, how winners and losers read the results as mandates for policy and action—these factors make even the most humdrum presidential contests worth examining. Every such contest also offers a chance to probe the state of the nation, particularly broad popular attitudes and larger trends. Some writers have compared these elections to freeze-frame photographs of people in motion. Others have likened them to medical diagnostic devices such as x-rays and magnetic resonance imagers that look beneath the surface of a body, in this case a body politic. The election of 2000, with its special qualities in "the leaving it," offers a particularly good opportunity to examine American politics and society at the beginning of a new century.

The favorite technique adopted by most commentators on this election, both scholars and media pundits, has been to compare it with different elections in the past. The most frequent comparison has been to one of the two nineteenth-century contests that Leuchtenburg cited in which a popular vote winner lost the electoral college, the election of 1876. This comparison is particularly apt because that election also produced a disputed result that was eventually resolved with the involvement of the U.S. Supreme Court. In 1876, besides Florida, two other southern states, Louisiana and South Carolina, were in doubt, and achieving a resolution to the post-election disputes and declaring a winner took almost four months, as opposed to five weeks in 2000. The Supreme Court became involved in that earlier election, but not as an institution in its constitutional role. Rather, individual justices served on the Electoral Commission that Congress established to deal solely with this disputed election. The main similarity between the 1876 and 2000 elections lies in the intensity of partisanship. Tensions and animosities across party lines ran higher in that earlier election mainly because it came only a decade after the Civil War. Likewise, many observers denounced Supreme Court justices in both instances for appearing to follow party lines. Finally, in both of these elections the Republicans showed a much stronger will to win. In 1876, with the passions of the Civil War as yet unquenched, their attitudes bordered on a determination to prevail at almost any cost.[3]

The other election of that era in which a popular vote winner fell short in the electoral count, 1888, has not drawn much comparison with 2000. Most commentators have simply mentioned it in passing as a second example of this phenomenon. The reason for the lack of interest seems obvious: There was no dispute over the outcome. In 1888, the Republican candidate prevailed clearly, although narrowly, in the electoral college, principally as a result of his party's having more efficiently concentrated its resources in a few swing states. Actually, this contest deserves more attention than it has received. For one thing, in 1888 the defeated Democrats also held the White House, and their incumbent candidate, Grover Cleveland, was not just vice president, but president. Moreover, the economy was booming. Much of the country was enjoying prosperity, and what discontent there was did not particularly focus on punishing the party in power. The challengers likewise picked a candidate with a name linked to a former president, although that link stretched back much farther than in 2000. Their nominee, Benjamin Harrison, was the grandson of William Henry Harrison, who had been elected president almost fifty years earlier, before the founding of the Republican party. Finally, as they had done twelve years previously, the Republicans displayed a near-fanatical zeal for victory. This time, they wanted revenge after having lost the White House in 1884 for the first time since 1860 and, up to then, the only time in the party's history.[4]

Those two elections account for most, but not all, of the comparisons between 2000 and earlier contests. One of the most interesting comparisons with a different race came not after but before the election, and not from a commentator but from a major participant. In August, the senior strategist of the Bush campaign, Karl Rove, expounded at length about how his candidate might win a victory comparable to William McKinley's in 1896. Waxing eloquent about plans to woo voters from the prospering "new economy," Rove foresaw the Republicans of 2000 repeating their predecessors' feat of 1896. Not only would they win this year with large popular and electoral margins, but they would also establish themselves as the majority party for a generation to come. Even discounting wishful thinking and fond hopes, Rove's comparison was noteworthy on several grounds. Symbolically, it was unusual and refreshing to have a late twentieth-century Republican spokesman invoke any previous party leader other than Ronald Reagan—who has become as much of an icon for Republicans as Franklin Roosevelt had been earlier for the Democrats—or, much less often, Theodore Roosevelt, who has served sometimes as a totem of swaggering nationalism and less frequently as a token for concern about the environment.[5]

What made Rove's comparison most interesting, however, was its familiarity with the most important interpretative concept dealing with the electoral dimension of American political history: "realignment." As originally formulated in the 1950s and 1960s by the political scientists V. O. Key and Walter Dean Burnham, this interpretation posits that certain presidential contests act as "critical elections" that produce shifts in the party allegiances of groups and regions that last for a considerable time, usually more than a quarter of a century, hence the term *realignment*. The 1896 contest between McKinley and his Democratic opponent, William Jennings Bryan, stands as the archetype of such critical, realigning elections, and Franklin Roosevelt's reelection in 1936 has been viewed in a similar light. The allure of realignment for the winners of such elections is their long-term profit. Both scholars and practitioners of American politics have argued about whether a true realignment has occurred since the time of Franklin Roosevelt and when one might occur. Hopeful Republicans and fearful Democrats alike speculated that Reagan had ushered in a realignment in 1980. Likewise, the Republican congressional sweep in 1994 prompted many to wonder whether a realigning presidential contest might soon be in the offing. The fortunes of both parties following those elections appear to indicate that such hopes and fears have not come to pass. Waiting for realignment became the late twentieth century's political analogue to waiting for Godot.[6]

The 2000 election disappointed Rove and others who hoped that a Bush victory would bring a decisive realignment in the Republicans' favor. Both the closeness of the outcome and its resemblance to the two preceding contests showed that no great changes occurred. But the ideas surrounding the concept of realignment do provide important insights into the current state of American politics. Even a cursory glance at the maps showing which states went for which candidates in 1896 and 2000 reveals a startling congruence in the extent of sectional loyalties. In both elections, political alignments contrasted starkly along sectional lines, as demarcated by the Potomac, Ohio, and Missouri Rivers. (See Figures 1.1 and 1.2.) Each time, one candidate carried almost every state south and west of those rivers, except on the West Coast. Conversely, his opponent won all or most of the states north and east of those rivers, along with all or most of those on the West Coast. Another glance at the maps reveals a glaring contrast. In 1896, the Democratic candidate, William Jennings Bryan, carried what he fondly dubbed "the Great Crescent" of southern and western states, whereas his Republican opponent, McKinley, won the geographically smaller but far more populous remainder. The 2000 results almost exactly reversed that outcome. The Republicans were dominant below and beyond the rivers, and the Democrats were ascendant elsewhere.

More than a century of population growth and internal migration has greatly altered the respective political strengths of these regional coalitions. Thanks to the booming of the "Sunbelt," two of the four most populous states, Texas and Florida, now lie within the Republican-leaning crescent; other states in the South and West have likewise gained people and electoral votes. This change has made those two sections much more formidable politically than they were in 1896. Together, they almost constitute a majority in the electoral college—almost, but not quite. Even with Florida awarded to them, the Republicans would have lost if they had not made a critical inroad into their opponents' territory. In one respect, the critical state in 2000 was Ohio, which bucked the trend in all but one of the other states of the Midwest by going Republican. The role played by Ohio made this election eerily reminiscent of the contest in 1916. Woodrow Wilson's reelection in that contest depended on his ability to detach Ohio from its usual Republican loyalty while also carrying another GOP stronghold, California, by fewer than 4,000 votes. In 1916, however, California commanded just over half the electoral votes that Florida did in 2000. The emergence of California as the leviathan of the electoral college has been the one aspect of the rise of the Sunbelt that has not favored the Republicans.[7]

The failure of either party to achieve realignment in 2000 also raises questions about the application of this concept to later elections. Did a realignment of the kind that occurred in 1896 ever

★ ★ ★ ★ ★ ★ ★ 1896 Presidential Election Results ★ ★ ★ ★ ★ ★ ★

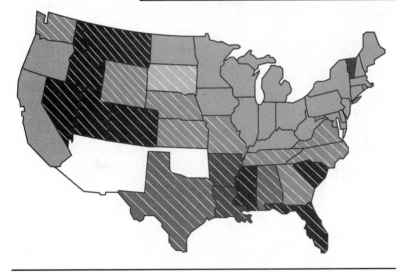

	Presidential Candidate	Vice Presidential Candidate	Political Party	Popular Vote		Electoral Vote	
■	William McKinley	Garret Hobart	Republican	7,108,480	51.01%	271	60.6%
▨	William Bryan	Arthur Sewall*	Democrat	6,511,495	46.73%	176	39.4%
	John Palmer	Simon Buckner	Natl Democrat	133,435	0.96%	0	0%
□	Joshua Levering	Hale Johnson	Prohibition	125,072	0.90%	0	0%
	Other	—	—	57,256	0.41%	0	0%

Key

< 50%		
> 50%		
> 60%		
> 70%	—	
> 80%		

Popular Vote   Electoral Vote

Election Notes: * Democratic electoral votes were cast for two Vice Presidential candidates: Arthur Sewall (149) and Thomas Watson (27).

Figure 1.1   1896 Presidential Election Results

★ ★ ★ ★ ★ ★ ★ 2000 Presidential Election Results ★ ★ ★ ★ ★ ★ ★

	Presidential Candidate	Vice Presidential Candidate	Political Party	Popular Vote		Electoral Vote	
■	George W. Bush	Richard Cheney	Republican	50,456,141	47.87%	271	50.4%
▨	Albert Gore, Jr.	Joseph Lieberman	Democrat	50,996,039	48.38%	266	49.4%
☐	Ralph Nader	Winona LaDuke	Green	2,882,782	2.74%	0	0.0%
	Patrick Buchanan	Ezola Foster	Reform	448,868	0.43%	0	0.0%
▥	Harry Browne	Arthur Oliver	Libertarian	386,035	0.37%	0	0.0%
	Other	—	—	232,398	0.22%	1*	0.2%

Turnout

100% 80% 60% 40% 20%

Key

< 50%
> 50%
> 60%
> 70% — —
> 80% —

Popular Vote **Electoral Vote**

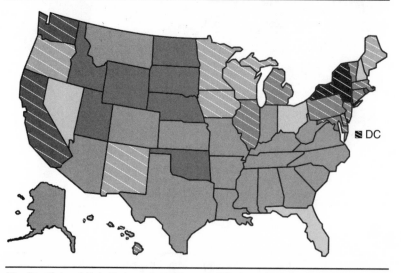

◄ DC

Election Notes: * Note that one Gore Elector in DC abstained from voting.

Figure 1.2   2000 Presidential Election Results

take place during the twentieth century? It is useful to examine the elections that seem to be likely candidates for that distinction. As already noted, 1980 does not seem to have made the grade. Neither Reagan's victory that year, which was an electoral but not a popular landslide, nor his reelection four years later, which was a landslide on both counts, altered the political landscape much. In 1980, Reagan did become the only presidential winner since Dwight Eisenhower in 1952 with coattails long enough to enable his party to wrest control of a house of Congress (the Senate) from its opponents. Otherwise not much changed. The Democrats held on to the House throughout Reagan's presidency and the term of his Republican successor, and they regained control of the Senate in 1986. In 1988, the Republicans did retain the White House, but both the electoral and popular majorities for their candidate, George H. W. Bush, the father of the winner in 2000, fell off sharply from Reagan's margins. The elder Bush's victory in 1988 also owed a great deal to the weakness of his Democratic opponent, Michael Dukakis, and he failed to win a second term in 1992.

Only one other presidential contest in the second half of the twentieth century has received serious consideration as a realigning election: 1968. Several scholars have maintained that this election witnessed the breakup of the previously dominant alignment, the "New Deal coalition" forged by the Democrats under Franklin Roosevelt. In a stunning reversal of Lyndon Johnson's 1964 popular and electoral landslide, the Republican nominee, Richard Nixon, won the presidency, and he and independent candidate George Wallace, who carried several southern states, captured more than 57 percent of the popular vote. Some commentators have called this result a "negative landslide," a massive repudiation of the Democrats and their vision of liberal, interventionist government. Subsequent events appeared to bear out that assessment. Even before Reagan's triumphs, Nixon's landslide reelection in 1972 had elicited pronouncements that the Republicans had risen to majority party status. For their part, the Democrats responded by retreating from their earlier embrace of activist government and the welfare state. Long before Bill Clinton declared in 1995 that "the era of big government is over," his sole Democratic predecessor since Johnson, Jimmy Carter, had partially reversed his party's course and initiated some of the conservative policies that Reagan pursued in the 1980s.[8]

But did the 1968 election really wreak feats of electoral and policy realignment? That seems to be the case only when it is compared to its immediate predecessor. Looking at this election in a broader context makes it seem much less unusual and consequential. In the third of a century since 1968, despite the Republicans' presumed majority, the Democrats have won three presidential races and retained control of at least one house of Congress for four-fifths of the time. Furthermore, 1968 seems even less noteworthy when it is compared to the elections of 1948 and 1960. Both of those earlier elections had also registered only popular pluralities for the winner and electoral margins that were less than spectacular. In 1960, John F. Kennedy's margin over his opponent, Nixon, was only 113,000 votes out of more than 68 million cast, less than two-tenths of a percentage point: the closest winning plurality since 1884. Kennedy's electoral college majority depended on exceedingly close and possibly tainted results in Illinois and Texas. Democratic defections and bolting candidates from the white South were nothing new in 1968. Running against President Harry S Truman as the "Dixiecrat" candidate in 1948, Strom Thurmond, then governor of South Carolina, carried four states in the Deep South, all of which, plus one more, the Republicans carried in 1964 despite Johnson's landslide. During this same period, other southern states such as Virginia and Florida entered the Republican column in 1952 and stayed there for the rest of the century, except for Virginia in 1964 and Florida in 1964 and 1976. Further Republican gains in the South, together with another close, questionable Illinois result going the other way, accounted for much of the difference between Nixon's loss in 1960 and his victory in 1968.

Democratic victories like those in 1948 and 1960 extend the question about electoral realignment farther back into the twentieth century. In fact, those results cast doubt on the strength and durability of the fabled New Deal coalition. Even during Franklin Roosevelt's presidency, Democratic majorities may have been much less secure than they appeared. Popular revulsion against the Republicans during the Great Depression gave Roosevelt an electoral, although not a popular, landslide in 1932. Four years later such continuing revulsion and his own gifts at public persuasion brought him a tremendous landslide in both the popular vote and the electoral college. Afterward, however, things grew much closer. In 1940 and 1944, Roosevelt won again comfortably but not spectacularly, and both of those victories depended in large measure on the particular circumstances of World War II. As Alan Lichtman has argued, the Republicans might well have won in 1940 if the Democrats had run anyone other than Roosevelt. Moreover, the Democrats' close call in 1942 and loss of both houses of Congress in 1946 and 1952 demonstrated the weakness of their control on Capitol Hill and their dependence on the continued loyalty of the white South.[9]

That loyalty was the weak link in the New Deal coalition. In the 1930s, African-American voters began to behave like other lower-income groups as they deserted the "party of Lincoln" to join the Democrats. The Roosevelt administration's occasional gestures toward racial equality discomfited many southern Democrats, despite lack of real action to promote civil rights. Truman's willingness to go further—to desegregate the armed forces, appoint a civil rights commission, and sponsor anti-lynching legislation—sparked the Dixiecrat revolt in 1948. Meanwhile, the growing power of African-Americans as an urban voting bloc in populous northeastern and midwestern states prompted Democratic leaders there to champion their cause. In the 1950s, the coincidence of the Supreme Court's school desegregation decision coming under a Republican-appointed chief justice and bipartisan support for modest civil rights legislation retarded the white South's defection from the Democrats. But in the 1960s continued pushes for desegregation and antidiscrimination measures by Democratic presidents, especially Johnson's wholehearted embrace of the civil rights cause, brought a parting of the ways. Strom Thurmond himself became a Republican in 1964, and he helped his new party carry southern states that year and in 1968, when Texas was the only state in the region not won by Nixon or Wallace. In 1976, regional pride helped Jimmy Carter temporarily recapture most of the South for the Democrats, yet from the mid-1960s onward white voters below the Potomac and the Ohio were making the South the Republican stronghold that stood out so starkly on the electoral map in 2000.

Such a checkered history of political success calls into question the proposition that any realignment comparable to the demonstrable case of 1896 ever occurred in the twentieth century. Even during their era of presumed majority party status (1932–1968) the Democrats never attained anything like the secure hegemony that the Republicans had previously enjoyed. On the contrary, the party's unbroken string of presidential victories from 1932 through 1948 and its rarely interrupted control of Congress from the 1930s to the 1990s seem to mask conditions that more closely resembled the late nineteenth-century era of minority presidents and closely balanced parties. Furthermore, viewed in even longer terms that take into account pre-Civil War party contests, those late nineteenth-century conditions, rather than realignment on the 1896 model, look more like the normal condition of the American two-party system.[10]

Such broader perspectives reinforce the unremarkable quality of the 2000 election. It departed from the norm only in how extremely close it was and in the unprecedented legal conflict it subsequently sparked. A closer look at the results underscores how much this election resembled its two immediate predecessors. Like many presidential contests, this one was a "battle of the bases." Rather than primarily seeking to detach votes from the opposition or make new converts, the two parties in 2000 strove to mobilize their core constituencies to the maximum. This is what the parties usually do. The clearest examples of this kind of campaigning occurred before the Civil War, in the late nineteenth century before 1896, and in the last part of the twentieth century. The exceptions to this practice have occurred when one party has suffered from an unfortunate turn of events, as the Republicans did in the 1930s; when one of them has nominated an exceptionally attractive candidate, as the Republicans did with Eisenhower in 1952 and Reagan in 1984; or, conversely, when one of them chooses an especially unattractive candidate, as the Republicans did in 1964 (Barry Goldwater) and the Democrats did in 1972 (George McGovern). Those conditions provide the stuff of which landslides are made. But landslides are the exception, not the rule. Moreover, as the sequels to 1936, 1964, and 1972 showed, landslides tend to have an ephemeral impact on political alignments.

Not surprisingly, the battle of the bases in 2000 most strongly resembled what had happened in the two preceding contests, 1992 and 1996. The political map in all three elections looked much the same. In 1992, the Democratic nominee, Bill Clinton, pulled off a coup by carrying four noncoastal states in the West (Colorado, Montana, Nevada, and New Mexico), thereby cracking a region that had been almost solidly Republican since 1948. That feat derived entirely, however, from Perot's unusually strong showing there. In Utah, Perot finished second, ahead of Clinton, and he trailed Clinton by fewer than 5,000 votes in Alaska and 7,000 in Idaho. The South was also less solidly Republican than usual in 1992. Clinton carried his home state of Arkansas, his running mate's home state of Tennessee, as well as Louisiana, Georgia, and the border states. But Arkansas was one of only three states in the nation where the Democratic candidate won a popular majority that year. Clinton lost the rest of the South, including its most populous states, Texas and Florida. In 1996, he did about as well as he had done previously in the West by adding Arizona to his column while losing Colorado and Montana. In the South, he pulled off another coup by becoming the first Democrat to carry Florida since 1976 and, before that, since 1964 and 1948. But he also lost Georgia and again carried no states in the South or West with a majority, except Arkansas, Louisiana, and West Virginia. Nationally, despite facing a weak Republican opponent in former Senator Bob Dole and a much-reduced showing by Perot, Clinton still fell short of a popular majority and fattened his electoral college margin by only nine votes.

A mirror image of that pattern in the South and West prevailed on the other side of the partisan-sectional divide. In both 1992 and 1996, Clinton lost only one state in either the Northeast or the Midwest—that perennial deviant, Indiana, which, except in 1964, has not gone Democratic in a presidential election since 1936. His only other popular majorities, a bare 50 percent apiece, came in Maryland and New York. Another northeastern state, Maine, delivered the same blow to the elder Bush that Clinton had suffered in Utah; he finished third there, behind Perot. That result was especially galling not only because Bush had carried the state in 1988 but also because it was the location of his family's long-time summer home at Kennebunkport. In 1996 Clinton carried all but two northeastern states by popular majorities and racked up his only showings above 60 percent there, in Massachusetts, New York, and Rhode Island. Elsewhere, he won popular majorities only in five midwestern states and two states on the West Coast, together with Arkansas, Louisiana, and West Virginia.

The results in 2000 look almost foreordained from the pattern of the two previous elections. Gore lost ten states that Clinton had carried four years before—Arizona, Nevada, Louisiana, Arkansas, Tennessee, Kentucky, Missouri, Ohio, West Virginia, New Hampshire—and, disputedly, Florida. Of those states, Clinton had won only three with popular majorities: Arkansas, Louisiana, and West Virginia. In 1996, Gore's native Tennessee had gone for the ticket that he shared with Clinton by only 45,000 votes, a plurality of two percentage points. Three of Clinton's other plurality states that switched in 2000—Missouri, New Hampshire, and Ohio—had all featured votes for Perot that exceeded his national average. In Florida, Gore outpolled Clinton's 1996 showing by more than 350,000 votes. Nationally, Gore's popular vote exceeded Clinton's 1996 total by nearly 5.5 million votes and fell short of his percentage by eight-tenths of a point. Judged by numbers alone, the only difference between Clinton's victory in 1996 and Gore's defeat in 2000 lay in the Perot vote. Perhaps the former vice president's vaunted shortcomings as a campaigner—which were so frequently contrasted to the former president's gifts—did not play so great a role in the 2000 result after all.

Numbers of votes ultimately decide elections, although in this one the outcome finally depended on who did the counting and when. But behind those numbers stood voters and their reasons for casting their ballots as they did. Even such a clear-cut sectional division as the result in 2000 requires more than simple geography to explain the outcome. Here, the comparison with the identical although partisan-reversed alignment of 1896 is also instructive. Back then, James Carville's famous dictum of 1992—"It's the economy, stupid"—held true with a vengeance. The division between the regions north and east of the rivers and Bryan's Great Crescent pitted richer and poorer sections of the country against each other. The cause of that disparity was economic development. The Northeast and Midwest had benefited from the Industrial Revolution of the nineteenth century vastly more than had the South and the West. By any pertinent measure—per capita income and wealth, industrial production, miles of railroad track and improved roads, population density and urbanization, numbers of schools and average levels of education, production and consumption of printed matter—the United States encompassed two different countries.

That earlier sectional division of the rich versus the poor had contained anomalies. The poorest and most disadvantaged group in the country, African-Americans, favored the Republicans, but because they lived mostly in the South, they were in the process of becoming almost totally disenfranchised. African-Americans did not acquire a measure of political power until they began migrating to northern cities in the early twentieth century. Conversely, lower-income groups in the Northeast and Midwest composed of recently arrived immigrants and industrial workers either remained outside the political process because of insufficient recruitment and perhaps cultural factors, or they recoiled from the Democrats' inflationist and low-tariff economic policies.

A century later, the sectional polarization stemmed from many of the same causes. The migration of industry away from the Northeast and Midwest and population shifts to the Sunbelt greatly narrowed disparities between those regions and the rest of the country. Yet even with those changes, the South and West remain the poorest, least-urbanized, and least-developed parts of the country, with the exception of the West Coast and newer urban centers in the South. The main change wrought under the New Deal coalition was to draw African-Americans and lower-income groups in the Northeast and Midwest decisively over to the Democrats, who became thereby a nationwide party of the less advantaged.

That fleeting achievement came at a cost. Almost as soon as African-Americans moved into the Democratic party, various groups of whites started to move out. That happened first and most tellingly in the South. No Democratic candidate since 1964 has won a majority of the white vote there, not even such native sons as Carter, Clinton, and Gore. The survival of the party in the South, and such successes as Carter and Clinton enjoyed there, depended heavily on lopsided majorities among recently re-enfranchised black voters in the region. Race also played a big part in pushing some lower-income whites outside the South to vote for George Wallace in Democratic primaries and as an independent candidate in the 1960s and 1970s, to swell Nixon's landslide in 1972, and to become "Reagan Democrats" in the 1980s. Those nonsouthern white defections do not seem to have been lasting, however, inasmuch as the Democrats started drawing these voters back in presidential races from 1988 onward.

It might seem strange that in 2000, unlike a century earlier, the poorest sections of the country lined up solidly behind the Republicans. This party has consistently attracted support from upper-income groups nationally and prided itself on being friendlier than its rival toward big business and high finance. Economic factors help to explain some, but not all, of this apparent incongruity. The South and West continue to harbor resentment at being outsider regions that enjoy less prestige and favor than metropolitan centers. At the beginning of the twentieth century those resentments fed desires to use government power to redress disadvantages of wealth and finance and gain a fairer shake for themselves. By contrast, at the end of the century those resentments had attracted voters to Ronald Reagan's appeal to "get government off our backs" and to favor more free-wheeling market capitalism and less fettered accumulation of wealth. Part of the change stems from the accelerating pace of economic growth in the Sunbelt after World War II. Many people in these regions have come to see a regulatory state and progressive taxation as hindrances rather than aids toward catching up with the better-developed parts of the country. Of these two self-styled outsider regions, the West preceded the South in this reversal of political roles. Except in 1964, no Democratic presidential candidate has carried more than an occasional scattering of noncoastal western states since 1948.

Still, explaining the shift of loyalties of the Great Crescent requires something more than economic considerations. Even race does not completely account for the transformation of the South. What are usually called "social" or "cultural" issues also merit attention. A common thread linking the different political directions that these outsider-region attitudes have taken is what has loosely been labeled *populism*. That term has been used to describe the complexes of resentment and embattlement on the part of people who have seen themselves as inhabiting what might be called both the cultural and the geographical "heartland" of the country. In their eyes, various kinds of outsiders—by turns, plutocrats and effete sophisticates; racial, ethnic, and religious minorities; urbanites and foreigners—have threatened to undermine values and ways of life that constitute the true core of Americanism. Some scholars have detected various forms of "populism" on the right-wing fringe since the 1940s. In the 1960s, the capture of the Republican party by the Goldwater conservatives in 1964 and the insurgent challenge of George Wallace brought many of these attitudes into the political mainstream.[11]

Various indicators from the 2000 vote make clear how strong these cultural divisions and populist attitudes remain. Political maps showing election results by counties (Figures 1.3 and 1.4) vividly illuminates several characteristics. One, again, is sectionalism. In the parties' respective stronghold regions, their opponents carried few counties at all. In Massachusetts and Rhode Island, Bush won no counties, and, despite his family's ties to Connecticut, which his father had won in 1988, he carried only one county there, and that only by a plurality. Conversely, in the West, Gore won no counties in Nebraska, Utah, and Wyoming, and only one each in Idaho and Nevada. Another factor that the county results highlight is the influence of race and ethnicity. In the South, Gore won a fairly large number of counties, including his highest percentage in the nation, 86.2 percent in Macon County, Alabama. But that county, like most of the others that Gore won in the South, has a high concentration of African-Americans; in effect, the map of strong Gore counties in the South largely replicates the contours of the Cotton (or Black) Belt, which reveals where the imprint of slavery fell most deeply on the landscape. Likewise, in Texas and the noncoastal West, nearly all the counties that went for Gore contained high percentages of Hispanics, especially Mexican-Americans.

Finally, the breakdown by counties reveals a fairly pervasive urban-rural split. Although Bush won only three states in the

Northeast and Midwest, he carried a greater number of counties everywhere in those regions except in New England and New Jersey. In those parts of the country and on the West Coast, the Democrats in 2000 remained, as they had been since before the New Deal, the party of the city. What has changed, however, is that they have also become increasingly the party of the suburbs. Such formerly renowned bastions of suburban Republicanism as Westchester County in New York, Fairfield County in Connecticut, and St. Louis County in Missouri all went Democratic in 2000, while Republican majorities in other similar counties declined. In part, this change reflects the economic and racial diversification of the suburbs, which has resulted from less-affluent and minority people leaving the cities. But it also reflects the influence of such social and cultural issues as abortion, school prayer, women's rights, homosexuality, and gun control, which have tended to sway suburban voters toward the Democrats.[12]

Polls conducted during the course of the 2000 campaign forecast and amplified the patterns revealed in the state and county results. Partisan breakdowns of likely voters underlined the "battle of the bases" nature of the election. Fewer than 10 percent of party-identifiers favored the opposing candidate, and independents tended to break slightly in favor of Gore. The main dissident candidates on the right and left, Pat Buchanan and Ralph Nader, each drew only 2 or 3 percent among partisans; Nader sometimes registered around 10 percent among independents. Age groups tended to split more or less evenly between Gore and Bush, although the Republican candidate did better among people over fifty-five, despite the Democrats' long-standing identification with Social Security. Income remained a good predictor of which party's candidate attracted people, with the Democrats predictably registering nearly 60 percent support among the lowest earners. To an extent, that support also reflected race and ethnicity, because minorities made up disproportionate shares of the poor. Among African-Americans Gore's support exceeded 90 percent, and it neared 75 percent

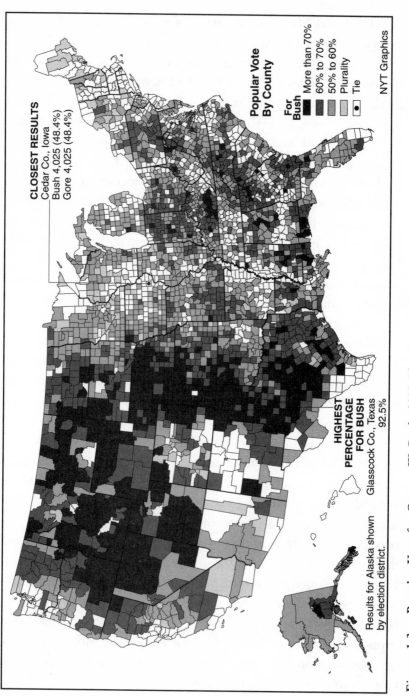

CLOSEST RESULTS
Cedar Co., Iowa
Bush 4,025 (48.4%)
Gore 4,025 (48.4%)

Popular Vote By County

For Bush
More than 70%
60% to 70%
50% to 60%
Plurality
• Tie

NYT Graphics

HIGHEST PERCENTAGE FOR BUSH
Glasscock Co., Texas
92.5%

Results for Alaska shown by election district.

Figure 1.3   Popular Vote for George W. Bush, 2000 Election, by County.
SOURCE: NYT Graphics

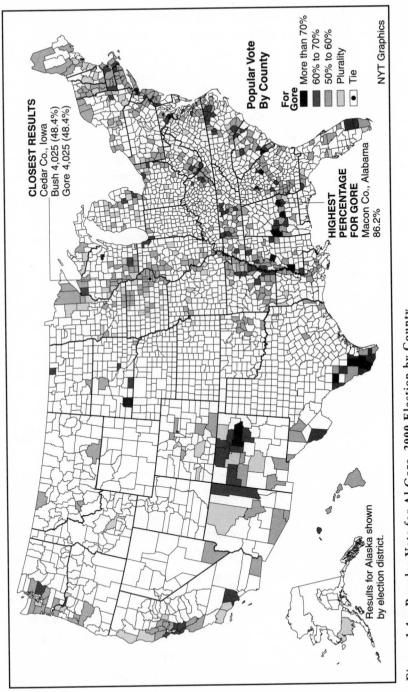

Figure 1.4 Popular Vote for Al Gore, 2000 Election by County.
SOURCE: **NYT Graphics**

among Hispanics. Interestingly, among Hispanics the Democratic candidate registered higher support among those naturalized since 1995 and lower among those naturalized before then. Among whites, Bush consistently led by over 10 percent.[13]

How much this lopsided minority support for the Democrats and the white tilt toward the Republicans reflected economic versus cultural concerns remains an intriguing question. The urban-rural breakdown was less clear-cut than might have been expected. Bush led strongly among rural residents and narrowly among small-city dwellers, whereas Gore prevailed strongly among inhabitants of large cities and narrowly among suburbanites. The long-standing gender gap persisted from earlier elections, at least among males. Bush usually led among men by more than 10 percent but broke more or less even among women. Working women favored Gore by about 10 percent, whereas those who identified themselves as homemakers leaned toward Bush by nearly 15 percent. More broadly, married persons favored Bush also by about 15 percent, whereas single persons went for Gore by nearly 25 percent. Along religious lines, Gore led among Catholics by a few points and among Jews by nearly nine to one; Bush prevailed among Protestants by nearly 10 percent. Those breakdowns suggest that questions of "family values" and notions of traditional mores associated with rural and small-town white Protestantism in opposition to urban secularism and diversity remain potent factors in political alignments throughout the country and especially in pushing apart the parties' respective stronghold regions.[14]

None of those divisions in 2000 came as any surprise. They had been present in varying degrees of starkness in preceding elections stretching far back into the twentieth century. What distinguished this election from its two immediate predecessors was the weakness of dissident candidates. In contrast to Perot in 1992 and to a lesser extent in 1996, neither Buchanan nor Nader generated significant support, although Nader's small showing in Florida almost certainly robbed Gore of victory there and thus, ultimately, the presidency. This weakness on the fringes did come as something of a surprise. Both Bush and Gore had initially faced strong challenges for their party's nomination from John McCain and Bill Bradley, respectively, and an undercurrent of disappointment with both nominees persisted throughout the campaign. It was true that neither Buchanan nor Nader possessed the deep financial pockets and idiosyncratic personal charm of Perot, but their poor showings derived mainly from the strength that both parties demonstrated in rallying core constituencies and attracting independents. The long-term decline of partisan loyalty has been something of a reigning truism among students of twentieth-century American politics, but the results in 2000 stunningly belied this denigration of parties.

The strength of the parties was no anomaly. Here is where "the leaving it" drama of the post-election conflict proves so revealing. The dispute over who really won Florida bared a central truth about the nature of the two parties and their roles in the country's political system. This truth contradicts another reigning truism about twentieth-century American politics, namely, that the two parties have become fundamentally similar, non-ideological collections of interest groups dedicated almost exclusively to the seeking and winning of office. Like other truisms, including the one about the decline of partisanship, this one also contains a few grains of truth. Certainly during the 2000 campaign both parties conspicuously championed major interest groups, especially economic interest groups. Organized labor played a big part in the Democratic campaign, as it has usually done throughout the twentieth century, especially since the New Deal. On the other side, major sectors of big business rallied behind the Republicans, as they have done with remarkable consistency since the realignment of 1896.[15]

Still, the rhetoric and behavior of both the campaign and the post-election controversy exposed the error of viewing the parties as divorced from ideology. Democratic attacks on Republican tax cut proposals as a subsidy for the rich and candidate Gore's "populist" pledges to fight for the "little people" drew Republican rebuttals as declarations of "class warfare." For all their pejorative intent, those charges conveyed important insights about the nature of the two parties. The Democrats were attempting, as they had done with equally remarkable consistency since 1896, to rouse the resentments of lower-income and economically insecure people against those who were better off, allegedly because of unfair advantages and special privilege. But this was not and never had been a simple case of pandering, much less "class warfare." Rather, the Democrats' central ideology has been one of economic opportunity and social mobility. In their view, pursuit of those goals requires vigilant, potent, sustained intervention by government to keep opportunity and mobility from being blocked by entrenched interests, especially big business and the wealthy and privileged. One might well wonder whether Gore was well-advised to invoke this rhetoric; he could just as easily have asked the familiar question, "Are you better off now than you were eight years ago?" But even so, his version of populism evoked familiar themes in the rhetoric and ideology of the modern Democratic party.

The post-election conflict brought this Democratic ideology to the fore even more clearly. Voters in Florida, the Democrats maintained, were being prevented from having their votes counted. What was more, these voters were plain, ordinary folk who labored against severe disadvantages. They included elderly voters in Palm Beach County, who had been misled by "butterfly ballots." They included less-educated Hispanics and African-Americans, particularly in Jacksonville and Miami, many of whom were unused to voting and had mistakenly failed to indicate their choices clearly on punch-card ballots. In the case of African-Americans, there were also charges of harassment and obstruction aimed at keeping them away from the polls or failing to vote. The Democrats presented a clear, simple message in their post-election campaign. It sprang from their core belief in themselves as a truly "democratic" party that celebrates and seeks to carry out the will of the majority in the face of great obstacles. One of the two wonders of the post-election conflict was that the Democrats' message did not ultimately enable them to prevail.

Instead, their opponents finally claimed victory for a variety of reasons. Circumstances obviously played a major part in landing Florida's electoral votes in the Republican column. That party's near-total dominance in the state government—holding the governorship, secretaryship of state, and strong majorities in both houses of the legislature—gave it a big home-court advantage. Tactical errors by the Democrats—such as failing to seek an immediate recount in every county or pursuing a re-vote in Palm Beach County—perhaps fatally hobbled their lawyers in the final arguments before the Supreme Court. Any one of those factors may have supplied the proverbial "for want of the nail" that piled up the consequences that caused the battle to be lost. But those immediate circumstances were not what made the post-election conflict so revealing or what lay at the heart of the behavior that allowed the Republicans to win.[16]

To Democrats, Republican rhetoric in the post-election conflict seemed the height of hypocrisy. Republicans repeatedly and vehemently accused their opponents of simply wanting to keep the recount going, without any fixed standard for evaluating ballots, until Gore finally secured a lead. The clear implication was that the ordinary citizens who could be observed on C-Span patiently examining chads were in reality the hired minions of a desperate conspiracy. Indeed, even to detached observers, that rhetoric, coupled with the Republicans' stance of having won and deserved to win, smacked of the biblical parable of the mote and the beam. They seemed so ready to impute the nastiest of motives to their opponents while blatantly ignoring their own questionable attitudes. Yet this Republican rhetoric and the behavior that it justified were not mere smokescreens of propaganda designed to cover high-handed tactics, nor did they reflect simple cynicism or hypocrisy: just the reverse. The Republicans' post-election behavior reflected their core belief and perception that they and they alone were the truly "legitimate" party that was committed to upholding the highest virtues and defending the deepest national values against the nefarious influences and threats of the opposition. The other wonder of the post-election conflict was that the Republicans purveyed their message so unselfconsciously and so resourcefully that they did prevail.

The two parties' rhetoric and behavior after the election glaringly exposed the central truth about their essential natures: namely, that fundamentally they are ideologically driven coalitions of both interest groups and true believers. Moreover, there is nothing new about this way of distinguishing the parties or of understanding the conflict between them. These definitions and perceptions can be traced to the origins of one party in the 1850s and to the earliest modern incarnation of the other party as far back as the 1790s.

"Legitimacy" has been the core ideology of the Republicans from the party's inception during the crises that led to the Civil War. The inescapable corollary to this defining element of the party's self-image has been its conviction that the other party does not truly share that essential virtue. Among Republicans, both the Civil War and the ensuing conflict over Reconstruction bred a near-total identification between their own political fortunes and their deepest values of religion and patriotism. Both the Republicans' will to win at all costs in 1876 and 1888 and their early designation of themselves as the "Grand Old Party"—even though they were junior to their opponents by two or even three generations—attested to their belief in themselves as by far the worthier and indeed the only legitimate party.

That Republican ideology waxed and waned in intensity over the course of the twentieth century. Success tended to mute Republicans' professions of exclusive virtue, although their alliance with big business did produce a tone of smugness during their ascendancies in the 1920s, 1950s, and 1980s. Any prolonged absence from the White House, however, brought out the darker side of their legitimist self-image. As early as the time of Woodrow Wilson—the first Democrat to shut the Republicans out of power for more than four years—they played the patriotic card by tarring Democratic policies at home and abroad as disloyal and "un-American." Red-baiting in the 1940s and 1950s infected both parties, although the Republicans caught the contagion far more than did the Democrats. Joseph Mc-Carthy was a Republican senator, and he went as far as he did largely because his party's leaders thought they saw political pay dirt in his rampages. Interestingly, too, it was in the 1950s that the Republicans acquired the lasting habit of slurring their opponents as the "Democrat party." The political environment of the immediate post-World War II era also spawned Richard Nixon, the later master of "dirty tricks" in search of victory at all costs. As the Democratic majority leader and later Speaker of the House, Thomas P. "Tip" O'Neill, lamented in 1973: "This ends-justifies-the-means attitude seems to persist within the Republican philosophy of government as if it were transmitted from one generation of candidates to the next like some malignant gene." Indeed, the embittered Republican partisanship on Capitol Hill in the 1990s, spearheaded by Newt Gingrich and his cohorts, looked like a reincarnation of those earlier campaigns, as did the moral obsession and lack of proportion evidenced during the Clinton impeachment.[17]

The Democrats, by contrast, have usually approached politics more like sports or business and less like war. From their earliest days, they tended to be more welcoming toward outsiders, at least toward immigrants from Europe, although not toward racial minorities until much later. Likewise, with the exception of the white South, Democrats traditionally leaned in the direction of cultural tolerance, with markedly less taste than their opponents for legislating morality. The Democrats acquired their modern shape in 1896, when they became the party of the economically worse off, at first mainly along sectional lines but later increasingly throughout the nation. The election that best illuminated the ideological character of this party occurred, curiously, not in 1896, but in 1912. This was when Wilson put forward the "New Freedom," which was a vision of economic competition and social mobility fostered by government intervention on behalf of the disadvantaged. Wilson's vision, with its underlying optimism about human nature and acceptance of individual and group self-interest, articulated the ideological course that the Democrats had been pursuing since 1896 and continued to pursue throughout the twentieth century.[18]

For the Republicans, 1912 was also ideologically illuminating, although in a less straightforward manner. That year, Theodore Roosevelt put forward the "New Nationalism," which was a vision of national interest and unity that transcended individual and group self-interest. In both his appeals to "legitimacy" and patriotic loyalty and his repudiation of what was latter dubbed "class warfare," TR was articulating the core Republican ideology. But in 1912, he bolted from the party and condemned what he saw as its subservience to big business and private wealth: He damned "the greed of the 'haves'" equally with "the envy of the 'have-nots.'" He exposed a fundamental tension within Republicans between their core ideology of "legitimacy" and their fondness for unfettered private enterprise and wealth. The party has been able to satisfy both tendencies during most of the twentieth century, although repeated insurgencies by "progressives" strained them in TR's era and later, as did the intraparty conflict of 1964. Most recently, John McCain's candidacy in the 2000 primaries again exposed the conflict between legitimist, nationalist appeals, on the one hand, and fealty to economic interests, at least in the area of campaign finance, on the other.[19]

These fundamental ideological identities help to explain why the two parties emerged as they did from the 2000 election. The Republicans' near lock on the South and noncoastal West owed as much to their appeals to legitimacy as it did to economics, perhaps more. These are the regions where cultural issues hold sway, even among comparatively economically disadvantaged people. From their birth as a party, the Republicans have shown strong affinities for yoking their legitimist nationalism to religion, evangelical Protestantism at first, but more recently conservative strains in Catholicism and Judaism as well. A shared view of human nature as flawed and sinful and in need of repression and authority has bound adherents to these persuasions together, especially when many of them have been mobilized by organizations such as the Moral Majority and the Christian Coalition. Race has obviously complicated this alignment, inasmuch as many African-Americans are also fervent evangelical Protestants but shun the Republicans. Both nationalism and authoritarian leanings also help to explain why the military has leaned so strongly toward the Republicans. In 2000, active and former members of the armed forces favored Bush by a sizable majority, even though Gore promised greater defense spending and owned a more impressive service record.

The Democrats' regional strength in the Northeast and on the West Coast and their appeal in cities and suburbs likewise owed as much or more to ideology as to plain economics. Here, too, cultural issues exert a strong appeal, often among economically better off people. The Democrats' long-standing distaste, outside the South, for mixing religion in politics and legislating morality has appealed to more secular, cosmopolitan types. A more optimistic, tolerant view of human nature has attracted diverse groups, although, with the exception of women's and anti-abortion organizations, they have been less readily mobilized than their adversaries. Ethnicity as well as race have muddled this picture. Like African-American evangelical Protestants, Hispanic Catholics have not shared a secularist orientation toward cultural issues. Thus far, however, both economics and the California Republicans' manifest unfriendliness toward immigrants in the 1990s have kept Hispanics leaning toward the Democrats.

These ideological identities also undermine another truism about the parties in the latter part of the twentieth century. This is the argument that disagreements over the size and scope of government have formed the major bone of contention in the political arena. To be sure, conservative Republicans began spouting limited government, states' rights views in the 1930s and seized ideological control of the party in 1964. Ronald Reagan made political hay out of such battle cries as "Government isn't the solution, it's the problem!" and "Get government off our backs!" In the face of this rhetorical tempest, many Democrats trimmed their sails. As noted previously, in the 1970s Jimmy Carter moved in the direction of deregulation and reduced federal domestic spending, and in 1995 Bill Clinton proclaimed: "The era of big government is over." The problem with this notion is not only that government at the federal level continued to grow and run up deficits until the 1990s but even more that anti-government rhetoric was always highly selective.

Mainstream Republicans should not be confused with free-spirited members of the Libertarian Party who want to limit the size and scope of government across the board. Republican anti-government rhetoric has referred almost exclusively to economic affairs; its aim has been to curtail regulation and social welfare spending and roll back wealth-redistributing taxes. Otherwise, Republican conservatives have favored both bigger military spending and such measures of government intervention as banning abortions and flag burning. Conversely, the Democrats have favored greater government intervention in the economy, progressive taxation, and more welfare spending, but they have harshly condemned government intrusions into abortion, flag burning, school prayer, and other matters involving freedom of speech and opinion. It was no accident that in 1988 the Republican candidate made an issue out of the Democratic nominee's one-time membership in the American Civil Liberties Union. The one anomaly among these cultural issues has been gun control, where Democrats have favored government intervention and Republicans have opposed it. In several states, however, Republican governors and legislatures have trampled on local rights to prevent municipalities from banning firearms. Congressional Republicans have similarly discussed federal legislation to prohibit states from enacting what they fear as overly strict gun control.

Given the emptiness of their anti-government rhetoric, the Republicans' post-election behavior in 2000 should have come as no surprise, either. They were willing to use superior government power to negate local and states' rights whenever they deemed it necessary. Their secretary of state in Florida attempted to prevent county canvassing boards from examining and counting discarded ballots. The legislature that they controlled repeatedly threatened to brush aside the popular vote and choose Republican electors on its own, even though its constitutional authority to do so was, to put it mildly, highly suspect. The party's national organization resorted to the federal courts and the U. S. Supreme Court to prevent the Florida Supreme Court and county canvassing boards from acting on their own. On the Supreme Court, five of the seven Republican-appointed justices resorted to tortured constitutional reasoning that contravened their own states' rights leanings in order to shut down the recount in Florida. Although those justices deserve the benefit of the doubt in interpreting the motives behind their decision, they did appear bent on having the election turn out in favor of their presumed partisan preference. Questions were raised about whether those justices would have acted the same way in order to have the other party's candidate prevail.

What the election of 2000 and "the leaving it" revealed was how divided the American electorate has been for the preceding century and seemingly remains. The divisions are not merely numerical and geographical. These divisions had been evident particularly in the two previous elections, but this election exposed them so starkly because the dissident candidacies of Buchanan and Nader fared so poorly. Behind the numbers and sectional contrasts lie powerful economic, social, ethnic, and cultural alignments that both feed and draw sustenance from the well-understood and sharply differentiated ideological identities of the two parties. All the concern during the campaign about the candidates' personal strengths and weaknesses and predictions about their blurring issues and hewing to the center proved to be misplaced; this was a party and issue election. That was not unusual or interesting in itself. Rather, it was "the leaving it"—the extreme closeness of the outcome and the parties' behavior in the post-election conflict—that unmistakably bared the depth and seriousness of the divisions in the country. It is doubtful that these divisions can be overcome by ritualistic invocations of "bipartisanship"—which is a flawed notion at its best—or "civility."

Only potent insurgencies within the parties and genuinely innovative and attractive reform agendas might overcome these divisions, assuming that they should be overcome. The poor showing of dissident candidates in the general election does not bode well for the prospects of insurgency and reform. The only intriguing straw in the wind in that direction was the brief flourishing of John McCain in the Republican primaries. He may yet prove to be a major force in the politics of the first generation of the twenty-first century.

NOTES

1. See Richard L. Berke, "G. O. P. Questioning Bush's Campaign," *New York Times*, November 12, 2000. For an example of the sports-type post-game rethinking, see the reports of talks by Carl Rove of the Bush campaign and Carter Eskew of the Gore campaign, *New York Times*, February 12, 2001.

2. See William E. Leuchtenburg, "The Election of 2000," *Organization of American Historians Newsletter* 29 (February 2001): 1, 22. Also available at http://www.oah.org/pubs/nl/feb2001/leuchtenburg.html.

3. The classic study of the 1876 election is C. Vann Woodward, *Reunion and Reaction* (Boston: Little, Brown, 1951). See also Keith Ian Polakoff, *The Politics of Inertia: The Election of 1876 and the End of Reconstruction* (Baton Rouge: Louisiana State University Press, 1973).

4. For one comparison between 1888 and 2000, see *Pittsburgh Post-Gazette*, November 5, 2000.

5. *Wall Street Journal*, August 31, 2000. On Rove and his position at the beginning of the Bush administration, see *New York Times*, February 18, 2001.

6. On realignment, see V. O. Key, "A Theory of Critical Elections," *Journal of Politics* 17 (1955): 3–18; and Walter Dean Burnham, *Critical Elections and the Mainsprings of American Democracy* (New York: Norton, 1970).

7. The only other states in the Northeast and Midwest that the Republicans carried in 2000 were Indiana and New Hampshire, both of which had also gone Republican in the two preceding elections. Assuming that they did in fact carry Florida, the only non-West Coast state that the Republicans lost in the South and West was New Mexico. In 1916, the only state besides Ohio in the Midwest or Northeast that Wilson carried was also New Hampshire, which he won with a fifty-six-vote plurality. On the 1916 outcome, see Arthur S. Link, *Wilson: Campaigns for Progressivism and Peace* (Princeton, N.J.: Princeton University Press, 1965), 160–164.

8. See Lewis L. Gould, Jr., *1968: The Election That Changed America* (Chicago: Ivan R. Dee, 1993).

9. See Alan Lichtman, *Prejudice and the Old Politics: The Presidential Election of 1928* (Chapel Hill, N.C.: University of North Carolina Press, 1979), esp. 225–226.

10. Some scholars have even begun to question whether Republican dominance between 1896 and the late 1920s was all that it seemed to be. Wilson's victory in 1916 may have been more than a fluke and may have foreshadowed shifts of voters in the Northeast and Midwest that occurred in the 1930s. Likewise, Republican ascendancy in the 1920s was not as strong as it had been twenty years earlier, and it appears to have owed as much to disarray among the Democrats as to positive appeals. On this point, see John Milton Cooper, Jr., "If TR Had Gone Down with the Titanic: A Look at His Last Decade," in Natalie A. Naylor, Douglas Brinkley, and John Allen Gable, eds., *Theodore Roosevelt: Many Sided-American* (Interlaken, N.Y.: Heart of the Lakes Publishing, 1992), 499–514.

11. On this broader phenomenon of "populism," see Michael Kazin, *The Populist Persuasion: An American History* (New York: Basic Books, 1995). On the right wing and attempts to link it to populism, see William B. Hixson, *The Search for the American Right: An Analysis of the Social Science Record, 1955–1987* (Princeton, N.J.: Princeton University Press, 1992).

12. According to some analysts, the suburban shift toward the Democrats has taken place mainly in the Northeast and Midwest, not in the South and West. See W. Drummond Ayers, Jr., "Republicans in Illinois Woo Suburban Voters," *New York Times*, March 12, 2001.

13. These results are taken from nationaljournal.com's subscription service, "poll track," which is an excellent source for polling during the campaign.

14. Polling results are taken from nationaljournal.com's subscription service, "poll track."

15. This challenge to the prevailing view of American parties and politics is similar to the brilliant, provocative argument advanced in John Lukacs, "American History: A Terminological Problem," *American Scholar* 61 (Winter 1992): 17–32. Lukacs contends that the two major political forces in the Western world, the United States and Europe, have been "socialism" and "nationalism," which the Democrats and Republicans, respectively, have represented. He also argues that nationalism is the more potent of the two forces and the one that can truly draw on "populism." This argument strikes me as rich and suggestive but not something that can be applied too stringently to twentieth-century American politics.

16. On the Florida situation and the two parties' tactics and actions, see Kevin Sack, "In Desperate Florida Fight, Gore's Hard Strategic Calls," *New York Times*, December 15, 2000; and the series, "Deadlock: The Inside Story of America's Closest Election," *Washington Post,* January 28–February 4, 2001. For a description of voting and recounting in Florida, see also Mark Danner, "The Road to Illegitimacy," *New York Review of Books* 48 (February 22, 2001): 48–51.

17. O'Neill quoted in John A. Farrell, *Tip O'Neill and the Democratic Century* (Boston: Little, Brown, 2001), 346. O'Neill was responding to a claim by Ronald Reagan, then governor of California, that the Watergate burglars were "not criminals at heart." On the use of "Democrat party," see William F. Buckley's comments repudiating this usage in *National Review* 52 (December 31, 2000): 18.

18. On Wilson's articulation of the New Freedom, see John Milton Cooper, Jr., *The Warrior and the Priest: Woodrow Wilson and Theodore Roosevelt* (Cambridge, Mass.: Harvard University Press, 1983), esp. 207–221.

19. On Roosevelt's articulation of the New Nationalism, see *ibid.*

2

Trust the People: Political Party Coalitions and the 2000 Election

HENRY E. BRADY*

THE ELECTION CAMPAIGN OF 2000 ENDED WITH THE nation seriously divided both politically and geographically. The voters of one party were in the towns and cities of New England; the Great Lakes states of New York, Pennsylvania, Michigan, Illinois, Wisconsin, and Minnesota; and the far western states of California and Oregon. Their standard bearer was a modern man who believed that new technologies would assure the future of the United States, but who also gained support from those voters who remembered the injuries of American slavery. The voters of the other party were found throughout the southern states of the Confederacy; the Great Plains of Texas, Kansas, Colorado, Nebraska,

*My thanks to Daniel J. Brady, Laurel Elms, and Richard Goulding for research assistance and to the American National Election Studies for their policy of releasing their biennial treasure troves of data in a timely and fully documented fashion.

39

Wyoming, South Dakota, and Montana; and the Great Basin of Utah and Nevada. Their standard bearer seemed more old fashioned and promised to bring religion and moral decency to the presidency. His appeal was rooted in American populism: He trusted the people, not the government, and he was widely regarded as an honest and decent man, although possibly not up to the job of being president.

These contrasting images are not a new story in American politics, although the ending has changed. In 1896, the presidential candidate who promised to trust the people, the Democrat William Jennings Bryan, lost decisively to the Republican William McKinley. In 2000, the presidential candidate who promised to trust the people, the Republican George W. Bush, won the election over the Democrat Al Gore by the narrowest of margins (and that only in the electoral vote). American populism, which seemed dead after Bryan's loss, seemed resurgent in 2000. But what a strange, topsy-turvy populism it is! Bush is a Republican, not a Democrat, even though his support is located geographically precisely where William Jennings Bryan found those populist voters who would not be crucified on a cross of gold. A glance at the electoral map for 1896 conveys an initial sense of familiarity because the same states cluster together in 1896 as in 2000—only six are discordant—but it ends with the unnerving realization that the partisan loyalties of the states have been almost completely reversed. In 1896 the South to the Mason-Dixon line and the West to the escarpment of the Sierra Nevada were Democratic, but they are now solidly Republican. Then the Northeast, upper Midwest, and far West were Republican; now they are Democratic.

Perhaps the political parties themselves have simply reversed places, causing the voters to switch as well. Bush, by this reckoning, is the William Jennings Bryan of our era and Al Gore is the William McKinley. But this simple substitution will not do. Bush's populism extends to his manner, his religion, his moral traditionalism, and his claim to hail from America's heartland, but his economic policies would be anathema to Bryan, whose credo was easy credit through the free coinage of silver, regulation of the trusts, and a better deal for American labor. Gore, not Bush, echoes Bryan's arguments for the regulation of business and help for labor. On economic matters, Bush and his party follow in the footsteps of McKinley, whose chief lieutenant, the Cleveland millionaire Mark Hanna, raised millions from industrialists who feared Bryan's sympathy for labor as much as his proposal to inflate the currency. Although Gore believes in new technologies, his belief pales next to McKinley's faith in steel, railroads, and coal, and Gore's environmentalism would be incomprehensible to McKinley. On economic issues, the parties have not reversed at all, and Bush resembles McKinley whereas Gore takes after Bryan. Except for the modern political consensus on the virtues of free trade and non-inflationary monetary policy, the economic perspectives of the Democratic and Republican parties of today are not that much different from the 1896 versions.

On the issues of race and moral traditionalism, however, the parties have changed completely, and in these areas George W. Bush, at least superficially, looks more like Bryan and Al Gore looks more like McKinley, although a century of rapid change makes these comparisons perilous. Gore and McKinley are both connected with the African-American struggle for emancipation from slavery. Through his father's leadership in the U.S. Senate and his own actions as a member of Congress, Gore is linked with the civil rights movement in Tennessee from the 1950s to the 1990s. McKinley's tie to emancipation was more direct through his service in the Civil War, but his involvement was fundamentally to ensure the preservation of the Union. As Jim Crow laws were promulgated throughout the South and parts of the North in the 1890s, McKinley demonstrated indifference to the needs of black Americans, even though blacks were usually devoted to the Republican party in the few places where they could vote. In the course of time, the Republican Party's inability to solve these problems set the stage for the Democrats to take the lead in bringing racial justice to the United States.

Bush's moral traditionalism includes a fundamentalist belief in the Bible like Bryan's, a professed tolerance for the creationist theories that Bryan defended in his last hurrah at the Scopes trial, and a rejection of abortion and homosexual unions that would surely resonate with Bryan's supporters. Gore, like McKinley, is also a religious man, but his support for abortion and homosexual rights signifies a triumph of liberalism over moral traditionalism that sets him apart from Bryan and Bush. In the late nineteenth century, liberalism wrestled, ultimately unsuccessfully, with the advocates of temperance such as William Jennings Bryan. Today the proponents of liberalism contest with conservatives over the proper relationship between religion and government in the supercharged areas of abortion, homosexual rights, prayer in the schools, and the provision of social services by religious organizations.

The parties, then, did not simply reverse positions. In economic policy, there is continuity, but in their attitudes toward race and moral traditionalism there have been great changes that are at the root of the reversal of the electoral map. This story is told in the following pages as I review how we moved from 1896 to 2000. After this quick jaunt through history, I describe in detail the current coalitions in the Democratic and Republican parties. I end with some difficult questions: Why do we have a two-party system that seems to be in such perfect, if unstable, equipoise that a few votes in Florida, or a shift in political allegiance of a single senator from Vermont, can completely upset it? What does this precarious balance mean for the future of American electoral politics?

HOW WE GOT HERE

Following the election of 1896, Republican presidents were elected decisively for all but eight of the next thirty-six years, the exception occurring when the Republican split of 1912 between the Bull Moose Progressive Party of Theodore Roosevelt and the old guard

Republicans of William Howard Taft permitted the election of Woodrow Wilson. Throughout this period, the Democratic Party seemed in disarray. It had been much stronger during most of the last quarter of the nineteenth century. The Democrats had closely contested or won presidential elections from 1876 to 1892, but the loss in 1896 showed that agrarian populism simply did not have the muscle to capture the presidency in an era of industrialization and urbanization. Yeoman farmers could not beat the trusts without organized labor. But labor organization was only in its infancy, and the workers in the American Federation of Labor preferred a form of business unionism that was committed to accommodation with capitalism without political engagements. More broadly, although Americans began to worry about the excesses of the unbridled laissez-faire capitalism of McKinley and his party, they retained a Jeffersonian skepticism of government, and they were fearful of European imports like socialism that supposedly offered solutions to the problems. The American middle way was the nostrums of the Progressives: more direct democracy in the political sphere through the initiative, referendum, primary, and nonpartisan elections and the amelioration of the worst excesses of capitalism through trust-busting, government regulation, and social programs like workers' compensation for injured workers.

Progressivism, basically an upper- and middle-class movement, replaced the peculiarly American mix of political populism and religious fundamentalism as the major reform movement of the early twentieth century. Populism seemed to enjoy its last gasps on the national stage with the passage of the Volstead Amendment in 1919, which launched the folly of Prohibition, and then with the 1925 Scopes trial, in which an aging Bryan's defense of creationism in Dayton, Tennessee, was mocked daily by H. L. Mencken's pungent dispatches to the *Baltimore Sun*. Populism lived on in the South and the Midwest, sometimes in a noble guise (the early Tom Watson and Huey Long) and sometimes in a vicious fashion

(George Wallace's career until the very end), but it was always anti-intellectual, and its national following was gone.

Progressivism had some successes in reforming state and local governments, but its achievements were limited to major industrial, upper midwestern, and western states until the disaster of the Great Depression forced governmental action on a national scale. Franklin Delano Roosevelt drew on the Progressive agenda to develop his New Deal program, including the Social Security Act of 1935, which established Social Security, welfare, and unemployment insurance, and the National Labor Relations Act of 1935 (the Wagner Act), which provided the basis for labor organization. More important for the Democratic Party, he created a new political coalition that involved the maturing labor movement (especially the new Congress of Industrial Organizations); immigrants and blacks in the northern cities; and the Democrats of the South, who, seventy years after the Civil War perpetuated by the party of Lincoln, would still rather vote for a yellow dog than a Republican. It was the addition of labor and blacks to the Democratic coalition that provided the political basis for thirty-six years of Democratic presidents from 1932 to 1968, interrupted only by war hero Dwight Eisenhower's victories in 1952 and 1960. The New Deal retained the South for the Democrats and gained support in industrial New England (Connecticut, Massachusetts, and Rhode Island), urban New York and Pennsylvania, the upper Midwest (Illinois, Michigan, and Minnesota), and the far West (California and Washington), where labor unions were strong and where immigrants or blacks were located in large cities.

In the 1960s, as a result of John F. Kennedy's support for Martin Luther King, Jr. and Lyndon Johnson's sponsorship of historic civil rights legislation, the Democrats gained the support of blacks throughout the country while beginning the process that would create a Republican South. By the mid-1960s, most of the major changes from 1896 had occurred. Workers had been brought into the Democratic Party through the New Deal. Blacks had moved from the party of Lincoln to the party of Kennedy and Johnson. The big government social welfare programs of Roosevelt and Johnson were resoundingly approved in the landslide election of 1964, rejecting Barry Goldwater's vision of a smaller federal government in favor of Lyndon Johnson's expansive legislative agenda, which led to the War on Poverty and Medicare. The Democratic Party's support for these expansive social welfare programs and for civil rights branded it the party of the poor, blacks, and big government, but the formula appeared to be working in the mid-1960s. Most of the states of the Northeast, the upper Midwest, and the far West were in the Democratic column, whereas the Great Plains states became Republican strongholds. Of Bryan's 1896 coalition, only the South remained Democratic, but it would not remain so for long.

In 1968, Richard M. Nixon began to make inroads among southern voters and among blue collar workers who lived, uneasily, with blacks in northern cities, by appealing to the "Silent Majority" who supported the Vietnam War and who opposed busing for integrating schools. Through his wooing of the evangelist Billy Graham, Nixon began the process of bringing conservative Christians, those who were "born again" and who believed in the inerrancy of the Bible, back into the mainstream of American politics. Christian fundamentalism had not gone away since Bryan's time, but it had no distinct national coloration because it was Republican in the Great Plains and Democratic in the South. Indeed, in 1976 Jimmy Carter, a southern Democrat, would garner significant support from Christian conservatives because of his forthright assertion that he was a "born again" Christian who found great sustenance in his Baptist faith. Nixon also linked his support for the Vietnam War with his rejection of the new lifestyles of the 1960s hippies and war protesters, and he denounced the Supreme Court's 1973 decision in *Roe v. Wade* that made abortion legal throughout the United States. As a result, cultural and moral issues began to coalesce into a platform for the resurgence of a political movement of Christian conservatives.

For voters in the South, the Democratic party's support of civil rights, its identification with the anti-war movement, and its support of the feminist movement and abortion were too much. Republican candidates began to succeed in the South. In 1968 Nixon won the electoral votes of fewer than half the southern states, but in 1972, thanks in part to the Democratic candidacy of George McGovern, which helped to highlight the differences between the parties, Nixon won all southern states but Virginia (whose electoral votes were split). In the aftermath of Watergate, Carter, with his roots in Georgia and his born again Christianity, came back to win all but one southern state in 1976, but Clinton, even though he was from Arkansas, carried only half the southern states in 1992 and 1996. By contrast, in 1980, 1984, 1988, and 2000, the Republican presidential candidates won all the southern states (except Jimmy Carter's Georgia in 1980). During this period, conservative Christians found that their natural home was the Republican Party.

AMERICAN POLITICS IN THE YEAR 2000

Most of the actors in the year 2000 electoral coalitions have now been introduced. They include African-Americans, union members, liberals, the poor, Christian fundamentalists, conservatives, business elites, and the well-off. It remains to explain the coalitions in the parties and the outcome of the election, which will take several steps. This section explains, by taking them apart, how the Democratic and Republican coalitions fit together. The dissection of a mechanism as complicated as a political party requires care lest one miss the operation of an important gear or lever or become distracted by an intriguing but minor aspect of the apparatus. My approach is to develop a schematic that describes the major features without delving into the minor contrivances that matter only to experts.

The schematic is very simple. Using data from the 2000 American National Election Study,[1] I characterize voters by their income and their religious attendance. There are, to be sure, many other ways of describing voters: by their education, age, residence, religious affiliation, and so forth. But people's income tells us a great deal about their economic interests and concerns, and religious attendance suggests a lot about their moral and social concerns. I will demonstrate how Democrats and Republicans differ in their incomes and religious attendance, and how the parts of each coalition differ in these respects as well. For the Democrats, I focus on blacks, Hispanics, the poor, union members, blue collar workers, and employees in the service and protective industries, who together constitute approximately two-thirds of the Democratic coalition. For the Republicans, I focus on Christian fundamentalists; those employed as executives, managers, or administrative personnel; professional workers; and the well-off. Together these groups constitute slightly less than two-thirds of the Republican coalition.

After completing this look at the characteristics of the major groups in each coalition, I turn to an examination of their policy differences. To explore the extent of these differences, I consider a number of issues that have come up in political campaigns over the past decade, and I show that they can be roughly organized along two dimensions. One comprises a set of issues regarding the relationship of government and the economy, which can be summarized by people's degree of economic liberalism or conservatism. The second dimension of moral conservatism summarizes a set of issues regarding the way that we should live. I show that these are quite distinct dimensions of concern, and I show that we can place Democratic and Republican groups along them in ways that reveal a great deal about the groups and the political parties.

Income, Religious Attendance, and
the Coalitional Structure of the Parties

Figure 2.1 describes the average location of all Americans, Democrats, Republicans, and various other groups on a simple two-dimensional picture. The vertical dimension is the frequency of attending religious services in the course of a year, which ranges from 15 times per year at the bottom to almost once a week (50 times a year) at the top. The horizontal dimension is household income in thousands of dollars. Thus, in the lower left-hand quadrant we find those groups that have low incomes and low rates of religious attendance. In the upper right-hand quadrant we have those with high income and high rates of religious attendance. The upper left quadrant is for those who have low incomes and high religious attendance, and the bottom right quadrant is for those with high incomes and low religious attendance. The letters on the figure represent groups described below. The upper dotted line runs through the Republican groups and the lower dotted line runs through the Democratic groups.

The large dot near the middle of the figure represents the average American (A) who attends religious services a little less than once every other week (23 times a year) and who has a household income of $52,400. To the left of this average person, there is the average Democrat (D), who goes to church about the same number of times but whose household income of $46,700 is $5,700 below the average for all Americans. To the right and toward the top of the figure is the average Republican (R), who attends religious services more frequently (30 times a year) and whose household income of $61,500 is $7,100 above the average. These differences are quite substantial, with Republicans going to religious services about 30 percent more often than Democrats, and with Republicans having about $14,800 more household income than Democrats.

An aphoristic description of these results is that the Republican Party represents the rich and the religious, whereas the Democratic

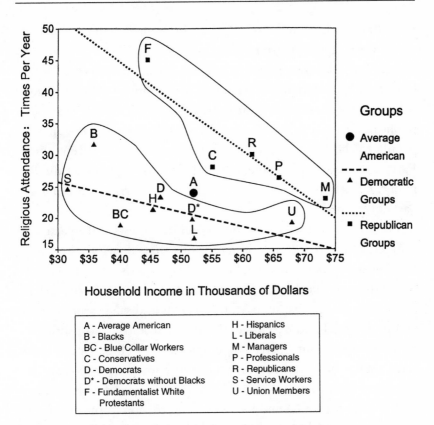

Figure 2.1   Groups by Religious Attendance and Income

Party represents the poor and the profane. There is some truth in this characterization, but both parties are complicated amalgams of diverse groups, which makes any single description too simple. For example, consider the claim that the Republicans are the party of the rich person. In the overall population, 35 percent of voting-aged Americans identify with the Democrats and 25 percent with the Republicans (40 percent are independents), giving the Democrats a substantial advantage. To say that a group can be identified with a party, the group must contain more identifiers of that party than these baseline numbers. Thus, among low income households (in the lowest quarter of incomes below $20,000 per year), 45 percent are Democrats, indicating that low income households are much more likely to be Democrats than the 35 percent of the party-identifiers in the population. Among high income households (all those in the upper quarter of incomes above $75,000 per year) 32 percent consider themselves Republicans, compared to the 25 percent in the population as a whole. High income people, then, contribute much more than their share of party-identifiers to the Republican Party, but the contribution is less than that of low income people to the Democratic Party. Attachment to the Republican Party does rise with income, but these results suggest that the Republican Party is not so much the party of the rich as it is *not* the party of the poor.

More can be learned about the economic interests of the parties by characterizing the occupational groups that identify with them. Each of these six occupational categories comprises one-seventh to one-fifth of the workforce: blue collar, service and protective, clerical and administrative support, technicians and sales, professionals, and managerial and executive. (Farming, forestry, and fishing account for only about 1 percent of employment.) These six categories form a status hierarchy in which those with lower education and incomes are at the bottom (blue collar and service workers) and those with higher education and incomes are at the top (professional and managerial workers). In addition, although technicians and sales workers are often lumped with clerical and administrative support workers into a "white collar" category, these groups differ in the amount of autonomy that they have on their jobs. Technicians and sales workers (and those groups above them in the hierarchy) typically have much more autonomy than clerical and administrative supporter workers and those below them in the hierarchy. Those groups with more autonomy have a different attitude toward work, often reflected in employers providing them with an annual salary rather than hourly wages, than those with less autonomy.

Since the New Deal, blue collar (BC) workers have been an important part of the Democratic coalition, and they are still disproportionately Democratic (39 percent), with average household incomes around $40,000 and low levels of religious attendance, as indicated in Figure 2.1. But the fraction of blue collar workers in the workforce has been cut by almost one-third over the past forty years, and their union membership has declined by well over one-half as manufacturing work in the North has either moved South or out of the country. As a result, blue collar workers are not nearly as important to the Democrats as they once were, although they still constitute about one-fifth of those identifying as Democrats. Service and protective workers, however, have become increasingly important as their numbers have grown, and they are now almost as important a part of the Democratic coalition as blue collar workers. The religious attendance of service (S) workers is similar to that of Democrats as a whole, but their average income of $31,600 is very low.

Union membership is still another way to describe economic interests. More than 46 percent of those from union households identify with the Democrats, and union households are still almost one-fifth of the Democratic coalition. But Democratic identification has declined among union members and households, as it has in the general population. Union households are still important, however, because they vote and participate in politics at a significantly higher rate than non-union members. In the 2000 election, for example, unions engaged in a large get-out-the-vote campaign that helped Gore narrow the gap between himself and Bush on election day. Union (U) households are also distinctive because of their low rates of religious attendance and relatively *high* incomes, which place them in the lower right-hand corner of Figure 2.1.

On the Republican side, managerial and executive workers are disproportionately Republican, and they constitute almost one-fifth of the Republican coalition. In Figure 2.1, they appear on the bottom right of the diagram (M) with very high incomes and relatively low religious attendance. As we shall see, this part of the Republican coalition coexists somewhat uneasily with the white, fundamentalist Protestants (F) who are in the upper left of Figure 2.1.

In addition, union households are surprisingly close to the managerial and executive workers in Figure 2.1. On the one hand, this location shows why union members, with relatively high incomes,
are vulnerable to the blandishments of the Republican party, but
on the other hand, the fact that the party identification of union
members is still distinctively Democratic compared to the Republican identification of managers shows that class differences based
on position in the work hierarchy, not just income, continue to
matter. Union members and managers may be neighbors in Figure
2.1, but there is a fence between them based on the authority that
managers wield over workers.

Another group that is important to the Republican Party is professionals (P), who constitute about one-quarter of the Republican
coalition. Professionals are more likely than any other group to be
independents, but they still include more Republicans than the
general population. They are located close to the average Republican in Figure 2.1. Professionals and managers are an important
source of resources, especially money, for the Republican Party.
The two remaining groups, technicians and sales workers and clerical workers, less clearly belong to either party, although clerical
workers lean Democratic and technical and sales workers lean
Republican.

Economic interests, then, in the form of income and authority
relationships in the workforce, help to explain why low income
people, blue collar and service workers, and union households
identify with the Democrats and why managers, professionals, and
high income people identify with the Republicans. The story is
simple and straightforward, and political cleavages based on these
economic interests persisted throughout the last century.

Despite these facts, American politics is often only faintly a politics of economic self-interest. Race and social issues have periodically riven American politics and sustained its most contentious
and animated episodes. Consider, for example: abolition and the
Civil War; the Anti-Saloon League, temperance, and the Volstead

Act; civil rights, the Black Power movement, and busing; and school prayer, women's rights, abortion, and homosexual rights. There are good reasons to consider groups whose allegiances to the parties depend as much, or more, on these factors as on economic self-interest. Considering them also helps to explain some of the anomalies in Figure 2.1.

A surprising aspect of Figure 2.1 is that the Democrats resemble the average American in their religious attendance. For a party that has so often been painted as the purveyor of "secular humanism" and even "Godless Communism," this fact seems surprising. More than anything else, it shows how religious Americans are and the simplicity of partisan stereotypes. But it also reflects an important feature of the Democratic Party that is not always noticed. One of the party's major constituent groups, African-Americans, attends religious services at a very high rate. Blacks (B) go to church as much as the average Republican. If blacks are removed from the Democratic Party, it moves to the position indicated by D*, and the average level of religious attendance is about 15 percent lower and the average income increases by $5,000. Blacks, who constitute about one-fifth of the Democratic coalition, are simultaneously among its poorest members and its most religious. Three-quarters of blacks either say that they are "born again" or that they believe that the Bible is the literal word of God, and two-fifths say both.

Blacks, with their strong memories of Democratic support for civil rights, are the Democratic Party's most loyal members, with almost 70 percent identification. (Only 3 percent identify with the Republican Party; 27 percent are independents.) Hispanics (H) are also linked with the Democratic Party because of its support of liberal immigration policies, but their rates of loyalty are nowhere near those of blacks. And some parts of the Hispanic community (Cubans in South Florida) are more Republican than Democratic.

Blacks are the major group of Christian fundamentalists within the Democratic Party. Within the Republican Party, the fundamentalists are almost entirely white Protestants who belong to Baptist, Pentacostal, Assembly of God, Church of God, or just "Christian" churches. White Protestant fundamentalists who say they are born again and that the Bible is the literal word of God constitute exactly the same fraction of the Republican Party as blacks do of the Democratic Party. This group is located in the upper left-hand corner of Figure 2.1 at F. They have low average incomes, and they attend church at very high rates, almost once a week throughout the year.

Altogether, these groups constitute the bulk of each party. About two-thirds of the Democratic Party come from low income people, blue collar or service workers, union households, and blacks and Hispanics. Slightly less than two-thirds of the Republican Party come from high income people, managers, professionals, and white fundamentalist Protestants. The lines on Figure 2.1 suggest the range of these coalitions for each party.

Two other groups, self-identified liberals (L) and conservatives (C), also appear in Figure 2.1. About half the population identify themselves as conservative and only one-third as liberal, and it is clear from Figure 2.1 that religious attendance has more to do with this self-identification than does income. Ninety percent of Republicans identify themselves as conservatives, but only 56 percent of Democrats identify themselves as liberals; in fact, 37 percent of Democrats call themselves conservatives. If we add liberals to the groups discussed previously that are part of the Democratic Party, we capture almost 90 percent of the party. If we add conservatives to the groups discussed previously that are part of the Republican Party, we capture more than 90 percent of the party.

Now that the major groups in each party have been identified and placed in Figure 2.1, we can interpret what it all means. There are two remarkable features of Figure 2.1. First, the groups are quite spread out for each party, and each coalition covers a great range of incomes and religious attendance. In political science parlance, American political parties are "catch-all coalitions" that try to accommodate all sorts of different groups. Second, the axis of the Republican party is sloped so that it includes white fundamentalist Protestants whose incomes alone would place them squarely in the Democratic Party and managers and high income people whose religious involvement alone would place them in the Democratic Party. The Republican Party has similar groups. The religious attendance of blacks alone would place them in the Republican Party. The incomes of union members alone would place them in the Republican Party. If income defined economic interests completely and these interests were the only motivation for identifying with a party, then white fundamentalist Protestants would be Democrats and union members would be Republicans. If religious attendance fully defined religious considerations and these considerations were the only motivation for identifying with a party, then blacks would be Republicans and managers would be Democrats. Clearly, both dimensions matter, and they provide parties with interesting coalitional possibilities.

Mapping Interests and Behavior into Attitudes

Political parties express the interests of their members and consolidate their coalitions through the political positions that they take. Consequently, we can infer the political positions of parties by finding out the opinions of their members. To do this, we must ask about a large number of politically important issues and identify those on which the partisans of the parties disagree. The 2000 American National Election Study included approximately two score issue questions on a large variety of topics. I chose to ignore those on defense and foreign policy because these topics, although sometimes very important in American politics, are not currently major issues.

The remaining questions were on spending, aid to blacks, government medical insurance, government provision of jobs, the environment, school vouchers, the death penalty, the role of women, social issues like abortion and homosexual rights, and gun control. A story can be told about each of them individually, but I have condensed them into two dimensions: economic liberalism-conservatism and moral liberalism-conservatism.[2] These two dimensions encompass most of the questions in the sense that if we know a person's position on economic liberalism, we know most of what there is to know about his or her position on the provision of government services, aid to blacks, government medical insurance, or government provision of jobs. And if we know the person's position on moral conservatism, then we know most of what there is to know about his or her position on abortion, homosexual rights, and the role of women. The two dimensions not only tell us a lot about each person's issue positions, they also do so very efficiently because both dimensions are needed to describe people's positions on these topics. Knowing someone's position on moral conservatism tells us almost nothing about that person's positions on economic matters, and vice versa.

There is an obvious relationship between these two dimensions and the income and religious attendance of people. We would expect, and we find, that those with higher incomes hold more conservative positions on economic issues, and those who attend religious services more often take conservative stances on moral issues. To see the implications of these connections between people's characteristics and their attitudes about issues, it is helpful to construct another figure that parallels Figure 2.1 but uses measures of moral conservatism and economic conservatism along each axis. (See Figure 2.2.)

Based on each person's answers to questions in the National Election Studies, I constructed a scale for economic conservatism and a scale for moral conservatism that ranged from 0 to 100, with higher values indicating greater conservatism. Then, for each of the basic groups in the party coalitions, I computed the average score on these two scales for members of the group. These scores were then plotted on Figure 2.2, the vertical dimension of which is moral conservatism and the horizontal dimension of which is eco-

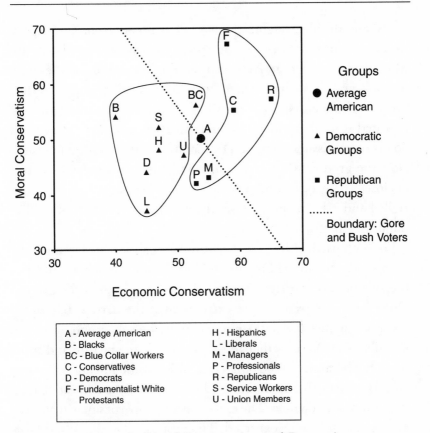

Figure 2.2   **Groups by Moral Conservatism and Economic Conservatism**

nomic conservatism. Those who are liberal on both dimensions appear in the lower left-hand quadrant, and those who are conservative on both are in the upper right-hand quadrant. Those who are morally conservative but economically liberal are in the upper left-hand quadrant, and those who are morally liberal but economically conservative are in the lower right-hand quadrant.

Ignore the line on the figure and the two oblongs for the moment, and concentrate on the D at the lower left, the A in the middle bottom, and the R on the right. These are the locations of the Democrats, the average American, and the Republicans respectively, and they lie roughly along a line that goes from liberal positions on moral and economic issues to conservative positions. Moreover, the average American is roughly in the middle, with Republicans somewhat farther away from the average person than are the Democrats. This result is nothing more than the oft-repeated story that today's Republican Party is farther away from voters on the issues than the Democratic Party is. The oblongs enclose the groups that are in each party. The left-hand side oblong encloses the groups that are part of the Democratic Party. The right-hand side oblong encloses the groups that are part of the Republican Party.

For both parties, the party-identifiers are almost always more extreme—farther to the bottom and left for the Democrats and farther to the top and right for the Republicans—than the groups. Only three groups are more extreme than the parties. Blacks (B) are more to the left than Democrats as a whole on economic issues, and liberals (L) are farther to the bottom of the picture and more morally liberal than the Democrats. White fundamentalist Protestants (F) are farther to the top and more morally conservative than Republicans as a whole. The extremity of the parties may seem surprising, but it is to be expected. The groups, after all, by and large consist of both Democrats and Republicans, so their average position on the two dimensions will be between the parties. The three exceptions—blacks who are economically liberal, liberals who are morally liberal, and white fundamentalist Protestants who are morally conservative—are very homogeneous and highly focused on particular issues.

By and large, the groups are where we would expect them to be. Union households (U), because of their high incomes, are relatively conservative on economic issues. Professionals (P), because of their high education levels, are more secular than we would expect, given their high rates of religious attendance. The biggest surprise is the very conservative positions taken by blue collar workers (BC) despite their relatively low church attendance and low incomes.

The roots of this conservatism probably lie in the low educational levels of blue collar workers and their competition with immigrants and black Americans for jobs. Indeed, among whites in all occupational groups, blue collar workers are more likely to agree that blacks should overcome prejudice without favors and that by simply trying harder they could be well-off. The location of blue collar workers in Figure 2.2 certainly reflects what we know about their declining Democratic identification and the hard-fought battles between the parties in states like Michigan for their support.

Challenges Facing the Parties

The positions of liberals and conservatives tell us some important things about the challenges facing both parties. Self-identified conservatives are morally conservative like Republicans, but they are much more moderate on economic issues than are Republicans. Self-identified liberals are just as liberal about economic issues as Democrats, but they are much more liberal on moral issues than are Democrats as a whole. Rhetorically, then, Republicans do themselves a great service by calling themselves conservatives because they disguise the extent of their economic conservatism (C is to the left of R) while choosing a position on moral conservatism that resonates with many voters in the middle of the income distribution who might not find their economic positions to be so acceptable. Democrats are by and large hurt by being called liberals because that label makes the party seem much less sympathetic to conservative moral issues than it is and does nothing to moderate the party's position on economic issues. In short, calling Republicans conservatives places them closer to the mainstream, whereas calling Democrats liberals places them farther away. The Democratic response to this is to emphasize the strength of Christian fundamentalists within the Republican Party, which places Republicans farther away from the center, but this response runs the danger of seeming to be disrespectful of Christians.

Another way to think of the challenges facing the parties is to consider subgroups within them that might be vulnerable to appeals from the other party. An obvious source of vulnerability comes from being cross-pressured by having characteristics that make members of the subgroup conservative along one dimension but liberal along another. There are four of these groups, two for each party. Each group is defined by considering people who are higher than the party average on one dimension but lower on the other dimension.

Consider, for example, Democrats who attend religious services more than do average Democrats but who have lower incomes than their fellow partisans. This subgroup is one-third black, and it is morally conservative but economically liberal. Its members are favorable to Christian fundamentalists[3] and feel no great sympathy with homosexuals. Their moral conservatism suggests that they could bolt to the Republican Party and join with white fundamentalist Protestants, but they are separated by the great gulf of race and their overweening concern for economic issues. They are very positive toward labor unions, poor people, welfare recipients, and blacks. Their only threat to the Democratic Party is that they might support the primary candidacy of someone like Jesse Jackson, who could hurt the party's image in general elections.

The other cross-pressured group in the Democratic Party consists of those who do not attend religious services very often and who have high incomes. They are by and large self-identified liberals, and they are morally very liberal and economically moderate. Their most salient characteristic is that they strongly dislike Pat Buchanan and Christian fundamentalists, but they feel favorable toward groups such as homosexuals. Members of this cross-pressured group might be receptive to appeals by the Republican Party, but only if it jettisoned Christian conservatives.

On the Republican side, one cross-pressured group is composed of those people who attend religious services frequently but who have low incomes. This group is composed of white, born again fundamentalist Christians who are very, very high on moral conservatism and whose economic positions are only slightly less conservative than those of the Republican Party. They like Pat Buchanan, Christian fundamentalists, and the Christian Coalition, and they dislike the women's movement, feminists, homosexuals, and Jesse Jackson. Although the average income of this group is quite low ($35,000), it is strongly attached to the Republican Party through its fundamentalism. The members of this subgroup, along with higher income white fundamentalist Protestants, are the "Main Street" wing of the Republican Party. The Main Street wing contributes a disproportionate share of time and effort to political campaigns, and it is the source of protesters, especially on issues like abortion. But the danger for the Republican Party is that this group will back a Pat Robertson or a Pat Buchanan, who will push an anti-abortion, moralistic agenda that will frighten away the independents who are needed to win elections.

The last cross-pressured group comprises Republicans who rarely attend religious services but who have high incomes. They are morally liberal like Democrats, but quite conservative on economic issues. This subgroup is the Wall Street Wing of the party. It contributes significant amounts of money to the party and to Republican causes. Its members do not like Patrick Buchanan or the Christian Coalition, but they are more worried about labor unions, poor people, people on welfare, Jesse Jackson, and Ralph Nader. They might be convinced to cast their lot with a New Democrat like Bill Clinton if the Republican Party were taken over by Pat Buchanan, but they voted overwhelmingly for Bob Dole in 1996 and George W. Bush in 2000.

Each party thus faces a distinctive set of threats. The Democrats must run away from the liberal label, avoid a primary challenge from a Jesse Jackson, and keep blue collar and union households within its ranks. They must stay away from issues like affirmative action, which split their own ranks by pitting blacks and liberals against union members and blue collar workers. Republicans must de-emphasize their conservative economic policies and rein in fundamentalist Protestants. They must avoid primary battles with social and moral conservatives like Pat Buchanan. They must stay away from strong and vocal opposition to abortion and the women's movement because these issues split their ranks while uniting the opposition. Both candidates and parties did these things very well in 2000, which partly explains the closeness of the election.

Vote Choice in 2000

The line running downhill from left to right on Figure 2.2 defines the boundary between Republican and Democratic voters in 2000. This line is based on a model of how moral conservatism and economic conservatism affected vote choice in 2000, and it splits the electorate in half, running right through the average voter. Those voters above the line were more likely to vote for Bush than for Gore, and those below it were more likely to vote for Gore than for Bush. The diagonal slope of the line indicates that both issues mattered for people's votes. Some Gore voters, for example, were moderate to conservative on moral issues but very liberal on economic issues (blacks in the upper left-hand corner of the figure), and other voters were liberal on moral issues but moderate to conservative on economic issues (union households, near the middle at the bottom of the diagram). Similarly, Bush's support came from people above the line who were moderate on moral issues but very conservative on economic issues (managers and high income people) and from conservatives on moral issues who were more moderate on economic issues. The placement of the line suggests even more strongly that some groups have only a tenuous connection with the political party for which they have the most identifiers. Blue collar workers are above the line in Bush territory, so the model predicts they should have voted for Bush. In fact, they were slightly more likely to vote for Gore, indicating that the model is missing something such as the long-standing relationship between labor and the Democratic Party. Similarly, professional workers are below the line, even though they voted for Bush.

WHY BUSH WON

Placing Bush and Gore in the Issue Space

Many factors affect who wins and loses a political campaign, but being near the voters on the issues is certainly the first rule for winning, a rule that Barry Goldwater in 1964 and George McGovern in 1972 ignored at their peril. Which candidate, then, was closest to the voters in Election 2000? In Figure 2.3 I have placed the candidates on the same two dimensions as in Figure 2.2. I have also arranged the figure so that the distances indicate how far each candidate was from the average voter and from those in his party. The average voter, as in the previous figures, is at A, and the candidates are perceived, by the voters, to be at G for Gore and B for Bush. The diagonal line, as before, is the dividing line between Bush and Gore voters, with Bush voters to the right and Gore voters to the left. I discuss the two vertical lines and the D and R later in this section.

The major conclusion to draw from this picture is that voters thought that Bush was closer to the average voter than Gore was. In the figure, Bush clearly has the advantage on economic issues, where he is much closer than Gore. On moral issues, he is farther away than Gore, but on balance, the simple alphabetical and arithmetical truth is that the distance from A to B is less than the distance from A to G. It is not surprising to find that Bush is farther away from the average voter than Gore on moral issues, but it is surprising, given what has been said so far, that Gore is farther away from the average voter on economic issues than Bush is. Figures 2.1 and 2.2 showed that Democratic partisans were closer to the middle than Republican partisans. Indeed, if we use the same information to place Democrats (D) and Republicans (R) in Figure

2.3, we get the same result again. Then why is Gore, a Democrat, perceived to be so far away from the mainstream? Luckily the American National Election Studies ask its respondents to place the parties as well as the candidates on some issues. They do not ask about any moral issues, but they ask about the same economic issues that were used to construct the rest of Figure 2.3. The two vertical lines indicate where the parties are perceived to stand. (The lines are vertical because people's perceptions of the parties' positions on moral issues could be anywhere along them. Happily, I do not care so much about these perceptions.) The Democrats are perceived to be far to the left of where the party-identifiers (D) place themselves and very close to where people place Al Gore. The same is not true of Republicans, who are perceived to be almost exactly where the party-identifiers (R) stand and where George W. Bush is perceived to be.

There are at least three possible explanations for this result. One is that Gore's populist economic rhetoric, which commenced with his acceptance speech at the Democratic Convention and continued throughout the campaign, led to a perception that he and his party were far to the left. Another possibility is that Democrats simply suffer from a preexisting presumption that they are much more liberal than their partisans. This presumption, needless to say, is fueled by Republican rhetoric, which focuses on "liberal Democrats." A third possibility is that Democratic identifiers, such as union members and blue collar workers, are much more conservative with respect to economic issues than their party, so they slant the overall position of Democratic partisans to the right. Whatever the explanation, Gore clearly had a disadvantage in terms of the perceptions of his economic positions.

Why Was the Election So Close?

Despite the disadvantage of being somewhat farther from the voters than Bush, Gore did win the popular vote by the substantial

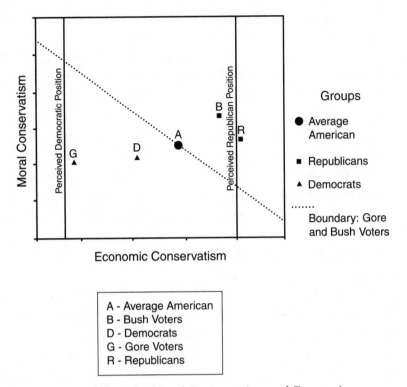

Figure 2.3   Candidates by Moral Conservatism and Economic
Conservatism

margin of over 500,000 votes, and he came within several hundred
votes of winning in Florida and winning the election. Indeed, the
evidence is overwhelming that more voters in Florida went to the
polls to vote for Gore than for Bush, but a significant number of
votes did not get properly recorded because of human and machine
errors. Moreover, recounts would not detect this fact because the
two major problems, the butterfly ballot in Palm Beach County
Florida and the use of outdated punch-card voting machines in
many Florida counties, either caused votes to be misallocated or
failed to record them. I have described these problems in detail
elsewhere,[4] but suffice it to say that Gore probably lost somewhere
between 10,000 and 30,000 votes because of these problems. All the
other difficulties that have been adduced to claim that Bush was

disadvantaged in other ways do not produce more than a few thousand votes under the most generous assumptions.

These facts make it hard to discuss "Why Bush Won?" without feeling that the question is ill-posed. Instead, it makes much more sense to ask why the race was so close. This question seems especially appropriate because many pre-election articles on the campaign mentioned political science forecasting models that predicted a clear-cut Gore victory based on the state of the economy. Indeed, it seemed hard to fathom why the voters would turn out a party that had presided over the greatest economic expansion on record. The statistical models of political scientists merely summarized this wisdom, although much less pungently than James Carville's famous sign in the 1992 Clinton headquarters: "It's the economy, stupid!"

The forecasting models are very simple affairs.[5] They take the incumbent party's share of the two-party vote (in 2000 that would be Gore's share) and observe how it has gone up and down with changes in a small number of factors deemed to be important determinants of the vote: the growth rate of the economy, the popularity of the president, whether the candidate of the incumbent party was closer to the electorate than the challenger, the number of terms that the party has been in power, and indicators for unpopular wars. The first three factors invariably increase the incumbent party's vote share. A better economy, a more popular president, and being closer to the electorate than the challenger all help the candidate of the incumbent party. In 2000, Gore enjoyed a very strong economy, and he had to bear a seemingly popular president according to the conventional measures. Gore might have been perceived to be farther away from the average voter than Bush, but the difference was not great. The last two factors considered by the models, protracted incumbency and wars, typically hurt the incumbent party. Gore did not have to worry about a war as did Adlai Stevenson in 1952 or Hubert Humphrey in 1968, but he did have to worry about the handicap of seeking a third term for the

Democrats. The wounds of incumbency inevitably reduce electoral fortunes.

Still, these models predicted that Gore would win handily, and he did not. Political scientists, like economists, find that their predictions always improve after events have occurred, and they have already weighed in with an explanation for their failure to predict the outcome in 2000. Larry Bartels and John Zaller[6] have shown that even before the election, a careful analysis would have revealed that it mattered how the growth rate of the economy was measured, and most models measured it wrong. The standard measure is Gross Domestic Product (GDP), which measures the total output of the economy. Bartels and Zaller argue that a better measure is Real Domestic Income (RDI), which measures the income received by people.

In most years, the difference between GDP and RDI is rather small, but when there are budget surpluses of several hundred billion dollars, the difference is considerable and can be felt by individuals because these surpluses represent money not available to individuals but held by the government. If several hundred billion dollars is split up among several hundred million people in the United States, it amounts to something like $1,000 for every person. If Clinton had decided to return this money in a tax cut or through additional spending before the 2000 election, it seems very likely that some voters would have been swayed to vote for Gore. The political science models that used the GDP, however, did not notice that this money was not available to voters, so they overestimated Gore's vote. When Bartels and Zaller re-estimated the models using RDI, they found out that they got a better fit to the historical data and a more realistic prediction for the 2000 election. If they are right, then Clinton's big mistake, especially in light of the fact that Bush immediately set out to give away the surplus anyway, was not to support a tax cut or immediate spending to help Al Gore get elected.

But Clinton was probably a problem for Gore in other ways. A whopping two-thirds of the population thought that the word *dis-*

honest described Clinton extremely well or quite well (compared to only 20 percent who thought that about Bush and 25 percent about Gore). Forty percent of the population thought that Clinton had made the moral climate worse, compared to only 3 percent of the population who thought that George Herbert Walker Bush (George W. Bush's father) had done so. And people also reported that Clinton made them angry much more often than did Gore and Bush. It is hard to believe that doubts and anger about Clinton did not hurt Al Gore. It is certainly the case that the Republicans ran many advertisements questioning Gore's honesty, and the public did consider him less honest than Bush. In past campaigns, character traits such as honesty have had little effect on popular voting, but in 2000 it seems likely that Clinton's behavior primed the public to be more concerned about this issue.

Finally, there is Ralph Nader, who won over 96,000 votes in Florida, and for whom exit polls indicated that a substantial majority of his supporters would have voted for Gore if Nader had not been running. The numbers here are compelling. Even if 90 percent of Nader's supporters had stayed home had he not run, the remaining 9,000 voters would have provided an ample margin for Gore even if they only split 60–40 for Gore over Bush. But it is worth noting that it is not clear that Gore would have picked up any other states. Bush won New Hampshire by about 7,300 votes, and 22,156 there voted for Nader. But 40 percent of these Nader voters were McCain supporters, and only about 60 percent of them said in exit polls that they would vote for Gore, which was not enough for him to win.

Why, then, was the election so close? One answer is that the parties chose candidates who satisfied their core constituencies while appealing successfully beyond them. Neither candidate could be called a mistake, from an electoral standpoint, like Barry Goldwater in 1964, George McGovern in 1972, or Michael Dukakis in 1988. Each appealed to the core of his party, but neither seemed so extreme as to frighten off independent voters. A second answer is that both parties avoided divisive primary seasons or conventions. John McCain and Bill Bradley provided significant challenges to Bush and Gore, but they did not arouse the fears that Pat Buchanan's Republican candidacy stimulated among Democrats in 1996 or Jesse Jackson's Democratic candidacy fostered in 1984 and 1988. Both candidates were also able to stay away from issues that divided their parties: abortion for the Republicans and affirmative action for the Democrats. Just as the Democrats had learned from their losing streak during the 1980s, the Republicans learned from their failures in 1992 and especially 1996. A third answer is that the economy, although strong, was a mixed blessing for Gore as long as Clinton had decided to save the surplus instead of spending it or giving it back to the voters. A fourth answer is that Clinton's lies and misbehavior dissipated the political benefits of the economic expansion and accentuated the tendency for voters to turn out incumbent parties. A final answer is that Ralph Nader took enough votes away from Gore to make the race close in Florida and elsewhere.

WHAT KIND OF VICTORY?

Bush's victory was consolidated, if not manufactured, by the Supreme Court of the United States, but he would have won even if the Court had not stepped in. Subsequent newspaper reports have indicated that statewide recounts would probably, although not certainly, have gone in Bush's favor. Even if the recounts had gone against Bush, the Republican Florida legislature or the Republican Congress would undoubtedly have used the constitutional methods at their disposal to make him president. Instead, in a much-debated opinion, the Court ended the election of 2000 with its December 12 opinion. If the Florida legislature and the Republican Congress had made the final decision, there seems little doubt that the 2002 elections would have revolved around their choice of president, with some voters deciding to reward their representatives and others deciding to punish them. To a political scientist like myself, that seems like a good way to do things.

It seems less clear to me that it was sensible for the Supreme Court to step in to make the decision, but it is not clear what the long-term consequences will be. We can say the following. The 2000 National Election Studies continued to conduct interviews for nearly two months after election day. Presciently, they added a question asking whether the election was fair. From the very beginning of the post-election interviewing, two-thirds of the Republicans thought that the election was fair, but Democrats and independents were in the middle, with somewhat less than half of them agreeing. During the period when the Supreme Court returned the first decision to the Florida Supreme Court on December 3 to when they made their final judgment on December 12, Republicans became even more sure that the election was fair (80 percent agreeing with this judgment) and independents and Democrats became less sure, with only about 40 percent believing it was fair.[7] It is not surprising that Democrats thought the result unfair and Republicans thought it fair, but the telling fact is that even independents thought the election was more unfair than fair.

In addition, the survey asked people to rate the Supreme Court on a "feeling thermometer" from 0 to 100. Again, around the first twelve days of December, people's feelings toward the Supreme Court dropped sharply by about five points, a drop of 7.5 points among Democrats, a drop of 5.7 among independents, and an increase of 4.3 among Republicans. It is hard to know whether this will have a lasting effect, but there is no question that people noticed that the Supreme Court intruded in the electoral process in a way that only partisan Republicans found acceptable.

The protracted election might also have an impact on people's feelings of efficacy and desire to vote. The data in the National Election Studies provide some evidence that Democrats and independents (but not Republicans) were more likely to think that people don't have any say in government after the Supreme Court became involved. But there is also evidence that people were more likely to think that their vote matters after the Supreme Court decision. It is hard to reconcile these two results, except to say that they indicate that people noticed what happened in Florida.

THE FUTURE OF AMERICAN POLITICS

Two issues about the future of American politics emerge from the 2000 election. One concerns the legitimacy of American electoral and judicial institutions; the other involves predicting what the next election will bring.

American institutions are remarkably durable. Doubtless the Republic will survive the debacle in Florida, but the outcome in *Bush v. Gore* will almost certainly have implications for future nominations to the Supreme Court, especially if the Democrats retain the control of the Senate that they fortuitously acquired in June 2001 when Senator James Jeffords, previously a Republican from Vermont, changed his identification to Independent, thereby giving the Democrats control of the upper house. It is even possible that some good things will come out of the events in Florida. New voting systems are already being installed in Florida, and other states are considering reforms as well. Political organizers will now be able to claim with some justification that single votes—or at least small numbers of votes—can matter. Perhaps that salutary lesson will encourage some segments of a disillusioned electorate to return to their polling places.

As for future elections, American politics appears to be in a period of extraordinary balance in which the presidency and the Congress will be up for grabs. Each party has substantial internal divisions and each is vulnerable to issues and to insurgencies from within, but each has also been able to control the issue agenda and its factions so as to win the presidency. It is always possible, of course, that social movements such as civil rights or Christian conservatism could disrupt one or the other of the parties, but problems of performance may be more devastating to the parties than anything else. George W. Bush has to worry most about economic downturns, foreign policy debacles, and the risk of political and personal scandals that has become so conspicuous a feature of American political culture since Watergate, Iran-Contra, Whitewater, and the Clinton impeachment. And he has to worry about them in a context in which his presidency and his power are precariously balanced on a few votes in Florida, in the House of Representatives, in the Senate, and in the Supreme Court.

NOTES

1. Nancy Burns, Donald R. Kinder, Steven J. Rosenstone, Virginia Sapiro, and the National Election Studies, *National Election Studies, 2000: Pre-/Post-Election Study*. (Ann Arbor: University of Michigan, Center for Political Studies, 2001).

2. The National Election Studies have a battery of four questions to measure "moral traditionalism." These questions ask whether new morals are causing societal breakdown, whether we should adjust our views to changed moral behavior, whether there would be fewer problems if we emphasized traditional family ties, and whether we should tolerate each other's morality. The index formed from these four items correlates very highly with the moral conservatism index.

3. In these paragraphs, all of the statements about which groups are favored are based on "feeling thermometers" in the National Election Studies, which ask respondents to say how warm they feel toward a group such as Christian fundamentalists or poor people.

4. Henry E. Brady, Michael Herron, Walter Mebane, Jasjeet Sekhon, Kenneth Shotts, and Jonathan Wand, "Law and Data: The Butterfly Ballot Episode," *PS: Political Science and Politics* (March 2001): 59–69; Jonathan N. Wand, Kenneth W. Shotts, Jasjeet S. Sekhon, Walter R. Mebane, Jr., Michael C. Herron, Henry E. Brady, "The Butterfly Did It: The Aberrant Vote for Buchanan in Palm Beach County, Florida," Working Paper, 2001, available at: http://elections.fas.harvard.edu/; Henry E. Brady and Laurel Elms, "Mapping the Buchanan Vote Escarpment in Palm Beach County, Florida," Paper presented at the meetings of the Public Choice Society. San Antonio, Texas, March 9–11, 2001.

5. James E. Campbell and James C. Garand, eds., *Before the Vote: Forecasting American National Elections* (Thousand Oaks, Calif.: Sage Publications, 2000).

6. Larry Bartels and John Zaller, "Presidential Vote Models: A Recount," *P.S. Political Science and Politics* (March 2001): 9–20.

7. The post-election interviewing by the National Election Studies does not create a random sample for every day, so the observed changes could be the result of the changing composition of the people interviewed. I have checked this possibility by extensive internal analysis of the data and by considering other published polls. The results reported in the text seem quite genuine. (My thanks to Richard Goulding for researching the other polls.)

3

THE RIGHT TO VOTE
AND ELECTION 2000

ALEXANDER KEYSSAR

THE ELECTION OF NOVEMBER 2000 LAUNCHED AN unprecedented rhetorical celebration of the right to vote. President Clinton got in on the act characteristically early, declaring on November 8 that voting was "our most fundamental right." The razor-thin margin of the election meant to the president that "No American will ever be able to seriously say again, 'My vote doesn't count'." As the legal and political battle over the Florida recount escalated, both the Bush and the Gore camps piously invoked the "sacred" right to vote (and in Gore's case, the right to have one's vote counted); their lawyers did likewise in briefs filed in numerous courts. The celebration was bipartisan and echoed everywhere by the pundits, who were everywhere. Not since the passage of the landmark Voting Rights Act of 1965 had the phrase "the right to vote" passed the lips of so many people in so short a time.[1]

The election also gave rise to an extraordinary number of complaints about people being deprived of their right to vote, making disfranchisement a more prominent subject than it had been at any time since the 1960s. Elderly Jews in Palm Beach county claimed that they had been disfranchised by the "butterfly ballot," which duped them into voting for Patrick Buchanan rather than Al Gore. Black voters reported that they had been intimidated en route to the polls and mistakenly told that they were not registered; Reverend Jesse Jackson, among others, linked their treatment to the South's sordid history of racial disfranchisement. Numerous Republicans, including former presidential candidate and war hero Bob Dole, railed against the potential injustice of depriving overseas soldiers of the franchise simply because their ballots lacked a postmark.

The rhetoric, the claims and counterclaims, testified to the presence of a broad democratic presumption in our political culture: Americans believe that everyone, or nearly everyone, has the right to vote and that it is wrong to prevent people from exercising that right. That belief is not merely self-congratulatory and patriotic, a verbal cloak draped around our eagerness to supervise other people's elections. Although strong anti-democratic currents have often swirled through American political life, most citizens believe that our governing institutions are—and ought to be—grounded in universal suffrage or something very close to it.

That conviction, a fundamental tenet of our political ideology, renders all the more jarring one of the stranger developments of the post-election conflict: the blunt expression of a legal argument denying that Americans actually possess a right to vote in presidential elections. This argument took its most dramatic form when the Florida legislature threatened, and indeed planned, to take matters into its own hands to guarantee the election of George W. Bush. If the legal wrangling had not ended by December 12, the Republican-dominated legislature intended to meet in special session and choose electors by itself. The justification for such an action stemmed from the wording of Article II of the United States Constitution, which specifies that "each state shall appoint, in such manner as the legislature thereof may direct, a number of electors" who would cast their ballots for president. According to Florida's Republicans, the legislature had the power to dispense with popular elections altogether.[2]

This perspective was not confined to the Sunshine State. It also appeared at the U.S. Supreme Court, beginning on Friday, December 1, 2000, when the Court heard oral arguments in the case of *George W. Bush v. Palm Beach County Canvassing Board*, the first of two cases decided by the nation's highest tribunal. Late in the hearing, Justice Antonin Scalia interrogated Al Gore's attorney, Laurence Tribe, about the knotty legal intersection of Florida statutes, the Florida constitution, and Article II of the federal Constitution, which provides for the election of the president. Florida's constitution did guarantee the right to vote of the state's citizens, Scalia acknowledged, but "in fact, there is no right of suffrage under Article II."[3]

Scalia's passing comment was reaffirmed and underscored in the Court's decision in the second case, *Bush v. Gore*. En route to handing the election to Bush, the majority opinion declared that "the individual citizen has no federal constitutional right to vote for electors for the President of the United States unless and until the state legislature chooses a statewide election as the means to implement its power to appoint members of the Electoral College." Going a step further, the majority observed that "the State . . . after granting the franchise in the special context of Article II, can take back the power to appoint electors." Under at least some circumstances, state legislatures thus possess the authority to bypass the electorate and determine on their own the identity of presidential electors.[4]

It is, of course, unlikely that a state legislature would ever utilize this authority, but if the 2000 election taught us anything, it is that the unlikely can happen. Most Americans, moreover, would be surprised—and perhaps outraged—to hear that this loophole in their right to vote even exists. (It's a reasonably safe bet that relatively few people actually read the dense verbiage of the decision in *Bush v. Gore*.) Indeed, based on a large, if utterly unscientific, sample of people I have spoken to since the election (including many encountered through the modern medium of radio talk shows), most Americans believe that the federal Constitution contains a clearly stated and affirmative guarantee of their right to vote in all elections, federal and state. This is not the case. The Bill of Rights protects our freedom of speech and conscience, our right to be secure from unreasonable searches and seizures, and perhaps even our ability to carry semi-automatic weapons, but it makes no mention of voting. The legal edifice of voting rights in the United States is, in fact, a complex and awkward structure, erected piecemeal in the course of a long and contentious history. That history is not a simple story of the steady and progressive enlargement of the franchise, but rather a more complicated and surprising narrative of retreats as well as advances, of efforts to restrict the suffrage as well as extend it to new claimants. The weight of that history was felt in diverse ways during election 2000.

I

The road to Tallahassee originated in Philadelphia in 1787. There, after a pointed but not very prolonged debate, the Founding Fathers decided not to embed a federal standard for suffrage in the Constitution. They chose instead to say little about the right to vote in federal elections and nothing at all about suffrage in state and local elections. The only direct mention of the subject came in Article I, Section 2, which provided that in elections for the House of Representatives "the Electors in each State shall have the Qualifications requisite for Electors of the most numerous Branch of the State Legislature." The right to vote in congressional elections was therefore yoked to the franchise in each state, but the states themselves set the standard.[5]

The decision to let the states decide who could and could not vote, even in federal elections, rested on pragmatic political considerations. Although Benjamin Franklin made an eloquent appeal for a broad national franchise, few of his much younger colleagues at the Federal Convention believed in anything close to universal suffrage (the phrase itself did not come into common usage until the 1840s); many thought that voting was a "privilege" rather than a "right"; and they disagreed among themselves about where to draw the line between voters and nonvoters. So did the states from which they came. By the time the federal Constitution was drafted, each state had already established its own suffrage provisions, and they differed significantly. Shrewdly—but perhaps lacking the foresight for which they are so renowned—the drafters decided to dodge the issue so that they would not jeopardize ratification of the Constitution itself. "The right of suffrage was a tender point and strongly guarded by most of the state constitutions," observed Oliver Ellsworth of Connecticut.[6] "The people will not readily subscribe to the national Constitution, if it should subject them to be disfranchised." James Madison made a similar point in *The Federalist*.

At the nation's birth, then, the only guarantees of a right to vote were inscribed in state constitutions, and their initial provisions were far from democratic. In all states except Vermont (then, as now—but not in the years in between—a radical stronghold), voting was restricted to property owners or taxpayers; women were excluded everywhere but in New Jersey; free blacks were barred in several states; and slaves, of course, had no claim on the franchise. The shape of the electorate, however, changed significantly during the first half of the nineteenth century, as pressures of various types—including shifting beliefs, a desire to encourage settlement, and the need to raise militias—led one state after another to remove property and taxpaying requirements from its constitution.

Indeed, in some states immigrants who had not yet become citizens were allowed to vote, on the assumption that the exercise of that right would act as an incentive to settlement and citizenship alike. But this impulse to democratize was not unalloyed: The scrapping of financial qualifications was often accompanied by the erection of new, more targeted barriers to voting, such as the addition of the word "white" to constitutional provisions everywhere outside of New England or the prohibition of voting by men who were declared to be "paupers." "Two steps forward, one step back," was, and continued to be, the rhythm of reform in suffrage law.

Indeed, in most states, the franchise was narrowed, along one axis or another, between the 1850s and World War I. This was a period when skepticism about, or hostility toward, democracy was growing among the nation's more elite and "respectable" citizens. In the South, white Democrats went to extraordinary and well-known lengths to disfranchise African-Americans whose ability to vote had been formally secured by the ratification of the Fifteenth Amendment in 1870. It is less well known that a similar, if more modest, movement occurred in the North, aimed largely at immigrants and industrial workers. Literacy tests (complete with grandfather clauses), lengthy residency requirements, cumbersome registration rules, taxpaying qualifications to vote for new offices, prohibitions of voting by people who received aid from the state: All of these devices and others were used to narrow the portals to the ballot box in states from New England to California. And nearly all of these legal provisions remained in force until the middle of the twentieth century. In the 1930s, several states prevented jobless relief recipients from voting on the grounds that they were technically "paupers." In New York, literacy in English was a qualification for voting into the 1960s.

For most of our nation's history, then, the shape of the electorate was determined by a crazy quilt of state laws that varied not only in their details but in some of their major substantive provisions. (The same was true of the procedural laws governing access to the ballot, the counting of votes, and election protests.) With few exceptions, moreover, the validity of those state laws was upheld by federal courts until the 1940s and even later. The courts indeed seemed so eager to keep Washington away from voting issues that they repeatedly upheld southern provisions, such as literacy tests and even the white primary, that were blatant attempts to circumvent the Fifteenth Amendment. Thanks to the legacy of the Founding Fathers, the federal government's involvement in suffrage law was belated, and even then it had to be superimposed on the existing fabric of state laws.

The federal government's first significant intervention, of course, came during Reconstruction, with the adoption of the Fourteenth and Fifteenth Amendments as well as legislation designed to enforce those amendments. The amendments themselves inscribed the phrase "the right to vote" into the Constitution for the first time, but, setting a critical precedent, they did not actually confer the franchise on anyone. What they did, instead, was to prohibit the states from denying male (and only *male* citizens) the right to vote on the particular grounds of "race, color, or previous condition of servitude."

That legal structure was replicated in the Nineteenth Amendment (1920), which prevented the states from discriminating based on sex. It was also the model for the immensely important wave of legal activity that effectively nationalized suffrage in the 1960s and early 1970s: the Twenty-fourth Amendment (barring poll taxes in federal elections); the Twenty-sixth (lowering the voting age to eighteen); the Voting Rights Acts of 1965 and 1970; and a string of critical Supreme Court decisions, including *Harper v. Virginia* and *Oregon v. Mitchell*. In these rulings, the Court concluded that various state limitations on the franchise, among them poll taxes and lengthy residence requirements, violated the Equal Protection Clause of the Fourteenth Amendment. Each step in this transformation and nationalization of suffrage law was achieved by placing specific restraints on what the states could do, rather than affirmatively granting the right to vote to particular groups. In 1963, an alternative approach, a proposed constitutional amendment to "establish a free and universal franchise throughout the United States," made little headway in Congress.

The United States did finally achieve something close to universal suffrage by the early 1970s, much later than is commonly believed, yet it did so without the polity ever formally embracing the principle of universal suffrage. The long, contested, and occasionally violent history of voting rights, moreover, reveals that there has always been a strong anti-democratic impulse in politics, that there have always been sizable numbers of Americans who have not believed that political rights should be shared by all citizens or who have doubted that large sectors of the population can competently exercise the franchise. (This latter view was resurrected during the turmoil in Florida in the form of the oft-repeated observation that people who weren't intelligent enough to fill out their ballots correctly did not deserve to vote in any case.) The force of these anti-democratic sentiments has not been constant, of course, and the numbers of those willing to profess their doubts has varied as well, which is why the trajectory of suffrage has not followed a neat linear path but has rather been marked by episodes of contraction as well as expansion.

II

The complex and variegated mix of state and federal laws that structure the franchise and election procedures helped to shape the legal drama of election 2000. The primary guarantee of the voting rights of Florida citizens was embedded in their state constitution, and the procedural laws governing the election, as well as its aftermath, were those of the state. This, of course, was why the state courts and state judges (not to mention Secretary of State Kather-

ine Harris) played such a prominent role in the dispute and why
the lower federal courts declined to get involved when first asked
to do so by the Republicans. Despite the nationalization of suffrage
law in the 1960s—yet also because of the particular, indirect structure of that nationalization—the role of the federal government
and the federal courts is limited to specific issues (particularly racial
discrimination), most of which were not at stake in the election dispute. It was for that reason that the Republicans and their judicial
allies, fearing that the Florida courts would not rule in their favor,
went to such lengths to find federal questions that a presumably
friendlier Supreme Court alone could adjudicate.

Justice Scalia's invocation, and interpretation, of Article II was
one way to do so. If Article II's reference to the role of state legislatures trumped the Florida constitution's guarantee of a right to
vote, then the case for federal intervention in a matter usually left
to the states was strengthened. (Such an interpretation also undercut the Florida Supreme Court's posture that all necessary steps,
such as recounts, should be taken to protect a basic right of
Florida's citizens, as specified in the state's constitution.) Making
this argument, as the U.S. Supreme Court acknowledged, meant
denying that the American people possessed the right to vote for
president, but what's a little disfranchisement among friends? A
similar goal underpinned the Republicans' surprising but ultimately successful claim that hand recounts raised an equal protection issue under the Fourteenth Amendment. The Equal Protection Clause, which made its first appearance in voting rights law in
a decision striking down poll taxes in state elections, provides the
most general, and unspecific, constitutional rationale for federal intervention in voting rights cases. It was mobilized by the Warren
Court as a means of extending the Fifteenth Amendment's explicit
ban on racial bars to other forms of discriminatory disfranchisement not expressly mentioned in any constitutional amendments.
Nearly all commentators believed initially that its applicability to
election 2000 was a stretch (to say the least), and several of the jus-

tices agreed, but in the end this claim enabled the final decision about recounts to be relocated from the Florida courts to the Republican-dominated tribunal in Washington.[7]

Other features of the post-election controversy echoed long-standing dynamics and patterns in the history of suffrage. One involved the voting rights of soldiers. Americans have long idealized the concept of the citizen soldier, but from the Revolution onward, the ranks of the military have been filled by recruits drawn from the unpropertied and uneducated classes and from minority groups, many of whom could not qualify for the suffrage. In part because of this clash between an ideal and the practice of politics, soldiers throughout American history have been in the vanguard of efforts to expand the franchise. During the American Revolution and the War of 1812, militiamen agitated successfully to lower property requirements so that men who fought for their country could vote; the enfranchisement of blacks during Reconstruction owed much to their service in the Civil War; African-American and Native American veterans of World War II were the point men in suffrage movements in the late 1940s and 1950s. (Nor should one forget that Congress approved the Nineteenth Amendment during World War I and that President Woodrow Wilson urged its passage "as a war measure.") It has, in effect, long been rhetorically and politically difficult to justify disfranchising individuals who were risking their lives for their country.[8]

Not surprisingly, then, soldiers constituted the one group of participants in Florida's election whose potentially illegal votes were all counted in the end. The issue arose amid claims that hundreds, perhaps thousands, of ballots cast by overseas military personnel were, or might be, disqualified because they lacked appropriate— and technically required—signatures or postmarks. Because members of the Armed Forces (particularly officers, who are more likely to vote) were presumed to be disproportionately Republican, the disqualification of these ballots was commonly regarded as potentially harmful to Governor Bush. Consequently, the Republicans filed suit to reinstate the ballots and clamored loudly about the injustice of disfranchising individuals who were protecting the nation. The clamor was effective: Faced with the unpalatable prospect of appearing to deny political rights to those "defending democracy" abroad, local canvassing boards became less punctilious about procedures, and the Democrats retreated, led by Senator Joseph Lieberman, who indicated that he "would give the benefit of the doubt to ballots coming in from military personnel."[9]

A second echo of deeper patterns in the evolution of suffrage was sounded far from Florida, in the liberal state of Massachusetts, which provided a remarkable contemporary illustration of the historical truth that the franchise in the United States does indeed contract as well as expand. Massachusetts was one of the few states where those convicted of crimes were never barred from the polls in the nineteenth or twentieth centuries. (This was true despite a quite illiberal history of franchise requirements in the Bay State: Massachusetts adopted a literacy test in the 1850s and barred paupers from voting for many decades.) But that distinction began to crumble more than a year ago, when politicians, led by Republican Governor Paul Cellucci, responded to the political activism of some prison inmates (who charged that the prisons were mismanaged and that death rates were abnormally high) by drafting a constitutional amendment to disfranchise men and women serving prison terms. The state legislature overwhelmingly approved the amendment, and on November 7, the Bay State's electorate did likewise, disfranchising roughly 10,000 individuals.[10]

III

Although convicted felons could still vote in Massachusetts in November 2000, they were already prohibited from doing so in nearly all the other states. Forty-seven states disfranchised felons who were serving prison terms; many extended the ban through periods of parole and probation; and roughly a dozen, including Florida, completely barred ex-felons, unless their rights were expressly restored by the state. In all, an estimated 3.9 million people were disfranchised by laws stripping political rights from those convicted of felonies. They constitute by far the largest group of citizens who are formally denied access to the ballot box in the United States.[11]

The history of laws disfranchising felons is long, complex, and, in some of its features, not well understood. These laws first appeared in some states as early as the late eighteenth century and seemed to be a continuation of a venerable European tradition of imposing "civil death" on those who committed serious crimes. Notably, they were first put on the books in the United States during a period when voting was commonly regarded as a "privilege" rather than a right. Equally notably, they were not universal. Before the Civil War, such laws were enacted in roughly two dozen states. (Why numerous states did not adopt them would be an excellent topic for a budding legal historian.) They became more commonplace in the late nineteenth century, and in the South the laws were generally rewritten to target "black crimes" and exclude as many African-Americans as possible. Alabama's 1901 constitution listed more than two dozen crimes that would result in disfranchisement, including bigamy and vagrancy.[12]

The rationale for these laws was always a bit problematic, particularly once voting came to be understood as a right. Disfranchisement did not effectively serve the conventional purposes of criminal punishment (such as prevention or rehabilitation), nor was there a clearly discernible link between the commission of a felony and undesirable political behavior. Late nineteenth-century politicians and judges groped for such a link, arguing that felons might band together and vote to repeal the criminal laws and that banning felons was necessary to "preserve the purity of the ballot box." But both arguments were conjectural at best.

Indeed, by the early 1970s the state laws disfranchising felons and ex-felons were being subjected to serious logical and judicial challenge. A federal appeals court noted that "courts have been hard pressed to define the state interest served by laws disenfranchising persons convicted of crimes," and the California Supreme Court concluded that California's law violated the Equal Protection Clause of the Fourteenth Amendment. This challenge was rebuffed by the U.S. Supreme Court in 1974 in *Richardson v. Ramirez*. The majority opinion, written by then-Associate Justice William Rehnquist, concluded that state laws disfranchising felons were sanctioned by a phrase of the Fourteenth Amendment that implicitly allowed suffrage exclusions for "participation in rebellion, or other crime." The weight of history was felt once again: Language drafted during the cauldron of Reconstruction and seemingly aimed at Confederate rebels was invoked to legitimize the disfranchisement of people who robbed grocery stores in the 1970s.

Since *Richardson v. Ramirez*, the number of convicted felons and ex-felons has grown substantially, and subsequent legal challenges have made little headway. By the year 2000, moreover, a majority of those disfranchised under the laws were African-American or Hispanic. In some states, including Alabama and Florida, between 15 and 30 percent of all black males were disfranchised because of their criminal records. Although convicted felons were unlikely to have voted in large numbers, those who did were certainly far more likely to have voted for the Democrats than for George Bush.

This fact was not lost on Republicans in Florida, one of the two states with the largest number of persons (more than 600,000) disfranchised by the felon exclusion laws. (Texas was the other.) Beginning in 1998, Republican officials in Florida went to substantial lengths to ensure that felons and ex-felons would not be permitted to vote. They purchased lists of convicted felons from private corporations, attempted to match the names on those lists with registered voters (a difficult process, with abundant opportunity for error, particularly since the state did not have social security numbers), and purged the voter rolls, often without notifying individuals that their registrations had been voided. The lists included the names of 8,000 men and women who had committed misdemeanors, rather than felonies, in Texas, as well as thousands of other persons whose political rights had been restored in the states where their crimes had been committed. Although many local election officials complained that the lists were filled with errors, and executives from the corporations providing the lists registered concern about the matching process, the state Division of Elections persisted. The upshot was that a large number, probably in the thousands, of perfectly legal would-be voters were not permitted to vote on November 7. Almost certainly, most of them were black. In Tallahassee, a black minister, Willie D. Whiting, was prevented from voting because election officials thought he was Willie J. Whiting, a convicted felon. Willie D. Whiting had no criminal record.[13]

IV

Laws governing the right to vote per se are part of a continuum or spectrum of election law that also includes statutes specifying registration and voting procedures as well as methods of counting ballots. The existence of this often voluminous body of laws illustrates a fundamental tension, even paradox, of democracy. Democratic theory is grounded in the assumption that the people can be trusted to use the electoral process to make competent judgments about the leaders who will exercise authority in their name. Yet the elaborate nature of our election laws also suggests that we do not wholly trust those who exercise power to conduct elections fairly and cleanly. Even in the eighteenth century, some political thinkers worried that officeholders or seekers would try to manipulate election rules to their own personal and partisan advantage.

As courts and politicians have long recognized, an individual's formal right to vote can easily be undercut by procedural obstacles to voting or by corrupt or biased counts. In northern cities in the late nineteenth century, political elites often winnowed the electorate by imposing cumbersome registration and residency rules, such as limiting the number of days on which one could register, requiring annual registration, and compelling immigrants to present their naturalization papers and migrants to provide written evidence that they had canceled their previous registration. Among the many methods of reducing the black vote in the South was the "eight box" system, which required voters to drop ballots for different offices into different boxes, which white registrars repeatedly shifted from one place to another, like a game of three-card monte, to confuse voters. The resulting invalid ballots would then not be counted.

State laws governing access to the ballot box are far more voter-friendly than they were a century ago, in part because of the interventions of the Warren Court and the passage in 1993 of the Motor Voter bill. Residency requirements are much shorter, registration periods are longer, and absentee ballots are far easier to obtain. Yet the glare of publicity generated by the closeness of election 2000 made clear that problems remain. In Illinois, Florida, and many other states, voters who had registered at motor vehicle bureaus discovered that their paperwork had never made it to voter registration offices. In Cleveland, thousands of would-be voters were denied the ballot because their polling places had changed, without notice. Voter rolls are swollen with the names of people who are dead or have moved, yet the periodic scrubbing of voter rolls deleted the names of bona fide voters. Men and women who arrived at polling places and were told they could not vote had difficulty getting assistance; poll workers spent endless hours on the phones getting busy signals as they tried to reach central offices to confirm information or get advice. (In Palm Beach County, overworked officials were unable to respond quickly to early indications that the butterfly ballot was causing chaos.) Some states and precincts permitted questionable voters to cast "provisional" ballots; others did not.[14]

The problems, as we all learned, extended to the counting of ballots. Throughout the nation, and especially in poorer neighborhoods, votes were counted by ancient machines with extraordinarily high error rates. Some of New York's machines are forty years old and have 27,000 parts; trained service mechanics are poorly paid and therefore scarce. (Disdain for funding the public sector is not conducive to the proper care and maintenance of voting systems.) Confusing ballot designs in Florida (not only in Palm Beach County) and elsewhere led scores of thousands of voters to cast ballots that would be voided. Optical scanners sometimes did not count an X (rather than a filled-in space or an arrow) as a valid vote; writing the name of a candidate, in addition to marking the right spot, also led to voided ballots. Relatively few polling places had technology that would alert voters to mismarked ballots and permit them to vote again; in some where the technology was present, officials turned the option off. Absentee ballots, it turned out, were often never counted at all.[15]

There was nothing necessarily partisan about these procedural glitches or the use of antiquated and poorly maintained machines. Theresa LePore, the designer of the "butterfly ballot" in Palm Beach County, was a conscientious Democratic election official who had no interest in trying to lure elderly Jewish residents into voting for Patrick Buchanan. Thousands of ballots in black precincts of Duval County were thrown out because sympathetic local activists mistakenly told voters to mark every page. Nonetheless, the imprecision, sloppiness, confusion, and quasi-formal indifference to voters seemed utterly incongruent with the goal of protecting the exercise of what President Clinton and others called "our most fundamental right." "You know why we never paid attention to this until now?" asked the co-director of the Indiana Elections Division. "Because we don't want to know that our democracy isn't really so sacred."[16]

What the confused procedures and mechanics reflect, in fact, is an electoral system that functions to serve the major parties rather than voters. The detailed laws governing election procedures in most states were not designed as a nonpartisan effort to make sure that the "voice of the people" was heard. They evolved instead as the rules of engagement between two hefty adversaries, each seeking to maximize its own turnout and minimize outright cheating by the other party. In New Jersey, in the late nineteenth century, for example, Republicans passed a law requiring prospective voters to register in person, on one of a few selected workdays. The law applied only to the seven largest cities and was clearly aimed at the Democratic machines. Several years later, the Democrats succeeded in revising the law to permit any registered voter, such as a party worker, to enroll others by affidavit. The upshot was that the well-organized major parties could easily register their own voters, while independents faced a burdensome and cumbersome procedure that frequently kept them from voting.[17]

It is not much of a leap from nineteenth-century New Jersey to Florida's Seminole County in the fall of 2000. In that heavily Republican county, election officials permitted Republican Party workers to come to the registration office and correct the misnumbered absentee ballot applications of identified Republican voters. The Democrats may or may not have been permitted to do the same thing (they failed to ask), but surely independent voters never had the opportunity, particularly since they were not notified of any errors. Such occurrences have long been commonplace; the rules are written by the major parties and administered by officials who are often party functionaries. Florida's Secretary of State and co-chair of the Bush campaign, Katherine Harris, was merely the highly visible, well-dressed tip of the iceberg. In most states, moreover, the rules make it particularly difficult for third parties to get on the ballot and challenge the hegemony of the Democrats and Republicans. In North Carolina, Ralph Nader was unable to get on the ballot because he lacked the requisite 50,000 signatures required by May 17, 2000. Because he was also not designated as an "official" write-in candidate, votes cast for him—and they were numerous—were, by law, not counted.[18]

V

It was precisely because the formal "right to vote" shades into matters of election procedures and vote counting that race became such a freighted issue in the 2000 election. Nationwide, the NAACP, working with other organizations including the Democratic Party, made a concerted and unprecedented effort to increase African-American turnout. It identified 2.8 million households that it bombarded with literature and phone calls. In Florida, which professionals in both parties knew all along would be a key battleground, these efforts were remarkably successful. There were 300,000 more black voters than there had been in 1996. Black voters, however, seemed to encounter far more than their share of difficulties actually casting their ballots and getting their votes counted. On election day itself, African-Americans registered numerous complaints that they had encountered intimidation on the way to the polls, discovered that their names were not on registration lists, were refused assistance, or were told that they were listed as convicted felons.

In the aftermath of the election, it became clear that the problem had a systemic dimension. Predominantly black precincts were understaffed (especially given the unusually high turnout) and more commonly equipped with older, error-prone punch-card voting machines. A study conducted by USA Today determined that ballots were four times more likely to be thrown out in majority-black precincts than in those that were predominantly white; the United States Civil Rights Commission concluded that African-Americans in Florida were ten times more likely than whites to have their votes discarded. Eighty-eight of the one hundred precincts with the largest number of discarded votes had black majorities. Similar, if less extreme, patterns were discerned elsewhere in the country, including St. Louis and Chicago. The Civil Rights Commission also found that some counties in Florida had failed to provide bilingual ballots to Hispanic and Haitian residents and that there was an apparent racial bias in the scrubbing of voter rolls. In Miami-Dade, the state's largest county, African-Americans constituted only 20 percent of the population but 65 percent of the voters whose names were purged.[19]

The African-American population, in Florida and throughout the nation, responded with outrage, seeing in the election abundant proof that racial discrimination at the polls had not ended with the passage of the Voting Rights Acts. Mass protest rallies were organized, charging that the Republicans had conspired to disfranchise blacks either because they were black or because they were an easily identified bloc of Democratic voters (or both); black members of the Florida legislature angrily attacked the legislature's plan to choose electors by itself; the NAACP sued the state of Florida; and the federal Commission on Civil Rights launched hearings to gather information. Indeed, six months after the election, with normalcy having returned to Washington, residual anger about the election seemed to be confined largely to the black community. The Congressional Black Caucus held its own hearings on election reform, partly to voice its ongoing distress and partly to prod congressional leaders who were stalling efforts to address the election debacle. In June, the Civil Rights Commission issued a draft report concluding that "injustice, ineptitude and inefficiency" in Florida had spawned "widespread disenfranchisement" that disproportionately affected minority voters. (Not surprisingly, perhaps, the two Republican members of the commission, as well as Florida's governor, Jeb Bush, denounced the commission's report.) Polls indicated that a large majority of the black community, which voted overwhelmingly for Al Gore, believed that racial discrimination had played a role in the election and that George Bush had been its beneficiary.[20]

The role that deliberate racial discrimination or partisan hard-ball played in the difficulties encountered by black voters, both in casting their ballots and in having those ballots counted, is unclear and may never be clear. But there can be no doubt that the response of African-Americans was both deeply felt and one more expression of the weight of history on the present. Being denied access to the polls or having one's vote tossed out because of mechanical failures inescapably had a different meaning, a more powerful resonance, for black Americans than it did for whites. African-American senior citizens in the South were young adults who were barred from the polls in 1960; they witnessed the beating and even killing of men and women who tried to register. Their children know the stories; their grandchildren know the history. African-Americans at the beginning of the twenty-first century are far more aware than whites that achieving universal suffrage was a long struggle, that our country, for most of its history, was far from democratic. Election 2000 was a sharp and painful reminder both of an ugly past and of the fragility of political rights in a nation with a long track record of discrimination.

VI

The unique legal drama that concluded election 2000 understandably overshadowed some of the election's less distinctive, but no less important, features. The popular vote was closely divided, as it had been in several recent elections, with neither major party displaying clear national dominance. A third-party candidate probably affected the outcome, as was also true in 1992, when Ross Perot's candidacy clearly contributed to Clinton's election. Minorities, especially African-Americans, remained firmly attached to the Democratic Party, as were unmarried women, and nearly two-thirds of the nation's white males voted Republican. The Republicans dominated the Sunbelt, whereas the Democrats ran well in the Northeast, the Pacific West, and along the Mississippi River. (The large red and blue television maps that showed a totally red—or Republican—heartland obscured the strength of the Democrats in the commercial and transportation hubs along the nation's primary waterway.)[21]

One other "routine" feature of the election was that half of the electorate did not show up at the polls. Nationally, turnout was 51 percent, up slightly from 1996 but four percentage points lower than in 1992. Variations among the states were substantial, ranging from Minnesota's high of 69 percent to a low in Hawaii of only 41 percent. Notably, the ten states with the highest turnout were all in the North, stretching in a band from Maine to Oregon (plus the far northern neighbor of Alaska); below-average turnout was concentrated in the Sunbelt. Although data linking social characteristics to political participation are not yet available, it is almost certain that the class skew in turnout that has been so prevalent in recent decades was present in November 2000 as well. The likelihood that a person will vote in the United States correlates directly with income and education. The poor are far less likely to vote than the wealthy; men and women with college and graduate degrees vote at twice the rate of those with a high school education or less. In 1996, turnout among citizens in families with incomes of less than $15,000 was 40 percent; for families with incomes over $75,000, the figure was 76 percent. The modern American electorate is not a random sample of the population.[22]

Turnout in American elections, of course, has been falling (with a few temporary interruptions) since the late nineteenth century, when 75 to 85 percent of eligible voters commonly went to the polls. The historical pattern is distinctively American, as is the class skew in participation. Precisely why this is so remains a matter of debate (the analysis of turnout has itself become something of a cottage industry), but it is surely not a coincidence that nonvoters come disproportionately from the same social groups that were, in the past, the targets of substantive and procedural restrictions on the franchise. Although relatively few Americans are now formally disfranchised, the burden of cumbersome procedures falls most heavily on the poor and less educated. In addition, the party system and political culture that evolved during the era of restricted suffrage continues to offer a relatively small, uninspiring range of choices to the nation's least well-off citizens. As the two-party system has been increasingly institutionalized, through ballot access rules and the public funding of already established parties, the ideological spectrum has narrowed, dissident voices have been harder to hear, and fewer Americans believe that the outcome of elections will matter much to them. Our recent patterns of nonparticipation have taken decades to solidify.[23]

Prior to the election, many pundits predicted that the apparent closeness of the presidential contest would yield a heavy turnout, perhaps the heaviest in thirty years. Obviously that prognosis was wrong, in part because of the discouraging dynamics of the electoral college: The outcome in many (even most) states, including California, New York, and much of the South, was no longer in doubt by early November. What is more interesting and perhaps significant is that the closeness of the election may have been less a stimulus to participation than a reflection of the same political practices and political culture that dampened turnout. This is so because the technique of contemporary politics, particularly presidential politics, is so heavily dependent on polling, which becomes more refined and sophisticated with every election cycle. Presidential candidates, coached by their teams of nonstop pollsters, deliberately aim for the center of the political spectrum. They avoid issues that are controversial (with high "negatives"), speak entirely in general terms about large matters (promising prosperity, for example), and only take stands that their pollsters tell them are attractive to the electorate. Because both major parties are using the same methods, a well-executed campaign should end up being close.

These practices would not necessarily have any impact on turnout if the pollsters considered the electorate to be the entire voting-age population of the nation. But they do not. The polling experts who work for political campaigns define the electorate as those men and women who are considered to be "likely voters," and "likely voters" are identified on the basis of their past voting behavior and socioeconomic characteristics. The felt needs and opinions of "unlikely" voters are disregarded or downplayed and rarely, if ever, make it onto a campaign's radar screen. Poor people who did not vote in 1996 may have been acutely concerned about job security, low wages, and the lack of health insurance, but they either were not called by pollsters or their responses were given little weight because they were unlikely to vote. The result of such practices, so visible in the presidential debates, was a concentration on narrow issues, such as prescription drug plans for senior citizens, that were of concern to targeted swing groups of "likely" middle-class voters. The vicious circle was completed, of course, when "unlikely" voters, faced with a campaign that ignored their most pressing needs, failed once again to show up at the polls. The practice of politics is, in effect, a mixture of self-fulfilling prophecy and calculated exclusions.[24]

There was also the role that money played in the election. Between January 1, 1999, and November 27, 2000, the two major parties raised nearly $460 million in "soft" or unregulated money, roughly double the total of four years earlier. This was in addition to official "hard" money contributions to presidential candidates and the hundreds of millions of dollars provided in federal funds. Election 2000 was the most expensive election in the nation's history (roughly $3 billion was spent on all races combined), and most of the funding came from people who could write checks larger than the median national income. Although the Republican war chest was bigger than that of the Democrats, it is unlikely that money played a decisive role in the outcome of the election. (Money did, however, play a key role in the selection of candidates. Primaries are in danger of becoming pro forma rituals to ratify the selection of candidates who have already won the fund-raising contest, such as George Bush.) But the role of big money is certainly a dispiriting fact to the average prospective voter, who is well aware that large donors have access and influence far greater than that possessed by most citizens. The very wealthy can trade large campaign donations for audiences with the president and cabinet members, nights in the Lincoln Bedroom, pardons, legislation affecting bankruptcy, and friendly appointments to the Federal Energy Regulation Commission.[25]

Money has long played an unseemly role in American politics, dating back at least to the middle of the nineteenth century, when almost all appointees to federal office were obliged to pay 2 percent of their salaries to the parties that got them their jobs. (An irony of the civil service reforms that banned such kickbacks is that both parties thereafter became more dependent on corporate funding.) But the raw and growing power of money in recent election campaigns threatens to undercut the value of the franchise itself, to transform egalitarian political institutions into hollow shells. A person's vote is his or her voice in selecting leaders and influencing policies, but the private financing of campaigns, particularly through unlimited contributions of soft money, permits some voices to be greatly amplified, to be easily heard above the chaotic hurly-burly of democracy. It is as though we had adopted a modern form of the archaic practice of plural voting, in which some citizens possessed one vote while others had four or five. Given the prominence of large donors in both parties, the recurrent spectacles of $10,000-a-plate dinners, the time and energy lavished on the rich at both the Republican and the Democratic conventions, it can hardly be surprising that most of the poor and the working-class stayed home on November 7.

VII

For most of us, election 2000 ended as it had begun: on television. We sat in our living rooms and watched reporters standing in the cold, outside the Supreme Court building in Washington, trying to figure out the import of the obliquely written majority opinion in *Bush v. Gore*. After an hour of uncertainty, it was over, ending with a legal whimper rather than a bang. Aesthetically unsatisfying and politically enraging as that denouement was to many, it did nonetheless testify to the stability of our institutions, to certain strengths in our political culture, and perhaps to the relative unimportance of politics in our daily lives. There was no looting or burning; no one physically attacked the Supreme Court; not a shot was fired at the relatively small number of demonstrators who did turn out to protest. Throughout the whole legal ordeal, there had never been mention of a coup d'etat by the military.

That said, election 2000 was not a pretty sight, and it is not likely to look any prettier in hindsight. The candidate who won the most votes did not take office. A popular, democratic process was taken over by high-priced lawyers making clever arguments under immense time pressure; the Republican legal strategy of stalling and delaying was effective. A majority of the justices of the Supreme Court voted in ways that were entirely consistent with their political ideologies and quite inconsistent with their recorded stands on legal issues. Critical procedural decisions in Florida were made by a secretary of state who was a partisan in the election, backed by a governor who was the brother of one of the candidates. The voting machines did not work, especially in poor neighborhoods. African-Americans were subject to discriminatory treatment and had their votes tossed out in unusually large numbers. The rich gave hundreds of millions of dollars to the two major parties, while the issues important to poor people were largely ignored. After several months of celebrating the quadrennial ritual of our political life, the highest tribunal finally said that the people did not have a right to vote for president anyway. As an updated portrait of democracy in America, election 2000 would not make Alexis de Tocqueville proud.

Moreover, the prospects for significant reform seem dim. Most states will likely get rid of their punch-card voting machines,

Florida has revamped its electoral procedures, and Congress may still pass a version of the McCain-Feingold campaign finance bill. But, thanks to the opposition of the small states, there is virtually no chance of abolishing the electoral college, despite significant popular support for doing so. Proposals for proportional representation and instant run-off voting, which would encourage third parties and inject new ideas into political life, meet a solid wall of opposition from mainstream politicians. A constitutional amendment to guarantee the right to vote in federal elections (a favorite of this author) would, at best, take years to enact. Ideas for making the process of registration and voting easier are countered by the (usually Republican) cry that they would encourage fraud. Although there has been more activity at the state level, the powers-that-be in Washington have generally stifled, rather than ridden, the reform energies unleashed by the election crisis. The men and women who have flourished in the current system have little desire to change it.

Yet our history suggests that we ought not to be too disheartened. The evolution of democratic institutions in the United States has never followed a straight line, and there have been many moments when democracy itself seemed to be in retreat. The voting rights of African-Americans were ripped from them between the 1870s and 1910; immigrants and workers also found it increasingly difficult to cast their ballots during those years. But those sharp and tragic injustices were eventually overcome. Democracy is not a fixed set of institutions and laws but rather a project, an ideal that we must constantly pursue, nurture, and revitalize. It takes imagination and work, and election 2000 has reminded us that there is much work to be done.[26]

NOTES

1. *New York Times*, November 9, 2000.
2. *New York Times*, November 23, 29, 30; December 1, 7, 9, 12, 2000.

3. *George W. Bush v. Palm Beach County Canvassing Board,* oral arguments, December 1, 2000, p. 55.

4. *Bush v. Gore*, 121 S. Ct. 526, 529 (2000).

5. The historical account in this section is drawn from my book, *The Right to Vote: The Contested History of Democracy in the United States* (New York: Basic Books, 2000).

6. Oliver Ellsworth, speech given on August 7, 1787, in Max Farrand, ed., *The Records of the Federal Convention of 1787* (New Haven, CT: Yale University Press, 1966), II: 201.

7. Keyssar, *Right to Vote*, pp. 271–273, 283–284.

8. All of these episodes and the general theme of voting rights for soldiers are discussed in *The Right to Vote*.

9. *New York Times*, November 20, 2000.

10. Massachusetts Department of Correction, *January 1, 2000 Inmate Statistics* (Boston, 2000), p. iii. Accounts of this initiative can be found in various publications of the Criminal Justice Policy Coalition. Available at www.state.ma.us/doc/.

11. For recent statistics, see *The Impact of Felony Disenfranchisement Laws in the United States,* a report by The Sentencing Project of Human Rights Watch, available at www.hrw.org/reports98/vote/usvot98o–01.htm.

12. The historical account here and in subsequent paragraphs can be found in *Right to Vote*, pp. 63, 162–163, 302–308.

13. John Lantigua, "How the GOP Gamed the System in Florida," *The Nation* (April 30, 2001): 11–17; *Washington Post*, May 30, 2001; John Lantigua, "Blacklisted in Florida," *Independent Weekly* (Durham, NC), May 9–15, 2001, pp. 23–29.

14. *Los Angeles Times*, December 11, 2000.

15. *Los Angeles Times*, December 11, 2000; *Washington Post*, May 31, 2001; *USA Today*, April 13, 2001.

16. *New York Times*, November 17, 2000; *Los Angeles Times*, December 11, 2000.

17. Keyssar, *Right to Vote*, pp. 105–116, 151–159.

18. *Raleigh News and Observer*, August 1, 2000.

19. *USA Today*, April 6 and 13, 2001; *Washington Post*, June 5, 2001; Commission on Civil Rights, "Confidential Draft, Executive Sum-

mary Points," dated June 5, 2001, reprinted in *Washington Post*, June 5, 2001.

20. *Washington Post*, June 5, 2001; *New York Times*, June 5, 6, 2001.

21. *New York Times*, November 9, 2000; *Washington Post*, November 8, 2000.

22. Keyssar, *Right to Vote*, pp. 320–322; *USA Today*, October 26, 2000. Turnout numbers for 2000 are from the Committee for the Study of the American Electorate.

23. Keyssar, *Right to Vote*, pp. 320–322.

24. This account is based on telephone discussions with several polling firms and a personal conversation with Peter Hart, the well-known political pollster.

25. *Washington Post*, November 6, 2000; other figures from *Common Cause News,* December 14, 2000, available at http://commoncause.org/publications/dec00/121500st.htm.

26. See Keyssar, *Right to Vote*, pp. 322–324.

PART TWO

THE COURT AND THE CONSTITUTION

4

THE SUPREME COURT
IN POLITICS

LARRY D. KRAMER*

From the character of the Supreme Court, I am sure the compromise in this particular, will be acquiesced in by the country. . . . The members of the Supreme Court are not politicians. They are born in a different atmosphere, and address themselves to different hearers.

**Senator Reverdy Johnson, supporting a bill
to bring the question of slavery in the territories
before the U.S. Supreme Court, July 25, 1848**

As both the nation's highest judicial body and also the one most removed from partisanship, the court can render a verdict that

---

*Thanks are due to a great many people for comments and conversation. I am especially grateful to John Ferejohn, Sanford Levinson, Michael McConnell, Pasquale Pasquino, Richard Pildes, Richard Posner, Robert Post, Jack Rakove, and Michel Rosenfeld.

all parties would be bound to respect as to how to resolve the
Florida vote.

Editorial, New York Times, November 25, 2000

BY THE EARLY 1850s, SOME MEMBERS OF THE U.S.
Supreme Court had apparently come to believe what many on
both sides of the slavery issue were saying, that the Court was the
only institution with the prestige and authority to solve the problem of slavery in the territories. They were wrong, and *Dred Scott
v. Sandford* is recalled as one of the worst missteps in Supreme
Court history: a foolish, failed effort to settle a highly charged political controversy. Chief Justice Roger Taney's career was ruined,
and the Court's reputation suffered wounds from which it took a
generation to recover.

The lesson of *Dred Scott* was not that the Court should avoid
controversial political disputes. Such disputes often threaten important constitutional values and present issues that the Court can
hardly ignore. The lesson was, rather, that the Court should tread
lightly when it ventures onto treacherous political ground. Conventional wisdom has thus long held that the Supreme Court *can*
decide highly charged issues, but that it should wait for a proper
case and do its best to present a united front. *Brown v. Board of Education* is the most famous example of this wisdom at work, and
the members of the Warren Court worked long and hard to
achieve unanimity before ordering the South to desegregate.

Viewed in this light, the Court's handling of *Bush v. Gore* is certainly odd. From the justices' early and unexpected willingness to
hear the case, to the bitterly divided final decision stopping any further recount in Florida, so much about the litigation seemed uncharacteristic, particularly coming from the Rehnquist Court.
Where was its oft-touted respect for states and state tribunals? How
can we explain the Court's decision to grant a last-minute stay?

Why did the five most conservative justices suddenly find new virtues in the Equal Protection Clause of the Fourteenth Amendment? Pointing to these and other surprising twists in the litigation, supporters of Vice President Gore decried the Court for casting law aside in the pursuit of partisan advantage. Supporters of the new president, in turn, defended the Court for its courageous intervention, while platoons of commentators dutifully lined up to applaud or berate the justices—invariably in accord with their own political loyalties. (Astonishingly, so far as I am aware, not a single conservative attacked the Court's decision, and not a single liberal defended it. Even impeachment produced at least a few maverick voices.)

The Court's handling of the case *was* peculiar in a number of respects. But given the high stakes and intense time pressures, that was inescapable and unsurprising. Still, we need to identify these peculiarities if we are to understand why the litigation unfolded as it did. For Bush supporters, the explanation is obvious: The crude effort of a runaway state court to award the presidency to Gore forced the Supreme Court's hand. Gore supporters offer a different, though equally damning, answer: The Court intervened because its conservative majority was willing to do whatever it took to secure a Republican victory. But could either of these explanations really be true? Taking a sober second look at this litigation is not easy when we are so close to the decision, with passions still swirling. Yet working through the case chronologically, retracing each step as if without foreknowledge of what came later, suggests a different and more plausible explanation, one that acquits the justices of the charge of staging a coup, but only by interpreting their conduct in a way that is just as alarming. For it suggests a Court fretting less about Democrats than democrats, worried less about whether Al Gore would be president than about allowing difficult problems to be handled by democratically elected institutions. The Court stepped in so aggressively, in other words, because, like the Taney Court, these justices, too, had deluded themselves into believing that only they could save us from ourselves.

Before we can interpret the Court's actions, we need first to re-count and explore them, one step at a time. This effort requires a patient review of the legal questions that the two supreme courts—Florida's and the nation's—faced.

ROUND ONE: THE PROTEST ACTION

The Florida Proceedings

The basic structure of Florida's election code is as follows: Each county canvasses the votes and files returns with the Department of State. A candidate or voter may "protest" a county's returns, but such protests must be filed with the County Canvassing Board before it certifies its results or within five days of the election, "whichever is later." If a protest is filed, the Canvassing Board must do certain things to correct for obvious possible problems. In addition, a candidate "may" request a manual recount—either before the county's results are certified or within seventy-two hours, again, whichever is later—and the Canvassing Board "may" then authorize a partial recount of three precincts or 1 percent of the total votes. If this recount indicates "an error in the vote tabulation which could affect the outcome of the election," the Canvassing Board must take appropriate action to identify and correct the error, including a countywide manual recount if necessary.[1]

After the Canvassing Boards file certified results with the Department of State, the secretary of state certifies the overall election result. According to Florida election law, the county returns "must" be filed with the Department by 5:00 P.M. on the seventh day following an election. Members of the Canvassing Boards are subject to fines for filing late returns, and the secretary "may" ignore these returns and rely solely on the results then on file.[2] A candidate whose protest is denied or who does not file a protest can still challenge the certified election result by bringing an action in state court to "contest" the certification. Grounds for contesting an election include the "rejection of a number of legal votes sufficient to change or place in doubt the result of the election."[3]

The closeness of the vote in Florida triggered an automatic machine recount, which, together with later-arriving overseas ballots, gave Bush a lead of 930 votes (out of almost 6 million votes cast). The Florida Democratic Party filed protests on Gore's behalf in four counties: Broward, Miami-Dade, Palm Beach, and Volusia. After conducting preliminary manual recounts, the Canvassing Boards in these counties determined that the standard for a full recount was satisfied, that is, that there had been "an error in the vote tabulation" sufficient to affect the election result. After complicated procedural maneuvering, the following situation emerged: The counties concluded that they could not complete full manual recounts within the seven-day deadline and asked permission to file late returns. Secretary of State Katherine Harris ruled that she would waive the deadline only if the problem requiring a recount consisted of fraud, "substantial noncompliance with statutory election procedures," or an act of God. She therefore indicated that she would not accept late returns from the four counties in question, which submitted what returns they had at the required time. Harris then certified Bush the winner in Florida. The Florida Democratic Party and Gore filed a lawsuit seeking to compel the secretary to accept amended returns to reflect completed recounts. After the trial court denied their claims, the Florida Supreme Court accepted an expedited appeal and ruled unanimously on November 21 that the secretary had abused her discretion by refusing to accept late returns. Invoking its equitable power to fashion a remedy, the court gave the four counties until November 26 to complete their recounts.

We need to examine the Florida Supreme Court's decision more closely to understand how events subsequently unfolded. There were two main issues in the case. The first was whether the County Canvassing Boards were permitted to authorize manual recounts under the circumstances. The Division of Elections, working under the supervision of the secretary of state, had issued an Advisory Opinion on November 13 stating that the phrase "an error in the vote tabulation" in the statute governing protests referred only to mechanical or software errors and did not include problems resulting from the manner in which voters had marked or punched their ballots. According to Bush, the Canvassing Boards thus acted improperly in undertaking manual recounts at all. The Florida Supreme Court rejected this argument, holding that "an error in the vote tabulation" referred to an error in the count and not merely the machines that did the counting.

It is tempting to brush this issue aside, because it played essentially no role in the subsequent appeal to the U.S. Supreme Court. It has, however, since attracted considerable attention from conservative commentators, who have insisted that the Florida court's interpretation was wrong. The argument reappeared, moreover, in Chief Justice Rehnquist's concurring opinion in the second go-around, where he listed the Florida court's reading of this language as an example of how badly the state tribunal had mangled Florida law. Noting that Florida instructs voters how to fill out ballots so that the machines will count them properly, the chief justice decided that "no reasonable person" could call it "an error in the vote tabulation" when the system functions as designed and simply fails to count ballots that are marked improperly. To rule otherwise, he mused, would be to assume that the system of machines used by the state "nonetheless regularly produces elections in which legal votes are predictably *not* tabulated, so that in close elections manual recounts are regularly required." This, he concluded, "is of course absurd."[4]

It is well known that many voters fail to follow directions and so mark their ballots improperly. Certainly a state could reasonably decide that a voter must not only get to a polling place but also mark his or her ballot properly for it to be counted. Some states accordingly limit manual recounts to instances of mechanical failure. But why is it unreasonable to adopt the opposite rule? It also seems perfectly rational for a state to recognize that many voters will innocently make mistakes of a type that a manual recount can correct. The decision to recover these votes obviously requires additional work, but in practice the question arises only in close elections, when such votes matter most. We thus have two plausible interpretations of the statute, and the choice between them is largely a matter of emphasis and attitude. If one is most concerned with avoiding messy controversy, "punishing" voters who mark their ballots improperly seems acceptable. But if one is instead concerned with maximizing the extent to which voters who attempted to cast votes have their votes counted, the messiness of an occasional hand recount seems like a small cost.

The Florida court chose the latter interpretation based on the structure and wording of Florida law. The statute in question refers to an error in "the vote tabulation," and a tabulation ordinarily refers to a count or a calculation. Moreover, nothing in the language of the statute suggested that a different or narrower meaning was intended. On the contrary, when the Florida legislature wanted to refer specifically to the machines that did the counting, it used phrases like "the vote tabulation system" or the "automatic tabulating equipment."[5] Finally, if any doubt remained about whether Florida law was concerned more with counting votes than with disciplining voters, the provision governing how returns should be canvassed stated that a mismarked ballot should be discarded only if "it is impossible to determine the elector's choice," and that "[n]o vote shall be declared invalid or void if there is a clear indication of the intent of the voter as determined by the canvassing board."[6] This had been Florida policy for nearly a century. So although it might not have been "absurd" to interpret the statute as Chief Justice Rehnquist did, the Florida court had the better argument and more plausible interpretation.[7]

In any event, the case ultimately focused more on a second question, namely, whether or under what circumstances the secretary of state could be required to accept late returns from a County Can-

vassing Board. This appeared easy at first, and two provisions of
Florida law implied that the answer was never. Section 102.111 of
the Florida statutes sets forth the duties of the County Canvassing
Boards and states that if returns are not received by 5:00 P.M. on the
seventh day following the election, "all missing counties shall be ignored." Similarly, section 102.112, which establishes penalties for filing late, plainly states that "[r]eturns must be filed by 5 P.M. on the
7th day following the . . . general election." According to Bush,
these provisions set a firm deadline that counties were required to
meet.

The Florida court identified two ambiguities in the statute
that led it to reject this interpretation. First, the command in
§ 102.111 that late filings "shall be ignored" conflicts with the final sentence of § 102.112, which restates the seven-day deadline
but provides that late returns "may be ignored," obviously signal-
ing that they do not *have* to be. Second, the court observed that
the provisions suggesting a firm seven-day deadline are in tension with the provisions regarding manual recounts in protest actions. As noted above, candidates may request a manual recount
until the later of two possible dates: when the Canvassing Board
certifies its returns or three days after an election is held. But recounts take time. So while the decision to recount is left to the
Board's discretion, should it deem a recount necessary, it might
well prove impossible to complete it within seven days, particularly in populous counties. An inflexible seven-day deadline
could thus be imposed only by partially gutting the manual recount provisions. It followed that, although the counties might be
required to submit returns on the seventh day, there must be circumstances when they can submit late returns, amended to reflect the results of a full recount.

These statutory ambiguities were unquestionably real, and the
court's resolution—rejecting an inflexible deadline and recognizing circumstances when late returns are acceptable—seems correct.
Not only did it better accommodate the provisions regarding man-

ual recounts, but it is also consistent with the language in § 102.112 that specifically contemplates late returns. To the extent this language seems inconsistent with § 102.111, the court explained, it must be read as superseding. Section 102.112 was added to the Election Code *after* § 102.111, based on experience suggesting a need for greater flexibility. And it is black-letter law that a conflict between a later, more specific statute and an earlier, general one should be resolved in favor of the former.

Ruling that late returns were permitted did not resolve the case, however, because the court still had to determine *when* such returns should be allowed. Advocates for Bush did concede that Florida law might leave room for filing late returns. However, they contended that decisions about whether and when to accept such returns were left to the discretion of the secretary of state, who in this instance had decided to reject the late filings. It is one thing, Bush argued, to say that the secretary "may" be authorized to excuse a Canvassing Board's tardy submission; it is quite another to say that she *must* do so.

Once again, the Florida Supreme Court disagreed, claiming to rely on conventional principles of statutory interpretation. Complex administrative schemes invariably call for someone to exercise judgment in applying the law. Rather than specify a solution for every contingency, legislatures typically confer discretion on the executive officials charged with enforcement. But such discretion can be dangerous, particularly in the hands of elected officials. So courts routinely limit its exercise, interpreting statutes to ensure that political officials do not misuse their authority. It was a long-established principle of Florida law—based not only on general political theory but on specific provisions of the Florida constitution—that the right to vote is fundamental. Judicial decisions stretching back more than sixty years had thus held, as the Florida court now reiterated, that "[b]ecause election laws are intended to facilitate the right of suffrage, such laws must be liberally construed in favor of the citizen's right to vote."[8] That being so, the court ruled, Secretary Harris could not exercise her discretion to ignore late returns in a manner that needlessly frustrates this right. The court recognized the legislature's concern with having counties file returns on time, but the device the statute used to achieve this goal was to impose fines on individual members of late-filing Canvassing Boards. Attempting to pressure the counties to be prompt by ignoring their returns, in contrast, "punishes not the Board members themselves but rather the county's electors, for it in effect disenfranchises them."[9] So although the secretary unquestionably has some discretion to disregard late returns, she abused that authority by forcing counties to complete their canvasses within the seven-day deadline. Because ignoring returns "is a drastic measure," the court added, it should be permitted only when including them would "compromise the integrity of the electoral process" in one of two ways: by making it impossible to bring a subsequent contest action or "by precluding Florida voters from participating fully in the federal electoral process."[10]

This second ruling was considerably more controversial than the first. The court's reasoning is potentially vulnerable in at least three respects:

- First, although the court did not eliminate the seven-day deadline entirely, it drastically reduced its role in the overall legislative scheme by requiring the secretary to ignore it in all but extreme cases and by limiting enforcement to the imposition of fines on board members.
- Second, by increasing the time available for counties to handle protests, the court shortened the time available if the loser subsequently chooses to bring a contest action in court. (Note that this is true only for presidential elections. In other elections, the contest could begin after certification and take as long as necessary, although it is obviously undesirable if such actions extend beyond the date when the winner should assume office. In a presidential election, state proceedings must be concluded before the electoral college

votes, because this is the constitutionally significant vote, and the Twelfth Amendment provides that if a state has not appointed electors by the designated day when the electors vote, the president shall be whoever receives the votes of "a majority of the whole number of Electors appointed.")

- Third, the court did not merely limit the secretary's discretion to ignore late returns; it all but eliminated that discretion altogether, leaving her room to exercise judgment in extremely narrow circumstances only.

The force of these arguments depends on one's theory of statutory interpretation. Deciding how to read and interpret statutes is among the most complex and unsettled subjects in law. Countless theories have been advanced over the years, and most courts use several different approaches, mixing and matching them as the context warrants. For present purposes, we need only focus on the difference between two common methods for determining what a statute means. According to one method, the meaning is found entirely within the confines of the statute itself, by examining its "plain language" or, some argue, its language and legislative history. Resort to other arguments or materials is warranted only if a question cannot otherwise be resolved.

Viewed from this perspective, the decision of the Florida Supreme Court is troubling, particularly the way it constrained the secretary's discretion. In effect, the court took a statutory scheme that presupposed that late returns would normally be ignored, subject to the secretary's judgment to make an occasional allowance, and turned it into a statute in which late returns must normally be included, subject to two narrow exceptions covering extreme circumstances. The court could have chosen a simpler way to deal with the secretary's decision to reject the late returns. For Katherine Harris had a conflict of interest that should have led to her recusal. The problem was not that she was a Republican, for most public officials are members of one of the major parties, and mere affiliation does not normally disqualify them from acting, even in matters that affect party interests. But Harris was also co-chair of Governor Bush's Florida campaign, a more serious conflict, and one that made it wildly inappropriate for her to remain in charge. On these grounds, the Florida court could reasonably have decided that her exercise of discretion did not deserve the usual deference. But the court chose to overlook the matter and instead rendered a general interpretation that seems hard to square with the statutory scheme viewed in isolation.

There is, however, another equally respectable approach to statutory interpretation that enables courts to bring certain a priori assumptions about legislative intent into the interpretive process, presuming that lawmakers meant to conform to these assumptions absent a clear statement to the contrary in the language of the statute. Once these presumptions, or "clear statement rules" as they are known in law, have been established, courts will assume the legislature took them into account in the drafting process and so expected their laws to be interpreted accordingly. The U.S. Supreme Court frequently employs this technique. It assumes, for example, that federal laws apply only to acts committed on U.S. territory absent unequivocal language to the contrary,[11] and also that Congress does not mean substantive regulation to apply to states (as opposed to private entities) unless the wording of a statute explicitly says so.[12] Nor will the Court find that Congress has conditioned federal benefits on a state's waiver of sovereign immunity unless the statute creating the benefit says so in language that is "unmistakably clear."[13] Most recently, the Court has refused to find congressional intent to regulate intrastate noncommercial activities, on the ground that they affect interstate commerce, because Congress did not say that it wanted to do so in sufficiently explicit language.[14] In all these cases, utilizing the first approach to statutory interpretation and reading the statutes without these strong background assumptions would have led to the opposite conclusion from that reached by the Court.

Obviously, the Florida Supreme Court adopted this second method in its decision, applying a clear statement rule presuming that, absent unequivocal language to the contrary, the Florida legislature wants every possible effort made to include each vote cast. Hence, the court ruled that manual recounts could be authorized for reasons other than mechanical failure, and it made the deadline flexible to accommodate efforts to examine the ballots while limiting the secretary's discretion to ignore returns. Seen in this light, the decision is hardly controversial. The clear statement rule invoked by the court was a matter of well-established Florida law that had previously been relied on to interpret election statutes, and the court's interpretations were not inconsistent with the statute's plain language. Certainly the state supreme court did no more violence to statutory text than did the U.S. Supreme Court in any of the cases mentioned above. All things considered, it was a relatively routine performance for a court relying on clear statement principles. As we shall see, this fact forced Bush to argue that the Florida court was constitutionally prohibited from employing such principles.

Proceedings in the U.S. Supreme Court

An aggrieved party seeks review in the U.S. Supreme Court by filing a petition for a writ of certiorari, commonly known as a "cert petition." Certiorari is an ancient common law device by which a superior court orders an inferior one to send it the certified record in a particular case. The decision to grant a writ is discretionary, and the Supreme Court uses it to choose the cases it wishes to hear. Denying a cert petition has no precedential force and is typically done without explanation or opinion. The writ of certiorari thus allows the Court to rid itself of cases without having to say anything about them.

The Florida Supreme Court handed down its decision on November 21; lawyers for Governor Bush filed a cert petition the next day. Legal experts confidently predicted that the U.S. Supreme Court would deny the petition, convinced that the justices would refuse to be dragged into a case so fraught with political risk. Instead, the Court immediately granted review and set the case down for expedited briefing and argument.

This should not have come as such a surprise. The Court was under an obligation to take the case and say something about it. Congress conferred certiorari jurisdiction to relieve the Court of having to decide unimportant disputes, enabling the justices to conserve their energy for cases genuinely needing review. Although the Court always retains this discretion, certain cases have such inherent public importance that the justices really must entertain them, whether they want to or not. *Clinton v. Jones* (the Paula Jones suit) was such a case. The Court did little other than to affirm the decision of the lower court, and some of the justices may have wanted to deny review on the ground that it was unnecessary. But other considerations come into play in such cases. When the president of the United States says that a lower court decision threatens his ability to perform in office, the Supreme Court has an institutional responsibility to hear this argument and offer its judgment, even if the decision ultimately does little more than agree with what was said below. The ambiguous silence of a cert denial is irresponsible where the stakes are so high. This understanding has deep roots in the institutional culture of the Supreme Court, making it unlikely that the justices would ignore a case like *Bush v. Palm Beach County Canvassing Board*.

What the Court would say once the case was before it was another matter. Denying cert, without more, may not have been an option, but the Court could have taken the case merely to state explicitly that there was nothing for it to do, that the election would have to be resolved in Florida and, eventually, in Congress. Indeed, most commentators, including many who were outraged by the decision in Florida, initially doubted that Bush would obtain relief from the high court.

One reason for doubting that Bush would prevail was that his legal arguments did not appear strong. The Bush petition set forth three questions for review. The first was whether the Florida court changed Florida election law in a way inconsistent with § 5 of Title 3 of the United States Code (3 U.S.C. § 5). Second, had the decision below "made" law in violation of the requirement of Article II of the U.S. Constitution that presidential electors be appointed by each state "in such manner as the Legislature thereof may direct"? Third, did the standards being used to conduct recounts violate the Equal Protection Clause? The Court originally agreed to hear the first two questions but declined to address the third. Critics of the ultimate decision cite this as evidence of partisanship. As of late November, they say, the justices did not think the Equal Protection argument even worthy of review; the conservative majority only reached for the issue after Bush's other arguments failed. But the Court may have declined to review the Equal Protection claim for a simpler reason. Although the Bush petition alleged that the recount process was "arbitrary, standardless, and selective," there was, as yet, no factual basis to know whether this was true. A proper record would be produced only during the trial held later, in the contest action. Furthermore, as Pamela Karlan suggests in Chapter 5, the petition presented only a sketchy version of the argument, which given concerns about standing (and time pressures), may have led the Court to overlook its potential significance.

The two claims that the Court did agree to hear on November 24 had serious deficiencies. The federal statutory claim was particularly weak. The statute in question was part of a congressional solution devised in the wake of the only previous election to present a similar controversy about the selection of electors. In 1876, several southern states produced competing slates, leading to a deadlock that was ultimately resolved by a special commission composed of members of both Congress and the Supreme Court. Although no one was happy with that approach, it took another decade to produce an alternative, currently codified in Title 3 of the United

States Code at §§ 1–15. According to Bush, 3 U.S.C. § 5 requires states to resolve disputes over presidential electors "exclusively by reference to 'laws enacted *prior to*' election day," an obligation the Bush people claimed that the U.S. Supreme Court had a duty to enforce.[15]

The problem with this argument was that the statute simply does not say anything like this. What it says is:

> If any State shall have provided, by laws enacted prior to [election day], for its final determination of any controversy or contest concerning the appointment of all or any of the electors of such State, by judicial or other methods or procedures, and such determinations shall have been made at least six days before the time fixed for the meeting of the electors, such determination . . . shall be conclusive, and shall govern in the counting of the electoral votes as provided in the Constitution . . . so far as the ascertainment of the electors appointed by such State is concerned.

That's a mouthful, but in ordinary English, what it says is that *if* a state resolves controversies over electors by a legal process created prior to the election (and finishes six days before the electors vote), then this resolution shall be binding on Congress, which has final responsibility for counting the votes. This presented Bush with three seemingly insurmountable difficulties:

- First, Florida *had* followed a process established by "laws enacted prior to" election day. According to the statute, to obtain its benefits, a state must have created a process before the election for resolving controversies "by judicial or other methods or procedures." Florida had done just this; its process, which included judicial challenges like the one at issue, had been established long before the election. Bush might not have liked the outcome of that process, particularly the Florida court's interpretation of state law, but the

process itself was unquestionably created and in place prior
to the election.

- Second, even supposing that the Florida court created "new
law" within the meaning of the statute, nothing in 3 U.S.C.
§ 5 prohibits a state from resolving disputes by laws enacted
after election day. The statute merely gives states an option:
If they resolve disputes under laws enacted before election
day, Congress will respect their determinations without further investigation; if not, the state risks a congressional in-
quiry reaching a different result.
- Third, even supposing that the statute had been violated, the
Supreme Court was not the proper forum in which to seek relief. Section 5 is part of a larger statutory scheme, which includes elaborate provisions in § 15 for "counting electoral
votes." These specify a process for raising objections and resolving disputes that makes Congress the arbiter and rather
conspicuously leaves courts out of the equation.[16] Whether an
aggrieved party should be permitted to mount a judicial challenge to the resolution reached by Congress presents a ticklish
question, but it seems hard to argue that candidates or voters
could seek judicial relief under § 5 *before* Congress has acted.

Bush's second argument seemed more plausible at first, although
on closer inspection, it, too, had some troubling defects. Pointing to
Article II of the U.S. Constitution, which provides that "[e]ach
State shall appoint [Electors], in such Manner as the Legislature
thereof may direct," Bush maintained that the Constitution vests
state legislators with absolute authority to regulate the choosing of
electors. As the case unfolded, two versions of this argument appeared, a strong one and a weak one. According to the strong version, this direct delegation of authority from the U.S. Constitution
means that nothing in state law, including the state constitution,
can interfere with the plenary authority of the state legislature. It
followed that, although the state court has authority to interpret

Florida election law, if it revised that law because it believed this was required by the Florida constitution, it would thereby violate the federal Constitution.

A weaker version of the argument focused on the relationship between the state's legislature and its courts. In this view, one could assume (without deciding) that the legislature might be prohibited from choosing electors in a manner that violated the state constitution, and even that a state court could so hold. But absent a finding that the state's election law is unconstitutional, state courts must enforce the legislative program as it was enacted and cannot modify that program in the interpretive process. It supposedly followed that the Florida court had violated the federal Constitution by relying on clear statement principles rather than following a plain language approach to interpreting Florida's election law.

The strong version of the argument—that Article II of the U.S. Constitution brooks no interference with the authority of state legislators to choose electors, even via the medium of a state constitution—is particularly farfetched. Two principles above all were sacred to the Founders of our Republic: first, that the people of a political society could speak for themselves and did so through their constitutions; and second, that the people's voice is always superior to that of their rulers. It was these ideas that led Americans to resist Parliament in the 1760s and to declare independence in 1776. The principle of popular sovereignty is the very foundation on which our Constitution rests, no less applicable within each state than in the nation as a whole. The notion that the Framers would have violated this principle by elevating the acts of a state legislature above the authority of a state constitution is wildly implausible. Certainly we would find lots of evidence on the subject had they purported to do this, for so controversial a step would have evoked intense discussion. Instead, there is nary a word, because in context everyone understood this clause as a simple delegation to states of power to choose electors pursuant to their ordinary legal process, whatever that might be.

So why does Article II read the way it does? Why does it refer to state legislatures rather than simply to states? In part, the answer is found in the convoluted drafting history of the particular clause, which saw the Framers try out numerous proposals before deciding to leave the process of selecting electors to the discretion of individual states. In part, the answer is that the Framers naturally assumed that election laws would normally be fashioned in the legislature. But the idea that this language was meant to deprive the people of a state of authority to use their constitutions to restrict what the legislature might do would have violated the most basic principle of the American Revolution. Anyone silly enough to have suggested such a thing would have been hooted down.

It may be tempting to say that the people of a state are not speaking when a court invokes the state constitution to modify or strike down legislation; all we really hear, one could say, is the voice of the court that interprets the constitution. But the U.S. Supreme Court could not say this without repudiating its own practice of judicial review, which—as Alexander Hamilton explained in *Federalist* 78—rests on precisely the claim that when the Court strikes down legislation, it gives expression to the people's voice as expressed in the text of a written constitution. If anything, the argument for judicial review is more compelling when it comes to state constitutions, which (like the Florida constitution) are periodically reenacted and so do not rest on the assent of generations long dead.

With these principles established, we can see that the weak version of the argument—that Article II requires courts to follow a plain language approach to statutory interpretation—is also unconvincing. Statutory interpretation is fundamentally a problem of separation of powers. Different theories allocate authority differently between the legislature and the courts, and the debate over which theory (or theories) to adopt is one about how to structure relations between the two branches. Hence, the weak version of the argument, no less than the strong one, ultimately rested on a claim that in referring to "Legislatures" in Article II the Framers meant permanently to alter the internal structure of state government, a claim utterly lacking evidentiary support or plausibility. (It is ironic that the three justices who eventually endorsed this argument— Rehnquist, Scalia, and Thomas—are the ones most often heard to complain about the need for strict adherence to original intent. Yet, here, so eager were they to reverse the Florida court that they did not even bother to inquire how or why the text took the form it did.)

A handful of Supreme Court decisions were potentially relevant to the issue. For example, Article V of the Constitution, which governs constitutional amendments, requires that a constitutional convention be called "on the Application of the Legislatures" of two-thirds of the states. In *Hawke v. Smith,*[17] the Court held that this language prohibited the states from calling a convention by any other means, including a plebiscite. Pointing to this decision, Bush argued that if Article V's reference to state legislatures was meant to be exclusive, the same word in Article II should be given the same meaning. But the Constitution contains other references to state legislatures. Article I, for example, provides that the manner of holding congressional elections shall "be prescribed in each State by the Legislature thereof," and Gore countered Bush's argument by pointing to *Smiley v. Holm,*[18] *Ohio ex rel. Davis v. Hildebrandt,*[19] and *Growe v. Emerson,*[20] all cases in which the Supreme Court ruled that this language did *not* prevent states from limiting their legislatures' discretion (with a gubernatorial veto in *Smiley,* a popular referendum in *Hildebrandt,* and state courts in *Growe*). Fortunately, we need not get lost in technical legal debate about whether or how to distinguish these various cases; it suffices to note that none is directly on point.

The closest case was *McPherson v. Blacker,*[21] an 1892 case in which the Supreme Court had to decide whether a state legislature could delegate to someone else its authority to choose electors. In the course of holding that it could, the Court asserted in passing that the words of Article II operate "as a limitation upon the state in respect of any attempt to circumscribe the legislative power."[22] Of course, when it came to reviewing the state court's interpretation of state law, the same opinion said "[w]e are not authorized to revise the conclusions of the state court on these matters."[23] Lawyers for Gore thus sought to distinguish *McPherson* by agreeing that Article II might make it a matter of federal and not only state law if the courts or governor tried to choose electors without legislative authorization, while arguing that Article II had no bearing on the power of state courts to interpret existing law. More important is the fact that the statement in *McPherson* is surplusage, what lawyers call "dictum," that has no precedential force because it was not necessary to decide the case.

In the end, existing legal authority did not decide the Article II argument one way or the other. What little authority existed offered some support to both sides, to the extent it supported anyone at all. In my view, the Article I cases cited by Gore seem more persuasive because they are actual holdings and not just dictum and because Articles I and II confer similar authority on state legislatures. Nevertheless, given the contrary holding in *Hawke* with respect to Article V and the dictum in *McPherson*, one cannot say that the issue was clear as a matter of precedent. The real problem with the Article II argument is simply that it makes no sense. It works only if one reads the words of the Constitution completely out of context and pretends that they were meant to do something they were not, and for no good reason. Forget about Bush and Gore and ask whether, behind a veil of ignorance, it makes sense to strip the people of the states of power to structure the process of choosing electors as they wish, whether by ordinary legislation or in their constitutions. The answer seems obviously to be no. Certainly no one in the Bush camp offered any reason why it should be yes, instead pointing to the text in a way that defied both history and context.

On December 1, the Supreme Court heard oral argument in *Bush v. Palm Beach County Canvassing Board*, and any thought that it had taken the case simply to clarify that it was not the place to seek answers abruptly vanished. Unlike the Burger Court, whose members tended to listen more than to speak, the Rehnquist Court is famous for bombarding lawyers with tough, rapid-fire questions. The election case was no different, except that the Court appeared even less interested than usual in using the hearing to figure things out. The justices seemed to have made their minds up already, and the main point of the argument was to signal their views and, indirectly, to argue with other justices who disagreed. At times, the lawyers must have wondered whether they had become children whose parents were not speaking to one another: "Tell your mother the sink needs fixing"; "tell your father I already did it." Counsel for the parties seldom had time to finish their answers, because no one really cared what they had to say. And when they answered poorly, one of the justices usually swooped in with a better response, couched as a follow-up question.

That the Court was divided was apparent from the start. Justices Stevens, Souter, Ginsberg, and Breyer were openly skeptical of Bush's arguments, whereas Rehnquist, O'Connor, and Scalia just as openly exhibited their support. Justice Thomas was mute as always, and Kennedy was difficult to read, but most observers assumed (reasonably enough) that they agreed with the other conservatives. As between Bush's two arguments, even the justices who were inclined in his favor showed more interest in Article II than in 3 U.S.C. § 5. The latter claim was discussed, but the questioning dwelt mostly on whether the statute presented a proper issue for federal judicial review, and the conversation became downright desultory when it turned to the actual merits of the argument.[24]

Interestingly, the conservative justices seemed most persuaded by what I have characterized as the strong version of the Article II argument, that state courts have authority to interpret their state's election laws but cannot hold those laws constrained by state constitutions. Much of the argument was thus devoted to debating whether this is what the Florida court had, in fact, done: Had it ruled against Bush on the ground that his interpretation of Florida's election law would have violated the state constitution? Or had it merely looked to the state constitution as a source of background interpretive norms in determining the intent of the legislature?

There were some interesting exchanges in this regard. Perhaps the most telling moment occurred during the questioning of Laurence Tribe, counsel for Vice President Gore. Chief Justice Rehnquist suggested that the state court had interpreted Florida election law narrowly to avoid striking it down as unconstitutional, thereby relying on the state constitution "in a way that the [*McPherson*] case says it may not in construing the statute."[25] Tribe answered (with assists from Justices Breyer, Souter, and Ginsberg) that the court had merely used the constitution "as a tiebreaker, as a way of shedding light on the provisions that are in conflict."[26] At that point, Justice Scalia interjected, "I would feel much better about th[at] resolution if you could give me one sentence in the opinion that supports . . . the proposition that the Florida Supreme Court was using the constitutional right to vote provisions as an interpretive tool to determine what the statute meant. I can't find a single sentence for that."[27] Tribe replied, "I can do a little better than find a sentence. The entire structure of that part of the opinion . . . would be incoherent if the constitution was decisive." When lawyers say "I can do better" in response to a specific request, it usually means that they cannot. In this case, however, Tribe could have quoted the following passage, located immediately after the Florida court's references to the state constitution:

> Because election laws are intended to facilitate the right of suffrage, such laws must be liberally construed in favor of the citizens' right to vote:
>
> > Generally the courts in construing statutes relating to elections, hold the same should receive a liberal construction in favor of the citizens whose right to vote they tend to restrict and

in so doing to prevent disenfranchisement of legal voters and the intention of the voters should prevail when counting ballots. . . . It is the intention of the law to obtain an honest expression of the will or desire of the voter.

State ex rel. Carpenter v. Barber, 198 So. 49, 51 (Fla. 1940). Courts must not lose sight of the fundamental purpose of election laws: The laws are intended to facilitate and safeguard the right of each voter to express his or her will in the context of our representative democracy. Technical statutory requirements must not be exalted over the substance of this right.[28]

One could hardly ask for a clearer explanation or more conventional application of the clear statement approach to statutory interpretation. The legislature is presumed to understand, and so to want, that its laws will be interpreted in accordance with deep-seated background principles. But Tribe's failure to quote this passage from memory is hardly blameworthy. A constant problem throughout the litigation was the lack of time for preparation. Lawyers and judges usually have months to prepare or decide a case, months in which to evaluate the record and frame their arguments, review their positions and check and cross-check every statement. Particularly with the stakes so high, the pressure of doing everything quickly was overwhelming and overbearing. It is no surprise that mistakes like this were made. On the contrary, given the circumstances, the lawyers and judges performed astonishingly well. Mistakes were nevertheless made, as Justice Scalia's misreading of the state court's opinion demonstrates.

After oral argument, the justices confer in secret, in a room with double doors where no one can enter or hear their conversation. We cannot know for sure how the conference in this case proceeded, but several points seem clear. The justices were not unanimous, and some number, probably a majority, were prepared to reverse the decision of the Florida court. Yet the justices were surely also acutely conscious of the risk to their institution and its reputation should they decide the controversy by a narrow, split decision. And perhaps they had not yet been drawn in so deeply as to have lost the ability to make concessions. So they compromised, finding a way to rid themselves of the case without either approving or disapproving what the state court had done. On December 4, they issued a brief opinion per curiam (meaning "by the Court") vacating the judgment below and sending the case back for the state court to clarify the basis for its decision.

It was a smart move. Remanding for clarification enabled the Court to avoid saying anything of substance about either of the two issues. With respect to Article II, the justices merely observed that the legislature "is not acting solely under the authority given it by the people of the State, but by virtue of a direct grant of authority made under Article II."[29] They then quoted the *McPherson* dictum, carefully noting that the case "did not address the same question petitioner raises here," and added:

> There are expressions in the opinion of the Supreme Court of Florida that may be read to indicate that it construed the Florida Election Code without regard to the extent to which the Florida Constitution could, consistent with Article II . . . "circumscribe the legislative power." . . . [W]e are unclear as to the extent to which the Florida Supreme Court saw the Florida Constitution as circumscribing the legislature's authority under Article II. [30]

A similar dodge was used with respect to the statutory claim. The Court observed that the Florida decision did not specifically address 3 U.S.C. § 5 and then reasoned:

> Since §5 contains a principle of federal law that would assure finality of the State's determination if made pursuant to a state law in effect before the election, a legislative wish to take advantage of the 'safe harbor' would counsel against any construction of the Election Code that Congress might deem to be a change in the law. . . . We are . . .

unclear as to the consideration the Florida Supreme Court accorded to 3 U.S.C. §5.[31]

In effect, the Court laid the issues out and decided nothing, because no decision was necessary or possible until the Florida Supreme Court had clarified its own positions.

By not saying anything substantive, the Court was able to render a unanimous opinion. Moreover, the justices surely expected the Florida Supreme Court to take the hint and handle the case on remand in a way that rendered further intervention unnecessary. Or perhaps they thought the contest phase could be dealt with in a manner that rendered the protest phase irrelevant. For at the expiration of the Florida court's extended deadline on November 26, the state election commission had certified George W. Bush the winner in Florida by 537 votes. Gore immediately filed a "contest" action, challenging the certification in three counties (Palm Beach, Miami-Dade, and Nassau). By the time the U.S. Supreme Court handed down its decision on December 1, a hearing had been scheduled for the next day before Judge Sanders Sauls. With a threat of reversal hanging over their heads, perhaps the Florida courts would handle the case in a way that enabled the high court to avoid further entanglement—or so, at least, the justices must have hoped.

ROUND TWO: THE CONTEST ACTION

The Florida Proceedings

Judge Sauls did his part, ruling against Gore on every issue after a two-day hearing. According to Sauls, the Democrats had failed to adduce evidence to cast sufficient doubt on the certified result, and thus offered him no reason to do any further recounting. Gore appealed, and on December 8, the Florida Supreme Court reversed by a 4–3 margin, ordering a statewide recount of "undervotes" (i.e., ballots read by the machines to contain no vote for president).

The legal issues in the contest phase were less complicated than those in the protest phase. Gore objected to the trial court's failure to include certain votes identified in protest-phase recounts, and he took issue with Judge Sauls's refusal to review approximately 9,000 Miami-Dade ballots that had never been manually recounted. The Florida Supreme Court agreed with most of Gore's charges, but this time it crafted an opinion carefully to suit the concerns expressed in Washington. The court thus introduced its analysis of Florida law by explicitly acknowledging that both it and the Florida legislature were "cognizant of the federal grant of authority derived from the United States Constitution and derived from 3 U.S.C. § 5,"[32] and the opinion meticulously turned to the statute for support at each step in the analysis. Gone were references to the state constitution or the fundamental right to vote, replaced by citations and quotes from the statutory language and legislative history.

The most intriguing aspect of this second Florida decision is that it made no explicit reference to the first one. Bush offered this as yet another of the Florida court's errors in his subsequent petition to the U.S. Supreme Court, arguing that the state court relied for some of its rulings in the contest phase on a judgment from the protest phase that no longer existed (because it had been vacated). As a technical matter, the argument was without merit. The state court did indeed order the inclusion of some votes recovered during protest-phase recounts, specifically between 176 and 215 votes from Palm Beach County (the precise number was still at issue) and 168 votes from Miami-Dade County. But it based this ruling on its independent statutory authority in the contest phase, without in any way relying on the first judgment. Under the statute governing contests, § 102.168, every ballot in a county whose certification is contested comes under the court's jurisdiction and supervision. If the court discovers legal votes that were not counted, it must add them to the total. The fact that these votes were discovered as part of a recount that was not or could not be included in an earlier protest is simply irrelevant. All that matters is that they are, in fact, "legal votes" under Florida law.

Making this argument nevertheless served its real purpose for the Bush team, which was to get the U.S. Supreme Court annoyed at the Florida judges for seeming to show disrespect. It remains a mystery why the state court proceeded in this manner. Given the press of time, perhaps the judges decided to deal with the more urgent case at hand before going back to clarify an earlier decision that no longer mattered. In any event, the Bush strategy worked, and at least some of the Supreme Court justices could not conceal their irritation during the subsequent oral argument.

Be all that as it may, the Florida Supreme Court ruled that Judge Sauls had made two fatal errors. First, he gave the certification decisions of the Canvassing Boards a presumption of validity, holding that they could be overturned only upon proof of "a clear abuse of discretion." The Florida Supreme Court disagreed. The Boards' actions "may constitute evidence in a contest proceeding," it said, but the trial judge must still make his own, independent determination of the merits (exercising what is known as "de novo review").[33] Second, Judge Sauls ruled that he would not reexamine any ballots unless Gore could show "a reasonable probability that the results of the election would have been changed" had any alleged irregularities not occurred. According to the state supreme court, this was the wrong legal standard, and a contestant needed to show only that irregularities occurred sufficient to place the result of the election "in doubt."[34]

The second of these rulings is plainly correct, and Bush did not challenge it. Prior to 1999, § 102.168 did not enumerate grounds for contesting an election, and courts had developed their own standard, requiring contestants to show, as Judge Sauls had done, that but for some claimed irregularity the result of the election would have been different. But the Florida legislature rewrote the statute in 1999 to replace this standard, adding § 102.168(3)(c) to permit a contest whenever a Canvassing Board rejects "a number of legal votes sufficient to change *or place in doubt* the result of an election."[35]

The Florida Supreme Court's other ruling—that the trial court in a contest action must exercise de novo review—seems more doubtful. The statute says nothing about this, although the state supreme court had given deference to Canvassing Board certifications in the past, at least when a board had stretched the law to *include* votes.[36] An interpretation that gives board certification some presumptive validity makes sense, too, given the overall structure of the Florida Election Code. Why bother to create a protest phase if the law attaches no special weight to what the Canvassing Boards do? Still, the statute is silent on the question, and one might ordinarily expect lawmakers to say something if they wanted courts to defer. Yet rather than narrowing judicial power, the statute provides in very broad language that "[t]he circuit judge to whom the contest is presented may fashion such orders as he or she deems necessary to ensure that each allegation in the complaint is investigated, examined, or checked, to prevent or correct any alleged wrong, and to provide any relief appropriate under such circumstances."[37] So although one can certainly disagree with the Florida Supreme Court on this issue, it is hyperbolic to characterize its ruling as an obvious flouting of clear legislative intent. There was no clear legislative intent. Indeed, two of the three dissenters wrote separately to say that they agreed with the majority on this issue, meaning six of the seven justices thought de novo review was the appropriate standard.

Having decided that Judge Sauls had applied the wrong standard, the state supreme court next asked whether Gore was entitled to relief under the right one. The court ruled first that a "legal vote" under Florida law "is one in which there is a 'clear indication of the intent of the voter'."[38] Chief Justice Rehnquist later cited this ruling as an example of how the state court "plainly departed from the legislative scheme." Florida statutory law, he insisted, "cannot reasonably be thought to *require* the counting of improperly marked ballots."[39] But it could, and it did. In § 101.5614—the provision specifying how votes should be counted—the legislature expressly stated that "[n]o vote shall be declared invalid or void if there is a clear indication of the intent of the voter," and it specifically provided for mismarked ballots to be discarded only if "it is impossible to determine the elector's choice."[40] Consistent with this language, Florida courts had for decades interpreted state election law to measure legal votes by whether there was a clear expression of voter intent.[41] Finally, lest anyone think this was an aberrant quirk of Florida alone, the state supreme court cited authority from other states employing the same "clear intent of the voter" standard.[42]

Applying what it viewed as the proper legal standard, the court found that Gore was entitled to relief. The unexamined Miami-Dade ballots alone, it reasoned, were enough to satisfy the statutory requirement for a successful contest. "On this record," the court explained, "there can be no question that there are legal votes sufficient to place the results of this election in doubt. We know this *not* only by evidence of statistical analysis but also by the actual experience of recounts conducted. The votes for each candidate that have been counted are separated by no more than approximately 500 votes and may be separated by as little as approximately 100 votes. Thousands of uncounted ballots could obviously make a difference."[43]

The court then turned to the question of appropriate relief. Bush maintained that if any recounting took place, it must be done on a statewide basis. The state supreme court rejected this argument, pointing to the language of § 102.168, which seems to envision countywide challenges and relief. With a worried eye on future elections, including elections for offices other than the presidency, the state court was obviously reluctant to find that a statewide recount would always be required. Nevertheless, given its broad statutory authority "to provide any relief appropriate under the circumstances,"[44] the court agreed that it would be fairer and more sensible in *this* case to order a statewide recount of undervotes.

But that decision created a further problem. It was already December 8, and any recount would have to be completed by December 12, if Florida was to get the benefit of the "safe harbor" in 3 U.S.C. § 5, or by December 18 at the latest, if Florida was to cast its electoral votes on the day designated by Congress. The time pressures to bring things to closure were immense, a factor the Florida Supreme Court explicitly acknowledged by observing that "the need for accuracy [in tallying votes] must be weighed against the need for finality. The need for prompt resolution and finality is especially critical in presidential elections where there is an outside deadline established by federal law."[45] Nevertheless, the court continued, these pressures offered no excuse for sacrificing the main consideration, which is to count all the legal votes:

> [A]lthough the time constraints are limited, we must do everything required by law to ensure that legal votes that have not been counted are included in the final election results. . . . While we recognize that time is desperately short, we cannot in good faith ignore . . . the appellant's right to relief as to their claims . . . nor can we ignore the correctness of the assertions that any analysis and ultimate remedy should be made on a statewide basis.[46]

At that point, the court dropped a footnote, adding:

> The dissents would have us throw up our hands and say that because of looming deadlines and practical difficulties we should give up any attempt to have the election of presidential electors rest upon the vote of the Florida citizens as mandated by the Legislature. While we agree that practical difficulties may well end up controlling the outcome of the election we vigorously disagree that we

should therefore abandon our responsibility to resolve this election under the rule of law.[47]

This portion of the state court's opinion merits quotation for two reasons. First, as we shall see, these passages are crucial in evaluating the propriety of the U.S. Supreme Court's final disposition of the case. But the state court's reasoning also highlights another critical factor that may explain how participants and commentators on both sides could so readily and fiercely believe that their interpretations of Florida law were right, and that their opponents were acting in bad faith. Disagreements about the meaning of Florida law may, more than anything else, turn on a difference in *attitudes*, a factor that goes unrecognized because it reflects something outside the formal canons of statutory construction.[48] Some people find messy elections scary and dangerous: contested results stir passions, create conflict and uncertainty, and threaten to undermine the legitimacy of office holders. To people of this disposition (who plainly include the conservative majority of the U.S. Supreme Court), it seems *obvious* that Florida law emphasizes a quick and orderly resolution, *obvious* that references to "voter intent" are subordinate to provisions for reaching a clear and speedy conclusion. Others feel differently. They worry less about the dangers from disorder and delay, and are willing to endure uncertainty in the interest of recognizing and recording the efforts of voters to vote. To people of this disposition (including the justices of the Florida Supreme Court), it seems no less clear and obvious that Florida law requires making every effort to count votes, even at the risk of confusion and unrest. In truth, the Florida Election Code reflects both concerns, with plenty of room in its multitudinous provisions to emphasize either one. It all depends on the disposition of the interpreter.

Of course, as a legal matter, interpreting Florida law is normally entrusted exclusively to the state's own courts. That federal judges—including justices of the U.S. Supreme Court—think the

Florida courts got it wrong, even grievously wrong, does not ordinarily entitle them to step in and impose their own views. This is why the Article II argument was so crucial for Bush. It offered him the only route to federalize what otherwise would have been purely a matter of state law, beyond the lawful reach of the federal judiciary. It is also why the U.S. Supreme Court's eagerness to embrace the argument, dubious at best, seemed so surprising and uncharacteristic, coming from a Court notorious for stretching the law to preserve state authority and limit federal intrusion.

The Stay

The Florida Supreme Court handed down its decision on Friday, December 8, sending the case back to the trial court for a statewide recount of undervotes. That very day, lawyers for Bush filed an emergency application asking the U.S. Supreme Court to "stay" (i.e., temporarily prevent the enforcement of) the Florida judgment pending appeal. The Court granted a stay on Saturday, and, treating the application as a petition for a writ of certiorari, also set the case down for argument on Monday, December 11. For lawyers especially, this was the single most electrifying moment in the proceedings. In part, this was because the stay made it impossible to finish a recount by December 12 and jeopardized the possibility even of completing one by December 18. But there was more to it than this. Stays are exceptional and rarely granted, even when the Court expects to reverse the judgment below. In the past, the justices have sometimes declined to grant a stay in capital cases even when this meant leaving the petitioner at risk of being executed before his case could be heard.[49] So to a legal audience, at least, this was an even more portentous development than it appeared to the nation at large. When Gore's lawyer, David Boies, heard the news while eating a late lunch, he reportedly leapt to his feet in disbelief and cried, "What is the irreparable harm?"[50] For Gore supporters, it was this action—even more than the final opinion—that demonstrated that the Court's conservative majority had cast law aside to assure Governor Bush's election.

One cannot fully understand this reaction—or why it may have been exaggerated and inappropriate—without knowing something about the law regarding stays. Appellate courts normally assume that a lower court's decision is correct unless and until it has been overturned. Moreover, because a stay is a form of injunction and injunctive relief is supposed to be difficult to obtain, applicants must make a special showing and persuade the court of several things. An applicant must show, first, that he has a "reasonable likelihood" of prevailing on the merits in the subsequent litigation. An applicant must also show that he will suffer "irreparable injury" unless a stay is granted. An injury is irreparable if it cannot be rectified by money or other relief after the fact. That my property may be destroyed does not usually make my loss irreparable, because I can be compensated by money damages and buy a replacement. It may become irreparable, however, if the property in question is unique and irreplaceable (say, a family heirloom).

It makes sense to require irreparable injury and likely success on the merits before granting a stay. A trial has been held. One party has prevailed and wants the benefit of its hard-earned judgment. This judgment may be upset on appeal, but the mere fact that the losing party can appeal is not itself a good enough reason to impose further delay on the prevailing party. This is true even if there is a reasonable chance that the judgment will eventually be reversed, assuming, at least, that any harm from allowing the judgment to be executed in the meantime can be compensated after it is overturned. But where the likelihood of reversal is coupled with irreparable injury, the balance shifts, and preventing the judgment from being executed seems reasonable.

Yet even this is not ordinarily enough to stay a judgment. After all, we do not know for certain whether the judgment will be reversed or affirmed on appeal, and the party who won at trial may also suffer from delay. Hence, once the applicant for a stay satisfies the two basic requirements of likelihood of success and irreparable injury, most courts ask yet a third question: Does the overall "balance of equities" favor granting the stay? If we grant the stay, how does the harm that will be suffered by the party who prevailed at trial (if the judgment is affirmed) compare to the harm that will be suffered by the party who lost below if we deny the stay (and the judgment is reversed)? Generally speaking, this last factor is analyzed on a kind of sliding scale: The more likely it is that the party seeking a stay will prevail on the merits, the less he need show that the balance of equities favors his position.

Many people reacted with outrage to the stay in *Bush v. Gore* because, like David Boies, they thought Bush had failed to show irreparable injury. Suppose the recount continues and Bush wins on appeal, they said. If a legally faulty recount showed Gore ahead, the Court could just vacate it and award Florida's electoral votes to Bush. No harm, no foul. Nothing about allowing the recount to go forward, in other words, threatened Bush's ability ultimately to prevail if he were legally entitled to do so. We do not know for certain why the Court rejected this argument, because (following their normal practice) the justices did not issue an opinion explaining their decision. Justice Scalia wrote a brief concurring opinion, however, in which he maintained that the Court had to be concerned about more than harm to Governor Bush alone; it also had to consider the harm that might be caused to the country "by casting a cloud" over the legitimacy of Bush's presidency.[51] This is an unusual argument, inasmuch as irreparable injury is normally measured exclusively in terms of harm to the party requesting relief. But the Court sometimes takes other concerns into account, and surely it would have been irresponsible not to consider the greater public good in a case of this magnitude and importance.

Most Gore supporters are willing to concede this much. But, they argue, there was eventually going to be a recount no matter what, carried out by academics or the media if not by Florida election officials. And if that recount showed Gore ahead, precisely the same shadow would fall over Bush's election. Granting a stay thus did not forestall the harm feared by Justice Scalia; it only spoiled Gore's chance of having a recount carried out while he could still be elected. Yet this assumes that a media-run recount done after the fact would have the same effect on public confidence as a state-run recount done before, an assumption that, although plausible, is hardly inescapable. Certainly the Court was not plainly wrong to conclude that the worst alternative (in terms of the election's legitimacy) was to have a faulty state-supervised recount proclaim Gore the winner only to be overturned by the U.S. Supreme Court.[52]

A more substantial problem with the Court's stay pertains to the balancing of equities part of the test. Conceding irreparable injury, one might argue (as Gore's lawyers did) that the harm to Gore from granting a stay was still greater, because it extinguished his ability to benefit from the December 12 "safe harbor" and made it substantially harder to complete a recount before the electors voted on December 18. Recall, however, that any balancing of equities must be done in light of the petitioner's probability of success. Given potential harm either from granting or from denying a stay, the likely outcome of the case becomes as important as the relative magnitude of the harm. So if the justices were very sure that Bush would win—as it appears they were—granting a stay was not improper. After all, Gore would suffer unwarranted harm only if the Court ultimately ruled that he was entitled to a recount.

Several conclusions follow. First, the problem, if there is one, is not with the stay but rather with the Court's eventual decision to halt any further recounting. If that decision was wrong, the Court was probably wrong to grant a stay; if not, a stay was proper. Yet having granted a stay under these circumstances, the justices who supported it were also effectively committed—as a matter of psychology if not of law—to halting any further recount, and this even before briefs were submitted or the case had been argued. Having ensured that Gore would be substantially disadvantaged, the justices would have looked exceedingly foolish to conclude that he was right after all. "Oops. We were wrong. Too late? Gosh, sorry, but you can always run again in 2004." This was not a posture any justice would be anxious to assume.

Proceedings in the U.S. Supreme Court

Unfortunately for the five justices who voted to stay the Florida judgment, it became apparent once the briefs had been filed that Bush's arguments were noticeably weaker this time around. As a formal matter, Bush raised the same three points as in his first petition, namely, that the Florida decision was erroneous under 3 U.S.C. § 5 and that it violated both Article II and the Equal Protection Clause of the U.S. Constitution. But the case had changed. To begin with, the justices had made pretty clear the first time around that they were not buying any theory that interpreted § 5 to require Florida to do anything. So Bush modified the argument, this time urging that Florida lawmakers must have meant to take advantage of the federal safe harbor, and that the Florida Supreme Court was "not free to disregard the Florida Legislature's decision to secure for the citizens of Florida the benefits of § 5."[53] Bush's federal statutory claim was thus reduced to a simple disagreement about the proper interpretation of state law, an argument about what the Florida legislature wanted, rather than what federal law required. As already noted, the U.S. Supreme Court cannot ordinarily overrule a state court's interpretation of its own law. Bush could point to Article II of the U.S. Constitution, which he was again arguing placed limits on the interpretive authority of state courts. But this collapsed Bush's § 5 claim into his Article II claim, converting the state court's supposed failure to give sufficient weight to 3 U.S.C. § 5 into just another instance of its alleged failure to respect the process created by the state legislature.

Thus revised, moreover, the argument bordered on frivolous. Florida election law made absolutely no reference to 3 U.S.C. § 5 or federal safe harbors or anything like that. As Chief Justice Rehnquist would later explain, under Bush's (and Rehnquist's) reading of Article II, "the text of the election law itself, and not just its interpretation by the courts of the States, takes on independent significance."[54] Yet the only state lawmaking body to say anything at all about 3 U.S.C. § 5 was the Florida Supreme Court, which the Bush team was otherwise busily denouncing for reading into Florida's statutes things that were not there. It was thus difficult, if not downright hypocritical, for Bush to argue that the Florida Supreme Court should have given greater importance to 3 U.S.C. § 5 when Florida's statute was utterly silent on the issue.

The Bush lawyers were similarly forced to modify their Article II argument in response to the second opinion of the Florida Supreme Court. In the protest phase the Florida court got into trouble by relying on "clear statement" principles drawn from the Florida constitution, which opened the door for Bush to argue that the state court had violated Article II by using the state constitution to limit the state legislature's discretion. Although that objection was questionable for reasons already discussed, the Florida court nevertheless sought to avoid it in the contest phase by resting its decision wholly on the statutory language and legislative history. This forced the Bush lawyers to offer yet a third version of the Article II argument. Now they argued that Article II did more than preclude Florida from limiting the power of its legislature in the state constitution, more even than forbid state courts from interpreting Florida election law in light of principles drawn from outside the statutory text. Article II now required the state court to interpret Florida law correctly, or, rather, not to misinterpret it badly. Of course, reasonable people often disagree about whether a particular reading of some statute is right or wrong, even clearly right or wrong. So the real effect of Bush's revised Article II argument was simply to shift final authority over state election law from state supreme courts to the U.S. Supreme Court. The high court in Washington would, in effect, become the highest court of the states on matters of state law affecting the selection of presidential electors—a remarkable proposition, made without even a scintilla of evidence suggesting that this is what the drafters of the Constitution intended (which it most assuredly was not), much less a persuasive argument as to why it is a good idea.

Bush did make one argument about how the Florida Supreme Court had violated Article II by relying on its state constitution. The Florida constitution formally creates the state's judicial system, and, among other things, it gives the state supreme court jurisdiction to entertain appeals from the lower courts. Bush argued that the Florida Supreme Court thus relied on the state constitution as the source of its authority to review the trial court's ruling in the contest action. "[B]ecause the Florida *Legislature* has conferred no role in reviewing contests over the results of a presidential election on the Florida Supreme Court," Bush explained, "the court below lacked authority to enter its judgment, and the judgment below must accordingly be reversed."[55] One has to believe this argument slipped into the brief by mistake, a product of the speed with which the work had to be done, because it is a kind of argument that only beginning law students usually make. When drafting an election code, or any law, for that matter, the state legislature obviously assumes certain things and takes for granted that they are incorporated by reference. It assumes that there *are* state courts, that only lawyers who are members of the state bar will appear in these courts, that the courts have rules of procedure to govern their proceedings, and so forth. It does not create the whole world over for each new law, because that would be a huge waste of time. And among the things the state legislature obviously takes for granted is that the normal process of appellate review applies. As Bush would have had it, Article II requires state courts to pretend that any detail not specifically delineated in an election code was deliberately *ex*cluded by the legislature, at least as respects the presidential election and no matter how nonsensical the resulting statute looks. If the Florida Election Code makes no reference to appellate review, then there should be no appellate review. Of course, as Gore pointed out in his brief, Bush could not explain why the Florida legislature would have given final authority to decide the election to a single trial judge, which is why even justices strongly inclined to rule in Bush's favor reacted incredulously. When pressed on this point by Justice Kennedy, Bush's lawyer Theodore Olson offered a half-hearted defense before sheepishly conceding that "[i]t may not be the most powerful argument we bring to this Court" (which elicited a bemused "I think that's right" from one of the justices).[56]

In any event, Bush mainly argued that the state supreme court had violated Article II by badly misinterpreting the Florida Election Code. In particular, he contended that the state court erred by ruling that Canvassing Board certifications should be reviewed de novo rather than for abuse of discretion. In addition, he argued that the Florida court erroneously allowed "dimpled" ballots to be counted, because the statute requires a "clear indication" of the intent of the voter. As explained above, Bush had a good point about the standard of review, and both of his arguments are certainly plausible. But neither argument is compelled by the statute, for neither rests on plain statutory language or a clear legislative command. Rather, both rely on debatable inferences drawn from the overall structure of the law, which fails to specify a standard of review in contest actions and leaves the meaning of "clear indication" undefined. So although Bush's two arguments were plausible, so, too, were those of the Florida Supreme Court. One might credibly believe, as Bush did, that the voter's intent on a punch-card ballot is not "clearly" indicated unless the hole is punched cleanly through. But one might also credibly conclude, with the Florida Supreme Court, that it depends on the rest of the ballot. A card on which the vote for president is dimpled but every other office cleanly punched is different from one on which there are dimples for every office; some dimpled ballots, in other words, plainly do contain a "clear indication" of voter intent.

The critical point is this: Where a statute is ambiguous, interpretation is unavoidable, and *someone's* choice among the plausible alternatives must prevail. But Article II cannot possibly be read to say that this someone should be the U.S. Supreme Court, certainly not unless the state court ignored clear and unambiguous statutory language, which simply was not the case here.

Bush's third argument was that the recount ordered by the Florida court violated the Equal Protection Clause. Because Pamela Karlan discusses this aspect of the case in her chapter, two brief observations will suffice here. First, Bush's lawyers plainly viewed this as their weakest argument, a not implausible assumption given that the Court had previously declined to address the issue. They devoted scarcely five pages to the point near the end of their brief, and Theodore Olson gave it equally short shrift in his initial presentation at oral argument. Second, Bush's legal team may have de-emphasized his Equal Protection claim because it would not give Governor Bush what they regarded as full relief. Unlike the Article II claim, which required outright reversal of the state court decision, a ruling that the Florida Supreme Court's recount plan violated Equal Protection would lead only to an order remanding the case back to the state for a recount to be conducted under proper standards. Or so everyone thought.

Oral argument in *Bush v. Gore,* or *"Bush II,"* was held on Monday, December 11, after what must have been a long weekend for all concerned. Everyone at the Court had worked literally round-the-clock to prepare, and visitors to the courthouse could glimpse bleary-eyed law clerks sitting wearily on the side. This was *the* moment, the final act of the strange 2000 election. Yet it lacked some of the drama and suspense of *Bush I.* Probably this is because everyone already knew the outcome (Saturday's stay having let that cat out of the bag). All that remained was to see how or whether the Court would split and what the grounds of its decision would be. The oral argument revealed little that was new, unless it was the surprising interest that several justices now demonstrated in the

Equal Protection issue. And sure enough, when the decision came down late Tuesday night, six and possibly seven members of the Court had voted to overturn the Florida decision on Equal Protection grounds. (The possible seventh was Justice Breyer, who recognized that serious equal protection concerns existed without actually stating that the Constitution had been violated.) Astonishingly, however, only two of them—Justices Souter and Breyer—thought the case should be returned to Florida to give the state court a chance to repair the damage and finish the recount. The other five—Rehnquist, O'Connor, Scalia, Kennedy, and Thomas—ruled that no further recounting would be permitted. On the crucial question to end the election, then, the Court had split 5–4, with the five most conservative justices reaching out aggressively to conclude matters once and for all.

Before turning to the Court's analysis, Chief Justice Rehnquist's concurring opinion, also joined by Scalia and Thomas, merits brief notice. It is a remarkably unself-conscious effort in which the Court's extreme conservatives say there are "additional grounds" for reversing the Florida Supreme Court and then berate the state court for misinterpreting its own law. The additional ground is Article II, of course, and so the arguments are by now familiar: The Florida court erroneously subjected Canvassing Board certifications to de novo review, it improperly allowed mismarked ballots to constitute "legal votes" (substituting a standard based on voter intent instead), and it inappropriately attached too little significance to the federal safe harbor in 3 U.S.C. § 5. The opinion's vexed tone is unfortunate. In a case of this magnitude, certain to be widely quoted and studied, and perhaps even read by the general public, a greater display of diplomacy and statesmanship would have been preferable. The same could be said of the choleric dissents by Justices Stevens and Ginsburg (although winners may have a greater obligation to show magnanimity than losers). It is a sign of how much the justices, too, were caught up in the events that they failed to exercise more restraint. Feelings were running high, no less for the justices than for the rest of us, and one suspects that they just could not help giving expression to them.

The chief justice's overwrought rhetoric is doubly unfortunate because his arguments are not very strong. Indeed, with the possible exception of the standard of review, the Florida court arguably had better interpretations on every issue. It is ironic to see the concurring justices lash out at the state court for ignoring statutory language while making arguments that are not supported by what the statute actually says or even positively inconsistent with its language (as in the case of defining "legal votes"). This might not have been so bad were the Supreme Court reviewing a lower federal court, in which case its authority to substitute its own preferred readings would have been clear. But in a case like this one, where the state court is supposed to have final authority and the Supreme Court's power to interpose rests on a novel (and dubious) construction of Article II, one would think any supposed misinterpretations should at least be very clear and obvious.

Justices Kennedy and O'Connor apparently felt this way, for they abandoned Article II and instead based their decision on the Equal Protection Clause. One of these two justices presumably drafted the Court's per curiam opinion, which acquired a majority through the additional votes of the three concurring justices. (Justices Souter and Breyer wrote separately and declined to join the majority opinion.) It is hard to miss the anomalousness of this line-up: Not only are the Court's two most liberal members, Stevens and Ginsberg, in dissent, but the five most conservative justices are found suddenly embracing Warren Court principles they have spent their entire careers trying to undo. And although one or another of these five has occasionally sided with the liberals in prior Equal Protection cases, it truly is unprecedented for all five to join an opinion expanding Equal Protection in this manner (unless it is for the purpose of limiting affirmative action). One suspects that Rehnquist, Scalia, and Thomas must have joined the per curiam reluctantly, and that their votes were gained only by O'Connor's and Kennedy's willingness to include the extraordinary announcement that the decision was "limited to the present circumstances" and should not necessarily be taken to establish precedent for any future case.[57]

The crucial part of the decision for our purposes is found in two short paragraphs near the end of the opinion, in which the Court ruled that no further recounting would be permitted. As noted above, the normal remedy for an Equal Protection violation of this sort would be to remand the case to Florida, so the state court could decide whether to revise its procedures and try again or declare the election over. But the five justices in the majority obviously had decided to take no more chances with the Florida courts; they were going to end this now, no matter what. And so they wrote:

> The Supreme Court of Florida has said that the legislature intended the State's electors to "participat[e] fully in the federal electoral process, as provided in 3 U.S.C. § 5. . . . That statute, in turn, requires that any controversy or contest that is designed to lead to a conclusive selection of electors be completed by December 12. That date is upon us and there is no recount procedure in place under the State Supreme Court's order that comports with minimal constitutional standards. Because it is evident that any recount seeking to meet the December 12 date will be unconstitutional for the reasons we have discussed, we reverse the judgment of the Supreme Court of Florida ordering a recount to proceed.
>
> Seven Justices of the Court agree that there are constitutional problems with the recount ordered by the Florida Supreme Court that demand a remedy. The only disagreement is as to the remedy. Because the Florida Supreme Court has said that the Florida Legislature intended to obtain the safe-harbor benefits of 3 U.S.C. § 5, Justice BREYER's proposed remedy—remanding to the Florida Supreme Court for its ordering of a constitutionally proper contest under the December 18 deadline—contemplates action in violation of the Florida election code, and hence could not be part of an "appropriate" order authorized by Fla. Stat. § 102.168(8).[58]

The Court would not remand the case, in other words, because the state supreme court had already told it that Florida law made reaching the federal safe harbor a paramount consideration; because no recount could be completed in time for that, the U.S. Supreme Court could simply halt the proceedings itself.[59]

Make no mistake: This is nothing less than a deliberate, bold-faced lie, for the justices knew perfectly well that the Florida court had said no such thing. On the contrary, while acknowledging the importance of trying to complete a recount that would secure the benefits of federal law, the Florida Supreme Court had given a higher priority to counting the votes at every stage in the proceedings. (Recall the passages quoted above from the Florida court's second opinion.) This was, moreover, the better interpretation of Florida's Election Code, which included numerous provisions stressing the need to count every vote and not a word about 3 U.S.C. § 5. The most the U.S. Supreme Court could possibly have said was that Florida law was unclear about what should happen in cases of unavoidable conflict between counting votes and finishing by December 12. The Florida court had, to be sure, given every indication that it deemed counting votes to be more important, but the state court had not yet actually faced the problem.

Here is why it mattered: Without the Article II argument, the U.S. Supreme Court had no constitutional authority to rule on what was purely a question of state law. If Florida law was unsettled, the Court was constitutionally required to return the case to Florida. Having determined to prevent that at all costs, the justices in the majority had no choice but to offer this pathetic, cynical claim to be following the lead of the Florida Supreme Court.

Ironies abound. Five justices accuse the state supreme court of exceeding its authority and of going outside the statutory text, and then proceed to reverse that court by flagrantly overstepping their own authority while relying on arguments found nowhere in the text. Three of five who agree that the Florida Supreme Court instructed them to give paramount importance to 3 U.S.C. § 5 attach a separate opinion accusing the same court of giving too little importance to the same federal statute.

WHY?

Initial reactions to the Court's decision in *Bush v. Gore* were predictable. Republicans and Democrats sniped angrily at one another while the rest of the country breathed a sigh of relief. But charges that a group of Republicans on the U.S. Supreme Court had made a "partisan" decision left an impression even among many who were content to let the Court settle matters. *Newsweek* reported that Sandra Day O'Connor's husband had been heard to complain that she would not be able to retire if Gore was elected, and critics of the Court charged the majority with improperly acting to choose their own successors. Yet as anyone familiar with the culture of the Court could attest, the justices almost certainly did not decide as they did for such narrowly partisan reasons. That simply is not how the Court operates.

Certainly partisan feelings may have played an unconscious role. The justices are people just like the rest of us, and the fact that some favored Bush and others Gore could not help but influence their judgment, affecting how they reacted to the unfolding events and what they understood the law to mean. But that is a far cry from saying that the justices deliberately set out to ensure that George W. Bush became the forty-third president of the United States. So what were they thinking?

At the end of its per curiam opinion, the Court added a short coda:

> None are more conscious of the vital limits on judicial authority than are the members of this Court, and none stand more in admira-

tion of the Constitution's design to leave the selection of the President to the people, though their legislatures, and to the political sphere. When contending parties invoke the processes of the courts, however, it becomes our unsought responsibility to resolve the federal and constitutional issues the judicial system has been forced to confront.[60]

These sentiments, coming as they do immediately after the Court's brute exercise of authority to halt the recount, have a "they doth protest too much, methinks" quality about them. Unsought responsibility?! Forced to confront?! Nothing kept the justices from ruling that the Supreme Court was not the proper forum in which to decide a presidential election. Nothing in the law, at least. After all, this was hardly the first time that the nation had faced a controversy of this sort. In 1800, the election remained deadlocked for months after Thomas Jefferson and Aaron Burr tied in the electoral college; in 1876, the nation experienced a preview of the 2000 election after several southern states sent competing slates of electors to Congress. Each of these controversies prompted a legislative response: the Twelfth Amendment after 1800, and the federal statutory scheme in 3 U.S.C. §§ 1–15 after 1876. And both of these responses deliberately and conspicuously excluded the courts, just as the original Constitution had excluded the courts from playing any role in selecting the president. If the justices truly were serious in their "admiration" of the Constitution's design, they could simply have allowed the process that had been created for precisely this sort of problem to run its course, in which case the dispute would eventually have been decided by Congress. But that would have left the Court on the sidelines, trusting other, more democratic institutions to solve the problem. And that is something these justices do not like to do.

We live in an age of contempt for democracy and democratic institutions. "The people" and their elected representatives are not to be trusted. They are too stupid or too irrational to govern. They have passions but no reason. This belief manifests itself in a surprising variety of forms. From the right, we get public choice and law and economics, cynically dismissing the possibility of faithful representation while trumpeting the invisible hand of the market as a better regulator than democratic institutions. From the left, we get "deliberative democracy," a philosophy that insists on stringent preconditions for self-rule, preconditions that it turns out can be satisfied only by small bodies as far removed from popular politics as possible.

Not surprisingly, judicial review has flourished in this environment. The Rehnquist Court is perhaps the most activist in American history. Without surrendering an inch of territory occupied by prior Courts, the Court has extended judicial control into a variety of new areas, using the Commerce Clause, the Tenth Amendment, the Eleventh Amendment (and the background principles from which it emanated), section 5 of the Fourteenth Amendment, the Privileges and Immunities Clause, the Takings Clause, and more. Seen against this background, there is nothing exceptional or unexpected about *Bush v. Gore*. It is merely an extreme instance of a regular pattern of judicial assertiveness that reflects the justices' mistrust of politics and their assumption that on most important questions they know better and that the rest of us are not to be trusted.

I began this chapter by suggesting an analogy between the *Bush* case and *Dred Scott v. Sandford*. Of course, the cases are not really comparable in terms of their significance for American history or even for the history of the Supreme Court. People were angered by the election litigation, but it aroused nothing compared to the passions inspired by slavery (which is as it should be). The comparison, rather, lies in the Court's attitude—in the arrogance that can lead a group of determined justices to conclude we need them to save us from ourselves, even if doing so requires them to bend the law.

NOTES

1. The procedures described in this paragraph are contained in Fla. Stat. tit. IX § 102.166.

2. Id. at § 102.111–112.

3. Id. at § 102.168.

4. Bush v. Gore, 121 S. Ct. 525, 537–538 (2000) (Rehnquist, C.J., concurring).

5. See, e.g., Fla. Stat. tit. IX § 102.166(3)(c), (5)(a).

6. Id. at § 101.5614(5), (6).

7. Noting that Secretary of State Harris had read the statute to apply only to mechanical errors, Chief Justice Rehnquist further criticized the Florida court for not deferring to her interpretation. Although it is true that deference is ordinarily owed to the reasonable interpretations of an executive official charged with enforcing a statute, this deference is reduced or eliminated when the interpretation in question is contrary both to long-established policy and to the apparent meaning of the statutory text, as was the case here.

8. Palm Beach County Canvassing Board v. Harris, slip op. at 31–32; the court cited State *ex rel.* Carpenter v. Barber, 198 So. 49, 51 (Fla. 1940); State *ex rel.* Whitley v. Rinehart, 192 So. 819, 823 (Fla. 1939); State *ex rel.* Landis v. Dyer, 148 So. 201, 203 (Fla. 1933); and Boardman v. Esteva, 323 So. 2d 259, 269 (Fla. 1975).

9. Palm Beach County Canvassing Board v. Harris, slip op. at 33.

10. Id.

11. See EEOC v. Arabian American Oil Co., 499 U.S. 244 (1991) (opinion by Rehnquist, C.J.).

12. See Gregory v. Ashcroft, 501 U.S. 452 (1991) (opinion by O'Connor, J.).

13. Edelman v. Jordan, 415 U.S. 651 (1974) (opinion by Rehnquist, J.); College Savings Bank v. Florida Prepaid Postsecondary Ed. Expense Bd., 119 S. Ct. 2219 (1999) (opinion by Scalia, J.).

14. Jones v. United States, 529 U.S. 848 (2000); Solid Waste Agency of Northern Cook County v. U.S. Army Corps of Engineers, 121 S. Ct. 675 (2001).

15. Brief for Pet. at 17, 19 (quoting 3 U.S.C. § 5) (emphasis added by Petitioner).

16. The pertinent language of § 15 provides:

> If more than one return or paper purporting to be a return from a State shall have been received by the President of the Senate, those votes, and those only, shall be counted what shall have been regularly given by the electors who are shown by the determination mentioned in section 5 of this title to have been appointed. . . . [B]ut in case there shall arise the question which of two or more State authorities determining what electors shall have been appointed, as mentioned in section 5 of this title, is the lawful tribunal of such State, the votes regularly given of those electors, and those only, of such State shall be counted whose title as electors the two Houses, acting separately, shall concurrently decide is supported by the decision of such State so authorized by its law. . . . But if the two Houses shall disagree in respect of the counting of such votes, then, and in that case, the votes of the electors whose appointment shall have been certified by the executive of the State, under the seal thereof, shall be counted.

It is worth noting that, had this process been followed, George Bush would almost certainly have been elected. In a worst case scenario, two slates of electors would have been sent to Congress, one based on a decision of the Florida Supreme Court, the other based on the slate certified by Katherine Harris after she decided not to accept late returns. The Republican-controlled House would presumably have backed the latter slate. Assuming that the presence of Gore and Lieberman in the Senate would have produced a deadlock between the two Houses, the tie-breaking rule would award disputed electors to the slate certified by the governor, and Governor Jeb Bush would already have certified the slate recommended by his secretary of state. Had the Senate managed to find a way around this rule, Gore still could have held on only if every single Democrat in the Senate adhered to the party line, including Gore and Lieberman themselves. And the odds of that happening were long indeed: Public opinion was already lining up in favor of a concession by Gore, pressure that would have continued to build (especially if Gore was hanging on only by virtue of his and his running mate's votes). As Republicans learned to their dismay during impeachment, party discipline in the Senate is well nigh impossible to sustain in the face of public opposition. If the much more disciplined Republicans could not come close to holding the line against Clinton, it seems extraordinarily unlikely that there would not have been even a single Democratic defection from Gore. Most likely, after a ballot or two, a substantial group of Democrats would have abandoned the party line, protesting the need to put public wishes above party needs.

17. 258 U.S. 221 (1920).

18. 285 U.S. 355 (1932).

19. 241 U.S. 565 (1916).

20. 507 U.S. 25 (1993).

21. 146 U.S. 1 (1892).

22. Id. at 25.

23. Id. at 23.

24. See Transcript of Oral Argument at 3–8, 45–50.

25. Id. at 52.

26. Id. at 52–61.

27. Id. at 61.

28. Palm Beach County Canvassing Board v. Harris, slip op. at 31–32.

29. Bush v. Palm Beach County Canvassing Bd., 121 S. Ct. at 471, 474.

30. Id.

31. Id.

32. Gore v. Harris, Pet. App. at 4a.

33. Id. at 12a–13a.

34. Id. at 18a–21a.

35. Fla. Stat. tit. IX § 102.168(3)(c) (emphasis added).

36. See Boardman v. Esteva, 323 So. 2d 259, 268 (Fla. 1975); Beckstrom v. Volusia County Canvassing Board, 707 So. 2d 720, 725 (Fla. 1998).

37. Fla. Stat. tit. IX § 102.168(8).

38. Gore v. Harris, Pet. App. at 22a.

39. Bush v. Gore, 121 S. Ct. 525, 537 (2000) (Rehnquist, C.J., concurring).

40. Fla. Stat. tit. IX § 101.5614(5), (6).

41. The court cited McAlpin v. State *ex rel.* Avriett, 19 So. 2d 420 (Fla. 1944); State *ex rel.* Peacock v. Latham, 169 So. 597 (Fla. 1936); and Boardman v. Esteva, 323 So. 2d 259 (Fla. 1975).

42. The court cited decisions from Massachusetts, South Dakota, and Illinois. See Gore v. Harris, Pet. App. at 22a.

43. Id. at 30a.

44. Fla. Stat. tit. IX § 102.168(8).

45. Gore v. Harris, Pet. App. at 30a–31a.

46. Id. at 31a–32a.

47. Id. at n. 21.

48. I am indebted for this point to my colleague Richard Pildes, who has developed it at length with respect to the U.S Supreme Court in Richard H. Pildes, Democracy and Disorder, 68 U. Chi. L. Rev. 695 (2001).

49. In Herrera v. Collins, 506 U.S.390 (1993), the Court granted cert (which takes only four votes) but denied a stay (which takes five). Herrera was kept alive long enough for his case to be considered only because of a subsequently issued state court stay. See generally Richard Revesz & Pamela Karlan, Nonmajority Rules and the Supreme Court, 136 U. Pa. L. Rev. 1067, 1074–1079, 1109–1117 (1988).

50. David Firestone, "Contesting the Vote," New York Times, Dec. 10, 2000, at p. A1.

51. Bush v. Gore, 121 S. Ct. 512, 512 (2000) (Scalia, J., concurring).

52. I should confess to being one of the people who was, at first, convinced that the law regarding stays favored Gore. I was persuaded to the contrary by my colleague Richard Pildes, who first suggested the argument made in the text above.

53. Brief for Pet., Bush v. Gore, No. 00–949, at 35.

54. Bush v. Gore, 121 S. Ct. 525, 534 (2000) (Rehnquist, C.J., concurring).

55. Brief for Pet., Bush v. Gore, No. 00–949, at 30 (emphasis in original).

56. Tr. of Oral Argument, Bush v. Gore, No. 00–949, at 5–6 (Dec. 11, 2000).

57. Bush v. Gore, 121 S. Ct. 525, 532 (2000) ("Our consideration is limited to the present circumstances, for the problem of equal protection in election problems generally presents many complexities.")

58. Id. at 533 (citations omitted).

59. Critics of the decision have wrongly accused the Supreme Court of setting a trap here, complaining that the main reason no recount could be completed by December 12 was that the U.S. Supreme Court itself did not finish with the case until 10:00 P.M. on the night of the twelfth, leaving a theoretical two hours to meet the deadline. Yet assuming the validity of the Court's Equal Protection analysis—which required Florida to develop a uniform standard for counting and to include both "overvotes" and undervotes—even a recount begun on December 8 probably could not have been completed by December 12.

60. 121 S. Ct. at 533.

5

EQUAL PROTECTION: *Bush v. Gore* AND THE MAKING OF A PRECEDENT

PAMELA S. KARLAN

ALEXIS DE TOCQUEVILLE HAD MANY FAMOUS THINGS to say about democracy in America, but none of these remarks is quoted more frequently than his observation that "[s]carcely any political question arises in the United States that is not resolved, sooner or later into a judicial question."[1] Even before de Tocqueville visited the United States in 1831, the Supreme Court had become embroiled in major issues of public policy. Sooner or later, the Court intervened in virtually every important question in public life, from racial segregation to economic regulation to free speech to the rise of the modern administrative state and the legitimacy of the New Deal. Yet the Court long steered clear of involvement in politics itself. More than a century after de Tocqueville's comment, faced with a claim by voters in Illinois that the use of congressional districts with vastly different populations violated the federal Constitution, the Court declined to "enter this political thicket."[2] Indeed, the Court used the phrase "political question" to describe controversies that lay beyond its power to resolve.

The determination of a presidential election might seem the archetypal political question for voters, not courts, to decide. In the wake of the disastrous election of 1876, some members of Congress proposed that, in the event of another deadlock, the matter should be "referred directly to the prompt and summary decision of the Supreme Court." But Senator John Sherman of Ohio—a sponsor of the Electoral Count Act of 1887 that still ostensibly governs the mechanics of how electoral votes are cast and counted—persuaded Congress to reject this course:

> [T]here is a feeling in this country that we ought not to mingle our great judicial tribunal with political questions, and therefore this proposition has not met with much favor. It would be a very grave fault indeed and a very serious objection to refer a political question in which the people of the country were aroused, about which their feelings were excited, to this great tribunal, which after all has to sit upon the life and property of all the people of the United States. It would tend to bring that court into public odium of one or the other of the two great parties. Therefore that plan may probably be rejected as an unwise provision.[3]

Ironically, Senator Sherman had also been a major architect of the Equal Protection Clause of the Fourteenth Amendment. The clause served as the vehicle first for the Court's active intervention in the political process in the 1960s and ultimately for the Court's resolution of the election of 2000. How the Equal Protection Clause turned the election of 2000 into a contest decided by one vote, and that vote taken not among the citizenry, by the presidential electors, or by the House of Representatives under the Twelfth Amendment, but by the U.S. Supreme Court, is the subject of this chapter.

THE CONSTITUTION AND
THE RIGHT TO VOTE

As the Supreme Court reminded us in *Bush v. Gore*—perhaps surprisingly—individual citizens have "no federal constitutional right to vote for electors for the President of the United States."[4] In fact, the original Constitution virtually ignored voting. The only branch of the national government that was elected directly was the House of Representatives. Article I, section 2, clause 1 provided simply that the House be "composed of Members chosen every second Year by the People of the several States, and the Electors in each State shall have the Qualifications requisite for Electors of the most numerous Branch of the State Legislature." The right to vote in federal elections was completely a creature of each state's decisions about who could participate in the state's own political process, and all states limited the franchise to only a subset of the population. The most widespread limitations involved age, sex, race, property ownership, and length of residence within the jurisdiction, but there were others as well. Throughout the nineteenth century, the Supreme Court reiterated that "the Constitution of the United States has not conferred the right of suffrage upon any one."[5] Professor Keyssar's essay in this volume traces the tortuous history of the franchise; suffice it to say for present purposes that, at least until Reconstruction, there was no plausible textual foundation for constitutional claims about the right to vote.

Reconstruction, however, dramatically changed the shape of the Constitution, and with it—at least potentially—the federal government's role in protecting the electoral process. Section 2 of the Fourteenth Amendment threatened to penalize states that disenfranchised blacks (or, arguably, other adult male citizens) by reducing the size of their congressional delegations, and thus their allotment of electoral votes as well. And the Fifteenth Amendment explicitly provided that the right of citizens to vote "shall not be denied or abridged by the United States or by any State on account of race, color, or previous condition of servitude."

During Reconstruction, Congress vigorously enforced notions of equality in the political process. For example, it used the Guaranty Clause of Article IV—which provides that "[t]he United States shall guarantee to every State in this Union a Republican Form of Government"—to deny readmission to southern states whose constitutions did not adequately protect black voters. And between 1869 and 1900, the House used its power under the Qualifications Clause—which makes each house the judge of the elections and qualifications of its members—to set aside results in more than thirty elections in southern states where black voters had been excluded by unfair registration statutes, fraud, violence, or intimidation. Finally, Congress used its power to enforce the Fifteenth Amendment to pass legislation making it a crime to interfere with the right to vote.

By contrast, the nineteenth-century Supreme Court gutted the federal government's ability to enforce political equality. In *United States v. Cruikshank*[6] and *United States v. Reese,*[7] the Court made it well-nigh impossible for federal prosecutors to secure convictions of defendants who interfered with citizens' voting rights. In *Williams v. Mississippi,*[8] the Court disingenuously turned a blind eye to Mississippi's admission that its 1890 constitution was intended to disenfranchise blacks. Finally, at the turn of the century, in *Giles v. Harris,*[9] the Court not only acceded to the movement to disenfranchise black citizens, but essentially removed the courts from any role in policing the fairness of the electoral process.

Giles involved a class of more than 5,000 black citizens in Alabama who alleged that registrars were improperly keeping them off the rolls. Justice Oliver Wendell Holmes's opinion for the Court distinguished between two sorts of claims. On the one hand, the courts were an appropriate arena for adjudicating claims by plaintiffs who claimed the denial of individual rights. On the other hand, courts could not intervene to provide "relief from a great political wrong"; for that, the injured must look to the state or to "the legislative and political department of the Government of the United States."[10] As the Court later explained, the plaintiffs in *Giles* "in effect asked the federal court 'to supervise the voting in that State by officers of the court.' What this Court called a 'new and extraordinary situation' was found 'strikingly' to reinforce 'the argument that equity cannot undertake now, any more than it has in the past, to enforce political rights.'"[11]

The legacy of *Giles* offers a powerful explanation for why the Supreme Court came to use the Equal Protection Clause to regulate the political process. In contrast to other possible sources of constitutional constraint, the Equal Protection Clause makes no mention of the right to vote. Rather, it simply provides that no state shall "deny to any person within its jurisdiction the equal protection of the laws." Thus, the clause focuses explicitly on the rights of individual *persons*, rather than on the structure or organization of government. As early as 1927, Justice Holmes himself distinguished a Texas statute prohibiting blacks from voting in Democratic primaries from the kind of law at issue in *Giles*:

The objection that the subject matter of the suit is political is little more than a play upon words. Of course the petition concerns political action but it alleges and seeks to recover for private damage. That private damage may be caused by such political action and may be recovered for in a suit at law hardly has been doubted for over two hundred years.[12]

For Justice Holmes, the Equal Protection Clause forbade this kind of classification and exclusion on account of race whatever the right at issue. By contrast, in *Colegrove v. Green*,[13] Justice Frankfurter once again invoked *Giles* for the proposition that any inequalities produced by the Illinois system of congressional apportionment were "not a private wrong, but a wrong suffered by Illinois as a polity," and therefore not amenable to a judicial solution.

EQUAL PROTECTION AND THE
REAPPORTIONMENT REVOLUTION

In 1962, when the Warren Court took its first steps into the political thicket, the Equal Protection Clause offered a way to get around the "political question" doctrine that seemed to bar courts from supervising the electoral process absent a violation of some explicit constitutional provision like the Fifteenth Amendment.

In *Baker v. Carr*,[14] the Court confronted a virtually identical claim to the one raised in *Colegrove*. Three-fifths of the way through the twentieth century, Tennessee continued to use an apportionment for its state legislature first adopted in 1901. Shifts in population—particularly the move from rural areas to the cities and the rise of the suburbs—meant that legislative districts had vastly different numbers of voters. Sullivan County had eleven times as many residents as Stewart County, but each had one seat in the state house. Roughly 15 percent of the state's voters lived in Shelby County (Memphis), but the county had only eight of the lower house's ninety-nine seats. Although the overall scheme in Tennessee might be a "topsy-turvical of gigantic proportions" and a "crazy quilt without rational basis," in Justice Clark's colorful description, it was not exactly random. Tennessee was typical of many states where representatives from underpopulated rural hamlets dominated the legislatures. By the early 1960s, it was clear that much of the Supreme Court's workload was an indirect consequence of malapportionment's hold on state politics. More moderate and progressive forces, based in growing cities and suburbs, found themselves outnumbered by more reactionary politicians who protected their own seats and the influence of their constituents by refusing to reapportion. Thus, it is not at all surprising that the plaintiffs in *Baker* were voters and city officials from Memphis, Nashville, Chattanooga, and Knoxville (the state's biggest cities) plus a voter from one of Nashville's suburbs.

The Court held that challenges to state apportionment plans were in fact justiciable, under the Equal Protection Clause. Equal protection claims, it decided, did not run afoul of the "political question" doctrine. "Political questions" implicate "the relationship between the judiciary and the coordinate branches of the Federal Government, and not the federal judiciary's relationship to the States:"[15]

> It is apparent that several formulations which vary slightly according to the settings in which the questions arise may describe a political question. . . . Prominent on the surface of any case held to involve a political question is found a textually demonstrable constitutional commitment of the issue to a coordinate political department; or a lack of judicially discoverable and manageable standards for resolving it; or the impossibility of deciding without an initial policy determination of a kind clearly for nonjudicial discretion; or the impossibility of a court's undertaking independent resolution without expressing lack of the respect due coordinate branches of government; or an unusual need for unquestioning adherence to a political decision already made; or the potentiality of embarrassment from multifarious pronouncements by various departments on one question.[16]

The Court concluded that none of these difficulties arose with respect to Tennessee's apportionment. Of particular importance, the Court held that the plaintiffs were not asking the Court "to enter upon policy determinations for which judicially manageable standards are lacking." To the contrary, judicial standards under the Equal Protection Clause were "well developed and familiar, and it has been open to courts since the enactment of the Fourteenth Amendment to determine, if on the particular facts they must, that a discrimination reflects no policy, but simply arbitrary and capricious action."[17] Having decided that the *Baker* plaintiffs' claim was justiciable, the Court then remanded the case, sending it back to the trial court to be decided on the merits.

Baker unleashed a torrent of litigation. By the end of 1962, cases challenging legislative districts had been filed in more than thirty states. When the Supreme Court actually reached the question of what the Equal Protection Clause required, it went far beyond the well-developed and familiar equal protection requirement that state action not be arbitrary or capricious. In its landmark decisions in *Gray v. Sanders*[18] and *Reynolds v. Sims*[19]—both of which were later cited in *Bush v. Gore*—the Court held that the touchstone of the Equal Protection Clause in the political process was the principle of "one person, one vote." That is, each voter within a state was entitled to be treated equally with every other voter.

The vice in both *Gray* and *Reynolds* was that the value of a voter's ballot depended on where he or she lived. *Gray* involved Georgia's use of a county-unit system for deciding primary elections for statewide office. The candidate who carried the popular vote in a county was considered the county winner and was given two "unit votes" for each seat the county was allotted in the state legislature. The winner of the primary was determined on the basis of unit votes rather than the popular vote. So the Georgia system resembled the electoral college. There were a set of winner-take-all popular elections within different geographic constituencies. The winner of each popular election received a set of unit votes. The winner was determined by the electoral, rather than the popular, vote. The plaintiff in *Gray v. Sanders* lived in Fulton County (Atlanta), which, with over 550,000 people, had roughly 14 percent of Georgia's population. But the state gave Fulton County only three house seats, and thus only six unit votes out of a total of 410. The smallest county in Georgia, Echols County, had a population of only 1,876, but it received two unit votes. Thus, each unit vote in Echols County represented 936 residents, while each unit vote in Fulton County represented 92,721. This meant, according to the Supreme Court, that "one resident in Echols County had an influence in the nomination of candidates equivalent to 99 residents of Fulton County."[20] Although the state modified its system while the case was pending, the relative influence of citizens in different parts of the state still differed dramatically. First, even the modified unit system left a majority of the unit votes in counties that together made up less than one-third of the state's population. Second, the winner-take-all feature of the unit vote meant that many voters' ballots became meaningless: If a candidate won the popular vote in a county with 10,001 voters by one vote, the votes of the 5,000 voters who preferred the other candidate would simply be discarded in determining who would be elected.

As the Court recognized, the result of the county unit system was to weight the rural vote more heavily than the urban vote and to weigh the votes of residents of smaller counties more heavily than the votes of residents of larger counties. The Court drew an analogy to the prohibitions on denying or abridging the right to vote on account of race or sex contained in the Fifteenth and Nineteenth Amendments:

> If a State in a statewide election weighted the male vote more heavily than the female vote or the white vote more heavily than the Negro vote, none could successfully contend that that discrimination was allowable. How then can one person be given twice or ten times the voting power of another person in a statewide election merely because he lives in a rural area or because he lives in the smallest rural county? Once the geographical unit for which a representative is to be chosen is designated, all who participate in the election are to have an equal vote — whatever their race, whatever their sex, whatever their occupation, whatever their income, and wherever their home may be in that geographical unit. This is required by the Equal Protection Clause of the Fourteenth Amendment.[21]

Thus, the Court struck down Georgia's county unit system as a violation of the Equal Protection Clause.

Reynolds v. Sims concerned the apportionment of the Alabama legislature. There, too, the existing plan involved substantial inequalities of population. There were population variances of over 40 to 1 in the state senate and 16 to 1 in the state house. And the Court recognized that these differences corresponded to the rural-urban-suburban political divisions within the state, with rural areas enjoying a "strangle hold"[22] over the process. The state's proposed post-*Baker* remedy made only modest changes. Under one plan, for example, the votes of citizens in the smallest senatorial district would still be worth twenty times the votes of citizens in Jefferson County (where Birmingham, the state's largest city, was located).

The Supreme Court, in an opinion that Chief Justice Warren (also the author of such blockbusters as *Brown v. Board of Education*) called the most important of his career,[23] held that the Alabama scheme violated the Equal Protection Clause. For our purposes, four aspects of the Court's opinion merit attention.

First, the Court adopted a broad, functional definition of the right to vote. Chief Justice Warren's discussion relied heavily on prior decisions involving criminal prosecutions of elections officials; these cases had held that the right to vote encompassed not only the right to cast a ballot but also the right to have that ballot properly tabulated and included in the official returns.[24] It concluded:

> There is more to the right to vote than the right to mark a piece of paper and drop it in a box or the right to pull a lever in a voting booth. The right to vote includes the right to have the ballot counted.... It also includes the right to have the vote counted at full value without dilution or discount. . . . That federally protected right suffers substantial dilution . . . [where a] favored group has full voting strength . . . [and] [t]he groups not in favor have their votes discounted.[25]

Second, the Court reiterated the principle of statewide equality. An apportionment scheme that "'contracts the value of some votes and expands that of others' is unconstitutional, since 'the Federal

Constitution intends that when qualified voters elect [representatives] each vote be given as much weight as any other vote.'"[26] In statewide elections, the Court identified a "basic principle of equality among voters within a State"; thus, "voters cannot be classified, constitutionally, on the basis of where they live, at least with respect to voting in statewide elections."[27] An apportionment system whose practical effect was to weight different voters' votes differently, depending on where they lived, was just as unconstitutional as a state law that explicitly provided that the votes of some citizens should be "multiplied by two, five, or 10, while the votes of persons in another area would be counted only at face value."[28] The Court concluded:

> Weighting the votes of citizens differently, by any method or means, merely because of where they happen to reside, hardly seems justifiable. One must be ever aware that the Constitution forbids "sophisticated as well as simple-minded modes of discrimination."[29]

Third, the Court stated that because the right to vote "is a fundamental matter in a free and democratic society . . . preservative of other basic civil and political rights, any alleged infringement of the right of citizens to vote must be carefully and meticulously scrutinized."[30] Unlike other government actions that classify citizens, which generally receive only minimal judicial scrutiny, government actions that treat citizens differently with respect to voting demand more skeptical judicial oversight. Given this heightened standard, the state's population deviations were unacceptable:

> To the extent that a citizen's right to vote is debased, he is that much less a citizen. The fact that an individual lives here or there is not a legitimate reason for overweighting or diluting the efficacy of his vote. The complexions of societies and civilizations change, often with amazing rapidity. A nation once primarily rural in character becomes predominantly urban. Representation schemes once fair

and equitable become archaic and outdated. But the basic principle of representative government remains, and must remain, unchanged—the weight of a citizen's vote cannot be made to depend on where he lives.[31]

Finally, when it came to the question of a remedy for the equal protection violation it had found, the Court counseled judicial circumspection and an appreciation for the difficult task of fashioning appropriate relief. Prospective relief—that is, an order ensuring that no further elections would be conducted under an unconstitutional plan—was virtually always appropriate. But when an "impending election is imminent and a State's election machinery is already in progress, equitable considerations might justify a court in withholding the granting of immediately effective relief" even though the current system was invalid:

> With respect to the timing of relief, a court can reasonably endeavor to avoid a disruption of the election process which might result from requiring precipitate changes that could make unreasonable or embarrassing demands on a State in adjusting to the requirements of the court's decree.[32]

The "Reapportionment Revolution" launched by *Baker v. Carr*, *Gray v. Sanders*, and *Reynolds v. Sims* was a smashing popular and jurisprudential success. It is by far the Supreme Court's most successful modern-day effort at fundamental legal and political change. Many of the Court's other transformative ventures triggered widespread resistance or revisionism: *Roe v. Wade* and abortion rights; *Furman v. Georgia* and the death penalty; *Miranda v. Arizona* and the criminal procedure revolution; and even *Brown v. Board of Education* and school desegregation. By contrast, one-person, one-vote attained "a truly extraordinary record of compliance with the constitutional mandate."[33] The principle, though bitterly contested as a matter of constitutional law in the early 1960s, has become an iconic feature of American democracy.

EQUAL PROTECTION, THE RIGHT TO VOTE, AND THE TIERS OF SCRUTINY

The heart of the Court's one-person, one-vote cases was its equation of vote dilution with disenfranchisement: "the right of suffrage can be denied by a debasement or dilution of the weight of a citizen's vote just as effectively as by wholly prohibiting the free exercise of the franchise."[34] The precedents on which the Court relied for this principle were a series of Fifteenth Amendment cases dealing with the disenfranchisement of black voters. Ironically, although the one-person, one-vote decisions radically transformed key aspects of the political system, they did nothing directly to vindicate the equality claims of black citizens.[35] In March 1965, as states scrambled to comply with *Reynolds*, only about one-third of blacks in the South were registered to vote; in Alabama and Georgia, the percentages were even lower: 19.3 percent and 27.4 percent, respectively.[36] One-person, one-vote provided substantial protection for the voting rights of registered voters, but it did nothing to expand the franchise.

Another line of equal protection cases, however, did address the question of individuals' right to participate. The key doctrinal development was the Court's decision that laws restricting the franchise should be subjected to particularly searching judicial review. In most situations, a state's decision to classify individuals in distinct categories and then to treat them differently would survive an equal protection challenge, "if the Court can conceive of a 'rational basis' for the distinctions made."[37] But the Court concluded that the assumption underlying that deference—that "the institutions of state government are structured so as to represent fairly all the people"—was itself at issue in cases involving claims of exclusion from the political process. So the Court held that only if "the exclusion is necessary to promote a compelling state interest" would it survive judicial review.[38] This strict scrutiny required that the state's means be narrowly tailored to the compelling goal: If there were less exclusionary means of accomplishing the same end, the classification would fall.

In Gerald Gunther's memorable phrase, strict scrutiny usually turned out to be "strict in theory and fatal in fact."[39] Whereas most laws, even some rather far-fetched ones, could survive rationality review, once courts decided to apply strict scrutiny, they struck down the law or practice at issue virtually every time.[40] Thus, the decision about which level of scrutiny to apply was, as a practical matter, the decisive question in many cases. To take one particularly salient example, in 1973 the Supreme Court upheld Texas's system of financing public education against an equal protection challenge.[41] The system allowed individual school districts to supplement state funds through local property taxes, resulting in vast disparities in per-pupil expenditures. Wealthy suburban districts had more to spend on each student, even using lower tax rates, than did poorer districts. The Court assumed that the Texas system could not withstand the strict scrutiny used in reviewing laws that infringed on fundamental constitutional rights, such as the right to vote. But the Court held that education, critical though it might be to a person's ability to function in modern society, was not a fundamental federal constitutional right.[42] Thus, the Court asked only whether Texas's scheme bore "some rational relationship to a legitimate state purpose,"[43] and concluded that states might permissibly pursue decentralization and local control over public education.

As the Court recognized, the seemingly inevitable consequence of invoking strict scrutiny did create a certain tension. On the one hand, the Court viewed voting in broad, functional terms. It recognized that many aspects of the political system, from decisions about legislative districts to ballot access restrictions to restrictions on participating in party primaries, affected the nature of a voter's ability to participate and elect the candidates of his or her choice. On the other hand, to treat the core constitutional right in this broad fashion would risk wholesale invalidation of virtually every aspect of a state's election code. If strict scrutiny were applied, it might be impossible for states ever to justify their election practices; the very variety among state laws might suggest that no particular procedure was *necessary* to the achievement of a compelling state interest. So the Court essentially confined strict scrutiny to claims of outright exclusion from the political process. For example, in *City of Mobile v. Bolden*,[44] the Court construed the Fifteenth Amendment's explicit protection of voting to guarantee only the right to "register and vote without hindrance."[45] Once again quoting the statement that "the Constitution of the United States does not confer the right of suffrage upon any one,"[46] the Court held that although the Equal Protection Clause "confers a substantive right to participate in elections on an equal basis with other qualified voters . . . this right to equal participation in the electoral process does not protect any 'political group,' however defined, from electoral defeat."[47] Thus, the city's decision to use at-large elections rather than district-based elections was not subjected to strict scrutiny, even though one foreseeable consequence was the dilution of black voting strength.

Interestingly, the one-person, one-vote cases finessed this issue. The Court had treated malapportionment claims as involving individual rights rather than group interests. The mathematical standard the Court laid out avoided the difficulty of deciding case-by-case whether particular apportionments were fair. Thus, claimants raising one-person, one-vote claims faced a lower barrier than claimants alleging other forms of vote dilution. Once a plaintiff showed a population deviation of more than 10 percent among state or local election districts (or any avoidable population deviation with respect to congressional districts), the burden shifted to the jurisdiction to show that the deviations were necessary to achieve a legitimate government purpose. Although there were "[a]ny number of consistently applied legislative policies [that] might justify some variance, including, for instance, making districts compact, respecting municipal boundaries, preserving the cores of prior districts, and avoiding contests between incumbent Representatives,"[48] courts have generally been skeptical of states' claims, because there often are ways of achieving these goals with less deviation from mathematical equality.

In any event, the interaction of one-person, one-vote and fundamental rights equal protection cases has meant that certain kinds of interference with the right to vote trigger extreme judicial skepticism, but the courts have focused that skepticism largely on areas where readily identifiable, objective rules are available and on formal rights to participate. Virtually always, the appropriate remedy under either strand of equal protection doctrine has been to expand, prospectively, the right to participate in the electoral process. At the same time, in the absence of statutory provisions such as the Voting Rights Act, courts have been extremely reluctant to act when intervention involves policing political results, such as who should win particular elections.

EQUAL PROTECTION AND THE COURT'S RELATIONSHIP TO CONGRESS

For individuals who came of age during the heyday or afterglow of the Warren Court, it is often surprising to recognize that even in areas where the Supreme Court was at the forefront of articulating principles of equality, real progress on the ground often occurred only after the political branches became involved. For example, ten years after the Court condemned de jure school segregation in *Brown v. Board of Education*,[49] fewer than 2 percent of black children in the South attended a school with even a single white student. Southern jurisdictions began desegregation in earnest only after the Department of Education threatened to withhold federal funds. Similarly, for all the Court's statements regarding the evil of racial discrimination in voting, it was not until Congress passed the Voting Rights Act of 1965, with its provisions suspending literacy tests and other restrictive registration practices, authorizing federal registrars for recalcitrant jurisdictions, and setting up a pre-clearance regime to prevent the adoption of new discriminatory practices, that black voters entered the political system in large numbers.

The text of the Fourteenth Amendment explicitly recognizes that Congress should play a central role in securing equality. Section 5 of the Amendment provides that "[t]he Congress shall have power to enforce, by appropriate legislation, the provisions of this article." Particularly given the circumstances surrounding its adoption in 1868, the amendment's recognition of a special congressional role makes sense. At the end of the Civil War, the Supreme Court was still suffering under the "self-inflicted wound" of its controversial and discredited decision in the *Dred Scott* case. Indeed, the first sentence of the Fourteenth Amendment was intended precisely to overrule the Court's holding in *Dred Scott* by affirming that "All persons born or naturalized in the United States . . . are citizens of the United States and of the State wherein they reside."

In *Katzenbach v. Morgan*,[50] the Supreme Court recognized an expansive role for Congress in enforcing the Equal Protection Clause. In *Morgan* and a later case, *Oregon v. Mitchell*,[51] the Court agreed that Congress could use its section 5 enforcement power to outlaw literacy tests broadly, without having to find that a particular jurisdiction's test was invidiously discriminatory. In later cases, the Court also upheld the Act's sweeping pre-clearance regime—which requires federal review before certain jurisdictions change their voting laws in any way and which forbids changes that have a racially discriminatory effect regardless of the purpose behind them—as appropriate uses of Congress's section 5 power.

In recent years, however, the reigning majority on the Rehnquist Court has expressed growing skepticism of Congress's invocation of its section 5 power. Beginning in 1997, the Court has struck down sections of the Religious Freedom Restoration Act and the Violence Against Women Act, as well as the extension of the Age Discrimination in Employment and Americans with Disabilities Acts to state employees, all as exceeding congressional enforcement power. A common thread in the Court's decisions is its skepticism of congressional ability to find facts adequate to support legislation under the Equal Protection Clause. In its cases regarding race-conscious redistricting, the Court has also expressed noticeable distrust of the executive branch's construction and enforcement of equal protection principles. Thus, when the Court came to confront equal protection issues in the election of 2000, it had already come to see itself as the only branch of government capable of interpreting the Equal Protection clause Faithfully.

THE ROAD TO *BUSH V. GORE*

Larry Kramer's contribution to this volume describes the backdrop against which the Supreme Court made its ultimate ruling: an agonizingly close election in which the margin of victory was within the margin of error and in which imperfections in the way machines record votes might determine the outcome. Three aspects of the developments leading to *Bush v. Gore* deserve special attention: the Supreme Court's initial refusal to hear Bush's equal protection claim; the Article II/Equal Protection Clause dilemma that the Court's opinion in *Bush v. Palm Beach County Canvassing Board* posed for the Florida Supreme Court; and the tactical and statutory issues governing the kind of recount ultimately ordered.

First, the Supreme Court originally declined to consider the equal protection implications of recounts. The first case to reach the U.S. Supreme Court was Bush's challenge to the Florida Supreme Court's November 21 decision requiring Secretary of State Katherine Harris to accept late-filed returns derived from manual recounts in the counties where the Democratic Party had filed protests. In his petition seeking high court review, Governor Bush raised the question "whether the use of arbitrary, standard-less, and selective manual recounts that threaten to overturn the re-sults of the election for President of the United States violates the Equal Protection or Due Process Clauses, or the First Amend-ment."[52] The petition alleged that "vote-counters . . . will divine the 'intent of the electorate' without *any* legislative guidance or uniform standards. The process therefore varies from county to county, and criteria for counting ballots as votes has [*sic*] changed repeatedly in each recount county."[53]

Although this argument was quite sketchy, the petition identified two forms of equal protection violation. The selective recounts treated voters differently "simply because they happen to live in dif-ferent parts of the State."[54] That is, whether a ballot would be counted at all might depend on whether a recount was ordered—a decision left to arbitrary choices by local canvassing boards—and if it was conducted, the standard used to discern whether the voter had intended to vote for a particular candidate was unclear. In addi-tion, the selective recount would "unconstitutionally dilute the votes of those who properly cast their votes on election day and those who do not live in the counties selected for a manual recount."[55]

The U.S. Supreme Court declined even to hear these equal pro-tection challenges, limiting its grant of certiorari to questions re-garding Florida's compliance with Article II, section 1 of the Con-stitution and the safe-harbor provision of the Electoral Count Act of 1887. In large part, as Larry Kramer suggests, this decision may have rested on the lack of a factual basis in the record for determin-ing whether different counties were employing different stan-dards. But the record surely was adequate for considering the sec-ond equal protection question: namely, whether in a statewide election, a scheme that limited manual recounts to only a few coun-ties treated similarly situated voters differently and unfairly. The Bush petition for certiorari was quite summary in its presentation of the equal protection argument, but a fuller explanation might go something like this: There are, in each county, some unknowable number of voters who intended to cast ballots in the presidential race but who, due to failure to follow the instructions, the interaction of human and machine complications, or other factors, failed to cast votes captured in the machine count. Some of these voters—those living in the counties that had decided to conduct manual recounts—would have their votes captured by a manual recount. Others—those living in the counties that decided to stick with the machine counts—would be denied this second chance. In a statewide election, where a candidate's votes could come from any precinct, the Florida scheme provided insufficient justification for recounting in some areas and not in others. Moreover, the failure to recount all votes might also injure voters whose votes *had* been recorded in the initial machine count. During the protest phase, the Democrats asked for recounts in four large, predominantly Democratic counties. They assumed (perhaps erroneously, as later media-conducted recounts suggested) that manual recounts in these counties would net additional Democratic votes. A Republican voter would be disadvantaged by this procedure, even if his or her vote had been recorded the first time around, because the votes of his compatriots would be less likely than Democratic votes to be captured in the recount process, since heavily Republican counties were not being recounted.

Even though the claim might conceivably be ready for review, the Court had good reasons not to hear it. They can be summed up within the concept of "standing." Article III of the Constitution permits federal courts to entertain claims only if the party pressing them is the appropriate one. That is, even the fact of a constitutional violation does not give every citizen a roving warrant to seek judicial enforcement. As the Court explained in *United States v. Hays,* a case involving the question of who could challenge allegedly gerrymandered congressional districts, standing requires that "the plaintiff must have suffered an 'injury in fact'—invasion of a legally protected interest that is (a) concrete and particularized, and (b) actual or imminent, not conjectural or hypothetical" and that "it must be likely, as opposed to merely speculative, that the injury will be redressed by a favorable decision."[56] Realistically speaking, George W. Bush would be injured by the recount process only if it changed the outcome of the election in Florida and did so in an unconstitutional fashion. Before the recounts were even conducted, that possibility seemed hypothetical at best. Moreover, whatever injuries Bush might suffer were not violations of the Equal Protection Clause: He was not being treated differently in any way from similarly situated individuals, namely, other candidates for president. Bush had the same right to file protests seeking recounts, but he had waived it for the obvious reason that he was ahead in the count. So if he were advancing an equal protection claim, it would be someone else's. Federal courts normally hesitate to resolve controversies on the basis of the rights of third persons who are not parties to the litigation. This rule is relaxed somewhat in situations where 1) the party before the court has suffered its own injury that gives it a sufficiently concrete interest in the outcome to ensure vigorous litigation, 2) the litigant has a close relation to the third party, and 3) there is some barrier to the third party's ability to protect its own interests.

George W. Bush was the only petitioner in *Bush v. Palm Beach County Canvassing Board*. Whatever else one might say, Bush was not himself a Florida voter. Thus, the question whether he could raise the equal protection claims of Florida voters would depend on whether he had a close relationship to those voters and whether those voters lacked the ability to protect their own interests. Neither criterion was clearly met. Moreover, Bush's ultimate strategic goal was not to have a fair recount; it was to prevent *any* recount. After all, he was ahead after the machine count and the margin of victory within Florida was wholly irrelevant. The problem with the voters' claims was that, with respect to the voters whose votes wouldn't be counted under the selective recounts, Bush was an inappropriate representative: He *wanted* to prevent their ballots from being counted. And with respect to the voters claiming dilution from the selective addition of manually recounted ballots, Bush was an appropriate representative only of those who cast votes for him. Finally, unless and until a recount would change the outcome and render Gore the winner, it was unclear, at best, whether Bush was suffering any injury in fact.

The second important element of the prelude to *Bush v. Gore* was a dilemma created by the Court's decision in *Bush v. Palm Beach County Canvassing Board*. As Larry Kramer points out, the Court's opinion remanding the entire case to the Florida Supreme Court allowed the Court to avoid saying anything substantive. But the tone of the opinion suggested that the U.S. Supreme Court was troubled by the possibility that the Florida Supreme Court was changing the existing law. Section 5 of the Electoral Count Act contained a safe-harbor provision. If a state sets out rules ahead of time for determining controversies over the appointment of its electors, and those rules produce a determination at least six days in advance of the day electors are supposed to vote, then the state's determination "shall be conclusive, and shall govern in the counting of the electoral votes as provided in the Constitution." In other words, if the state uses already established procedures for deciding who its slate of electors should be, Congress would not revisit the question when the time came for counting electoral votes.

> Since §5 [of the Electoral Count Act] contains a principle of federal law that would assure finality of the State's determination if made pursuant to a state law in effect before the election, a legislative wish to take advantage of the "safe harbor" would counsel against any construction of the Election Code that Congress might deem to be a change in the law. . . . We are . . . unclear as to the consideration the Florida Supreme Court accorded to 3 U.S.C. §5.[57]

The opinion in *Bush v. Palm Beach County Canvassing Board* was thus a warning shot across the Florida Supreme Court's bow: Don't make any new law in overseeing the 2000 election.

This placed the Florida Supreme Court in an awkward position. The Florida Election Code spoke in vague terms, both about the standard for deciding when a ballot is legally cast and about the remedial powers of state courts in election contest proceedings. With respect to the former question, the Election Code provided that "[n]o vote shall be declared invalid or void if there is a clear indication of the intent of the voter as determined by the canvassing board."[58] With respect to the latter issue, Florida law provided that "[t]he circuit judge to whom the contest is presented may fashion such orders as he or she deems necessary to ensure that each allegation in the complaint is investigated, examined, or checked, to prevent or correct any alleged wrong, and to provide any relief appropriate under such circumstances."[59]

In contrast to states like Indiana, where the legislature elaborated on the clear intent standard by directing that "a chad that has been pierced, but not entirely punched out of the card, shall be counted as a vote," whereas a chad "that has been indented, but not in any way separated from the remainder of the card, may not be counted as a vote,"[60] Florida's Election Code provided no subsidiary rules for deciding voter intent. That is hardly unusual; as Justice Stevens later noted, a majority of the states use a similarly general standard. But it meant that any delineation, within the context of a remedial decree affecting the 2000 presidential election, of more precise subordinate rules for discerning a voter's intent might be attacked as "new law." On the other hand, as long as the principle was described in such general language, it remained quite possible that different vote counters would disagree on whether a ballot reflected a clear indication. Thus, if the Florida Supreme Court avoided the Scylla of Article II and the Electoral Count Act, it might find itself sucked into the whirling Charybdis of the Equal Protection Clause.

The third piece of the prelude was that everyone—parties and courts alike—was operating under extreme time and information constraints. The Gore forces assumed that their best chance of picking up votes was to capture "undervotes" in heavily Democratic counties. So when they filed their "contest" lawsuit—called *Gore v. Harris* as it worked its way through the Florida courts—the relief they sought was a manual recount of ballots in two counties where they had originally filed administrative protests, and in those counties alone.[61]

Judge Sanders Sauls, the trial court judge assigned to hear the contest proceeding, ruled against Gore. The primary basis for his ruling was a holding that Gore had failed to show by a preponderance of the evidence that the certified outcome of the election would probably be different if the disputed ballots were counted. Of particular salience to the equal protection issue, Judge Sauls added that the proper remedy for a statewide election contest

> would necessarily have to place at issue and seek as a remedy with the attendant burden of proof, a review and recount on all ballots, and all of the counties in this state with respect to the particular alleged irregularities or inaccuracies in the balloting or counting processes alleged to have occurred. . . . There is in this type of election, one statewide election, and one certification. Palm Beach County did not elect any person as a presidential elector, but, rather, the election with the winner-take-all proposition, [was an election] with the winner dependent on the statewide vote.[62]

On appeal to the Florida Supreme Court, Gore continued to press for a partial recount. The defendants, in part no doubt as a tactical matter, argued not only that the recount should extend statewide but also that the recount should reexamine all ballots, surely a formidable undertaking in the short time remaining before December 18, when the electors were to cast their votes.

On December 8, the Florida Supreme Court issued its opinion in *Gore v. Harris*, and it took an intermediate position. The contest provision, § 102.168, identified "rejection of a number of legal votes sufficient to change or place in doubt the result of the election"[63] as a basis for contesting an election. The Court interpreted that language to mean that only contested ballots should be examined in a recount order pursuant to § 102.168. Counting uncontested votes, it observed, would be irrelevant to determining whether legal votes had been rejected. Thus, it refused to order a statewide manual recount of *all* ballots.

At the same time, the Florida Supreme Court found that it was "absolutely essential in this proceeding and to any final decision, that a manual recount be conducted for all legal votes in this State . . . in all Florida counties where there was an undervote, and, hence a concern that not every citizen's vote was counted:"[64]

> The demonstrated problem of not counting legal votes inures to any county utilizing a counting system which results in undervotes and "no registered vote" ballots. In a countywide election, one would not simply examine such categories of ballots from a single precinct to insure the reliability and integrity of the countywide vote. Similarly, in this statewide election, review should not be limited to less than all counties whose tabulation has resulted in such categories of ballots. Relief would not be "appropriate under [the] circumstances" if it failed to address the "otherwise valid exercise of the right of a citizen to vote" of all those citizens of this State who, being similarly situated, have had their legal votes rejected. . . . [A] final decision as to the result of the statewide election should only be determined upon consideration of the legal votes contained within the undervote or "no registered vote" ballots of all Florida counties, as well as the legal votes already tabulated.[65]

Given the press of time, the Florida Supreme Court ordered the Leon County Circuit Court, the trial court responsible for hearing statewide election contests, "to order the Supervisor of Elections and the Canvassing Boards, as well as the necessary public officials, in all counties that have not conducted a manual recount or tabulation of the undervotes in this election to do so forthwith, said tabulation to take place in the individual counties where the ballots are located."[66] In short, it ordered that the recount process be farmed out, in the first instance, to the individual county canvassing boards.

The court-ordered recount began the next morning (Saturday, December 9), but in the late afternoon was stayed by the U.S. Supreme Court.[67] The stay clearly foreshadowed the ultimate outcome of the case. Having stopped the recount process with roughly seventy-two hours to go before the safe-harbor window of the Electoral Count Act was to close, it seemed highly unlikely that the Court would permit the process to start up again. Four of the five justices who voted to stay the recount were silent as to their reasons; the fifth, the often voluble Antonin Scalia, provided at least a hint that the Court would be receptive this time to the equal protection argument it had earlier declined to address. He noted that one issue in the case "is the propriety, indeed the constitutionality, of letting the standard for determination of voters' intent—dimpled chads, hanging chads, etc.—vary from county to county, as the Florida Supreme Court opinion, as interpreted by the Circuit Court, permits."[68]

Although Bush devoted relatively little space in his brief to the equal protection argument, the issue seemed to preoccupy several members of the Court at oral argument. They seemed particularly troubled by the lack of any sub-standards to guide counters in applying the "clear intent of the voter" standard, as well as by the candid admission of Gore's counsel that ballots might in fact be counted differently by different tabulators. And ultimately, the per curiam opinion joined by five members of the Court concluded that the recount ordered by the Florida Supreme Court violated the Equal Protection Clause.

THE SUPREME COURT'S
DECISION IN *BUSH V. GORE*

The Court's analysis of the equal protection issue started on a jarring note, as the Court reiterated the nineteenth-century principle that

> [t]he individual citizen has no federal constitutional right to vote for electors for the President of the United States unless and until the state legislature chooses a statewide election as the means to implement its power to appoint members of the Electoral College. ... The State, of course, after granting the franchise in the special context of Article II, can take back the power to appoint electors.[69]

One might wonder why this gratuitous observation seemed necessary. My suspicion is that it paved the way, perhaps unconsciously, for the Court's ultimate decision on the question of remedy. If the Court had viewed the right to vote and have one's vote counted in presidential elections as a fundamental constitutional right, it would have been hard pressed to explain why that right could be infringed to meet a statutory deadline set far in advance of the date on which the Constitution itself would require the election to be decided. Put in terms of the strict scrutiny framework discussed previously, it might be hard to conclude that attainment of the safe-harbor provision of the Electoral Count Act was a compelling state interest sufficient to justify disenfranchising otherwise qualified voters. Even if Florida lost the benefit of the safe harbor, there was never any realistic possibility that the state would lose its electoral votes altogether: Congress surely would have accepted *some* slate, whether the already filed one certified by Secretary of State Harris, the legislatively selected one then being discussed by the Florida legislature, or one produced by the judicially required recount. As the per curiam opinion itself observed in another context, "The press of time does not diminish the constitutional concern. A desire for speed is not a general excuse for ignoring equal protection guarantees."[70] Nor is it an excuse for ignoring the Due Process Clause's protection of fundamental constitutional liberties.

The equal protection question posed by the Court may reflect a similar dynamic. "The question before us," the Court announced, "is whether the recount procedures the Florida Supreme Court has adopted are consistent with its obligation to avoid arbitrary and disparate treatment of the members of its electorate."[71] Normally, of course, the standard for claims involving denials of the right to vote is not the "no arbitrary treatment" standard of rationality review, but the more skeptical "no distinction unless it's necessary to the achievement of a compelling government purpose" standard of strict scrutiny. Again, the Court's formulation foreshadows the ultimate outcome, focusing more on whether voters are treated equally than on whether their votes are actually counted.

The Supreme Court's opinion focused on two problems. First, the Florida Supreme Court failed to provide "specific standards" or "uniform rules" to ensure equal application of the basic "clear intent of the voter" standard. The Court believed that when dealing with inanimate objects, like ballots, "[t]he search for intent can be confined by specific rules designed to ensure uniform treatment."[72]

> The want of those rules here has led to unequal evaluation of ballots in various respects. As seems to have been acknowledged at oral argument, the standards for accepting or rejecting contested ballots might vary not only from county to county but indeed within a single county from one recount team to another.
>
> The record provides some examples. A monitor in Miami-Dade County testified at trial that he observed that three members of the county canvassing board applied different standards in defining a legal vote. And testimony at trial also revealed that at least one county changed its evaluative standards during the counting process. Palm Beach County, for example, began the process with a 1990 guideline which precluded counting completely attached chads, switched to a

rule that considered a vote to be legal if any light could be seen through a chad, changed back to the 1990 rule, and then abandoned any pretense of a per se rule, only to have a court order that the county consider dimpled chads legal. This is not a process with sufficient guarantees of equal treatment.[73]

Second, the Court saw an equal protection issue in the fact that the already conducted manual recounts in Broward, Volusia, and Palm Beach Counties were not limited, as the newly ordered statewide recount was, simply to undervotes, but had included all ballots:

> The distinction has real consequences. A manual recount of all ballots identifies not only those ballots which show no vote but also those which contain more than one, the so-called overvotes. Neither category will be counted by the machine. This is not a trivial concern. At oral argument, respondents estimated there are as many as 110,000 overvotes statewide. As a result, the citizen whose ballot was not read by a machine because he failed to vote for a candidate in a way readable by a machine may still have his vote counted in a manual recount; on the other hand, the citizen who marks two candidates in a way discernible by the machine will not have the same opportunity to have his vote count, even if a manual examination of the ballot would reveal the requisite indicia of intent. Furthermore, the citizen who marks two candidates, only one of which is discernible by the machine, will have his vote counted even though it should have been read as an invalid ballot.[74]

The Court analogized these disparities to the disparities condemned in cases such as *Gray v. Sanders* and *Reynolds v. Sims*, identifying the constitutional vice in those cases as differential treatment of voters based on where they lived.

On one level, the analogy holds. If, for example, Florida had enacted a statute providing that "punchcard ballots where the chad is only partially detached shall count as valid votes if cast in Broward

County but shall not count as valid votes if cast in Palm Beach County," that statute would face grave constitutional difficulty. It would be hard to see any justification, let alone a compelling one, for treating two physically identifiable ballots differently based on the residence of the voter who cast them. Similarly, a statute providing that manual recounts in one category of counties shall reexamine all ballots while recounts in the remaining counties shall reexamine only undervotes would also seem to draw an arbitrary distinction among voters depending on where they lived.

But if such statutes had been on the books, three other things would have been true as well. First, the statutes could easily be challenged prospectively, that is, before their application in a particular election contest, when the effect on the ultimate outcome would be clear to the reviewing court and the public. It would thus be possible to ban recounts under the constitutionally suspect procedures while not foreclosing a recount altogether. Second, if such statutes were challenged prospectively, it would throw into sharper relief the real equal protection problem: There is something troubling about there being different probabilities of a voter's ballot actually being counted depending on where the voter votes. This would then raise the issue the Supreme Court mentioned only in passing: Irrespective of the recount process, citizens in Florida had significantly different likelihoods, ex ante, of having their ballots counted. As Henry Brady has noted, the Accuvote optical scan voting systems used in sixteen Florida counties have an undervote rate of about three votes per thousand and an overvote rate of between three and four votes per thousand, whereas the punch-card systems used in twenty-four other Florida counties have an undervote rate of around fifteen per thousand and an overvote rate of about twenty-five per thousand! Thus, voters in punch-card counties are far less likely to have their votes counted in the machine-counting round than voters in Accuvote counties. This difference greatly exceeds the differential rate at which ballots were being recaptured in the manual recounts. It seems hard to believe that a court confronted with these issues could cavalierly declare, as the per curiam did, that "[o]ur consideration is limited to the present circumstances, for the problem of equal protection in election processes generally presents many complexities. The question before the Court is not whether local entities, in the exercise of their expertise, may develop different systems for implementing elections."[75] When it comes to statewide elections, it is hard to see why local entities, in the exercise of their expertise (or more likely their differential frugality) could use different election systems if the results were to make some voters' votes far more likely to count than others. The fact that the Court disclaimed any interest in this problem raises the suspicion that the Court is not nearly as committed to equal protection principles as it claims.

But the analogy to the one-person, one-vote cases breaks down at a deeper level still. The problem in *Gray* and *Reynolds* was not the random, one-time-only differential weighting of individuals' votes, but the systematic degradation of identifiable blocs of citizens' voting strength. Malapportionment froze the existing political order into place and undermined the possibility of truly representative government. That is why the Warren Court repeatedly pointed to the fact that the challenged systems allowed a small numerical minority to control the outcome of a statewide election or the composition of the state legislature. By contrast, whatever the vices of the recount ordered by the Florida Supreme Court, it neither produced a systematic, repetitive dilution of any citizens' vote nor did it risk enabling a numerical minority to tie up the political process.

More significantly, the Supreme Court's ultimate remedy for the equal protection violation it found—namely, to stop the recount altogether—completely separates its decision from the Court's earlier equal protection jurisprudence. Consider, again, the two problems the Court identified with the recount: the different standards used within counties and the reexamination only of undervotes.

With respect to the problem of different standards for deciding a previously uncounted ballot's validity, there are two groups of voters who might be injured. First, a voter might be injured if she lived in a county where vote-counters during a manual recount rejected ballots like hers instead of living in a county where such ballots were included. Second, a voter whose preferred candidate's support was concentrated in counties with restrictive views of what counts as a clear intent might claim that the overall voting power of that identifiable group was diluted by the use of different standards. In either case, however, the equal protection claim is one in which the voters involved would be seeking to have votes *counted*, rather than to have votes *excluded*.

Moreover, the per curiam opinion's implicit assumption that inconsistent evaluation of ballots should be cured through the declaration of "specific rules designed to ensure uniform treatment"[76] ignores a very different method of ensuring equality, namely some form of centralized review of line-level decision making, that is, the decisions that election officials have to make when they assess the meaning of a single mark that a voter has placed next to the name of an individual candidate. And when it comes to elections, there may be powerful reasons to prefer this "procedural" form of harmonization to the "substantive" form that rigid rules might produce.

To understand this point, consider the world we had for the latter part of the nineteenth and first part of the twentieth century when it came to elections, and which still exists in some states: a world of official printed paper ballots, which obviously must be counted manually, even in the first round of counting.

One could, of course, have very rigid rules for whether to include such ballots. Consider Illinois, for example. When it came to paper ballots, the Illinois Election Code expressly required that voters mark their paper ballots by making a cross (an "x") in the space next to the candidate of their choice.[77] Applying this hard-and-fast rule, Illinois courts held that votes would not be counted "unless two lines intersect in a cross in the appropriate place on the ballot, even if the voter's intent is clear."[78] Thus, in one case, the court refused to count ballots which the voter had marked with a check, rather than a cross, or ballots on which the voter had written the word "yes" rather than marking the box with an "x."[79] In other cases, lines that did not actually cross within the box were held not to constitute a legal vote,[80] as were circles made within the circle next to a candidate's name.[81]

If the rules are rigid enough, it probably does not matter who counts the ballots, because any vote-counter acting in good faith is likely to be able to distinguish between a cross, a check mark, or the word "yes," except in some truly odd cases. But this uniformity comes at a significant price: It can result in throwing out a substantial number of ballots where there is no real disagreement about a voter's intent. It achieves equality at the price of exclusion.

But many jurisdictions using paper ballots did not have these kinds of rigid rules. So it was up to the line-level canvassers in the first instance to decide which ballots were valid and which were not, using some kind of intent-of-the-voter standard.

So how could (or did) such jurisdictions ensure uniformity, which is what the Supreme Court has now intimated is required? They did it procedurally, rather than substantively. There were various protest, contest, and appeals processes, which ultimately placed disputed ballots before a single arbiter. The procedural solution creates uniformity not through the application of rigid rules but by channeling disputes into an arena where those disputes could be resolved consistently. That, in effect, is how *most* states' systems operate today. They do not have rigid rules but rather employ procedural solutions for dealing with disagreements over what counts as a valid vote. That was one of the key premises of the dissenting opinions that Justices Souter and Breyer delivered: They thought that the Florida *courts* were the appropriate mechanism for making sure ballots were treated uniformly. And that solution generally works, unless time is too short to permit orderly procedures—a source of sharp disagreement within both the Florida and U.S. Supreme Courts—or unless one is so skeptical of judicial integrity that one thinks state judges will count a checkmark if it is next to Candidate X's name but not if it is next to Candidate Y's.

A similar analysis of the underlying injury applies to the Florida Supreme Court's order to recount undervotes but not overvotes. First, the citizen who casts an overvote but whose intent was clearly discernible—for example, a voter who both punched out the chad or marked the optical scan box next to a candidate's name and also wrote in the candidate's name on the write-in portion of the ballot (and perhaps thousands of voters in Florida did just that)—is injured because her overvote will not be captured by the recount process. That voter is denied the opportunity to have her vote recovered that is accorded to citizens who cast undervotes.

There is something disquieting about the fact that although the Court focused largely on the claims of excluded voters, the remedy it ordered simply excluded more voters yet. And there's something disquieting as well about the Court's allowing George W. Bush to raise the claims of excluded voters, since he wanted their votes to remain excluded; he wanted no recount at all. As I have pointed out elsewhere, George W. Bush makes a strange champion for undervoters in heavily Democratic Palm Beach County, who presumably want their votes counted. And yet, neither Al Gore's counsel nor the Court ever addressed the threshold question of standing and whose rights were being remedied.[82]

Indeed, the remedy the Court ordered distinguishes *Bush v. Gore* from every other voting rights case and virtually every other modern equal protection case as well. Faced with a finding of unconstitutional inequality, especially in an area that touches on a fundamental right, courts generally "level up," that is, they order that the previously excluded group receive the benefit already accorded to everyone else. They almost never "level down," ordering the withdrawal of the benefit from everyone. But *Bush v. Gore* took precisely this leveling down approach: If Florida could not conduct a manual recount in which all voters' ballots were treated identically, then it could not conduct a manual recount at all. This meant that the U.S. Supreme Court's order left *more* presumably legal ballots uncounted than the Florida Supreme Court's ruling had. If anything, then, the remedy exacerbated the equal protection problem that some citizens' votes were recorded while other citizens' were not.

Moreover, the Court's growing distrust of Congress's ability to construe and appropriately enforce the Equal Protection Clause may also resonate in the decision to stop the recount. The Constitution and the Electoral Count Act seem to identify Congress, rather than the federal courts, as the venue for arguing about states' decisions regarding their electors. Had the Court allowed the recount to proceed, and had the recount resulted in Gore's being declared the victor in Florida, the question of who should receive Florida's electoral votes surely would have ended up before Congress. It seems difficult to believe that George W. Bush would simply have conceded the election and returned to Austin.

Had Congress faced the issue, it surely would have debated whether the Florida recount process treated all voters fairly. It clearly could consider equal protection values in deciding which slate of electors' ballots to count. Yet the Court strained mightily to avoid the possibility that Congress might be called upon to play its constitutional and statutory role under Article II, the Twelfth Amendment, and the Electoral Count Act. Why? Given the Court's recent treatment of Congress's output, especially its handiwork under the Fourteenth Amendment, one answer springs immediately to mind: The Court mistrusted Congress almost as much as it distrusted the Florida Supreme Court. To throw the question into Congress risked chaos and sloppy thinking. The Court decided that only it could save us from ourselves.

In the end, of course, the decision to stop the recount had virtually nothing to do with the Equal Protection Clause. It essentially smuggled in through the back door the Article II rationale advanced explicitly by Chief Justice Rehnquist's concurrence: that the Florida Supreme Court's remedial order had contravened the legislature's directives in setting out the manner by which the state's presidential electors should be selected. So why did the per curiam insist on relying on the Equal Protection Clause to explain the constitutional infirmities in the Florida recount process?

I think it is precisely because one-person, one-vote has been such a stunning popular and jurisprudential success that the Court attempted to wrap its decision in *Bush v. Gore* in the mantle of *Gray* and *Reynolds*. Consider how the joint opinion of Justices O'Connor, Kennedy, and Souter in *Planned Parenthood v. Casey*—the case in which the Supreme Court reaffirmed the central right to reproductive autonomy recognized in *Roe v. Wade*—wrapped itself in the mantle of another iconic Equal Protection Clause case, *Brown v. Board of Education*. The *Casey* joint opinion noted a special dimension "present whenever the Court's interpretation of the Constitution calls the contending sides of a national controversy to end their national division by accepting a common mandate rooted in the Constitution."[83] It identified only two such occasions "in our lifetime, . . . the decisions of *Brown* and *Roe*."[84] And it then explained the need to stick by its analysis in *Roe* this way:

> [T]o overrule under fire in the absence of the most compelling reason to reexamine a watershed decision would subvert the Court's legitimacy beyond any serious question. Cf. *Brown v. Board of Education*, 349 U.S. 294, 300 (*Brown II*) ("It should go without saying that the vitality of the constitutional principles [announced in *Brown I*,] cannot be allowed to yield simply because of disagreement with them").[85]

In *Bush v. Gore* as well—one hopes yet another once-in-our-lifetime decision—the Court was asking the nation to end its close division by accepting a common mandate rooted in the Constitution. And as between the Equal Protection Clause—source of some of the Supreme Court's finest moments, in cases such as *Brown* and *Reynolds v. Sims*—and Article II, § 1—the central pillar of *McPherson v. Blacker,*[86] a nineteenth-century case concerning how Michigan selected its electors—there's no contest. If the Supreme Court was going to stop the recount process, and thus decide, in effect, who would be the next president of the United States, it had to use a constitutional provision with some pedigree. The Equal Protection Clause provided exactly that. Moreover, it allowed the Court to invoke the specter of unfairly disenfranchised voters, whereas the other available constitutional contenders protected either the prerogative of state legislatures (Article II, § 1) or, even worse, the interests of candidate George W. Bush (the Due Process Clause).

The decision in *Bush v. Gore* was unprecedented in the colloquial sense of the word. To my mind, it was also unprecedented in a normative sense of the legal concept; the precedents on which the Court relied did not support the overall result it reached. But it is unfortunately not unprecedented in a more descriptive sense. *Bush v. Gore* represents only the latest, and perhaps most extreme, manifestation of what I call "structural" equal protection. In a structural equal protection case, the Court uses the clause to regulate the institutional arrangements within which politics is conducted, rather than to protect the rights of specific individuals or groups, especially those who cannot protect themselves through the normal political process. In these cases, which include the race-conscious redistricting cases about which I have written extensively elsewhere,[87] the Court steps into the political process in the service of a highly controversial and contestable vision of how politics should work. And it tends to consider the question of equality in very narrow terms, focusing on a discrete practice, race-conscious districting or manual recounts, for example, without ever considering the broader context within which that practice is embedded. In the end, the Court now has so much confidence in its own ability to domesticate the political thicket that it has completely forgotten the dangers that lurk there—to its own reputation as well as to the vibrancy of robust democratic politics.

NOTES

1. Alexis de Tocqueville, Democracy in America 290 (Vintage ed. 1945) [1848].

2. Colegrove v. Green, 328 U.S. 549, 556 (1946).

3. 17 Cong. Rec. 817–818 (1886).

4. Bush v. Gore, 121 S. Ct. 521, 529 (2000).

5. See, e.g., United States v. Cruikshank, 92 U.S. 542 (1875).

6. 92 U.S. 542 (1876).

7. 92 U.S. 214 (1876).

8. 170 U.S. 213 (1898).

9. 189 U.S. 475 (1903).

10. 189 U.S. at 488.

11. Lane v. Wilson, 307 U.S. 268, 272 (1939).

12. Nixon v. Herndon, 273 U.S. 536 (1927).

13. 328 U.S. 549, 552 (1946).

14. 369 U.S. 186 (1962).

15. 369 U.S. at 210.

16. Id. at 217.

17. Id. at 226.

18. 372 U.S. 368 (1963).

19. 377 U.S. 533 (1964).

20. 372 U.S. at 371.

21. Id. at 379–380.

22. 377 U.S. at 570.

23. G. Edward White, Earl Warren: A Public Life 337 (1977).

24. Reynolds, 377 U.S. at 554 (citing United States v. Saylor, 322 U.S. 385 (1944); United States v. Classic, 313 U.S. 299 (1941); United States v.

Mosley, 238 U.S. 386 (1915), and *Ex parte* Siebold, 100 U.S. 371 (1879)). These cases involved election officials who either "lost" the ballot boxes from particular precincts, stuffed ballot boxes, or improperly altered ballots lawfully cast by voters.

25. Reynolds, 377 U.S. at 555 (quoting South v. Peters, 339 U.S. 276, 279 (1950) (Douglas, J., dissenting)).

26. Reynolds, 377 U.S. at 559 (quoting Wesberry v. Sanders, 376 U.S. 1, 7 (1964)).

27. Reynolds, 377 U.S. at 560.

28. Id. at 562.

29. Id. at 563 (quoting Lane v. Wilson, 307 U.S. 268, 275 (1939); Gomillion v. Lightfoot, 364 U.S. 339, 342 (1960)). Both *Lane* and *Gomillion* were Fifteenth Amendment cases involving claims of intentional racial discrimination.

30. Reynolds, 377 U.S. at 561–562.

31. Id. at 567.

32. Id. at 585.

33. White v. Regester, 412 U.S. 755, 779 (1973) (Brennan, J., dissenting).

34. Reynolds, 377 U.S. at 555.

35. In the long run, by dislodging reactionary rural legislators who had enjoyed a stranglehold on the political process, one-person, one-vote did contribute to the election of more moderate legislative bodies. But it is hard to tease out this effect from the contemporaneous dramatic expansion of the franchise discussed in the text.

36. Bernard Grofman, Lisa Handley & Richard G. Niemi, Minority Representation and the Quest for Voting Equality 21, 23 (1992).

37. Kramer v. Union Free School District, 395 U.S. 621, 628 (1969).

38. Id. at 627.

39. Gerald Gunther, The Supreme Court, 1971 Term–Foreword: In Search of Evolving Doctrine on a Changing Court: A Model for a Newer Equal Protection, 86 Harv. L. Rev. 1, 8 (1972).

40. For example, the Supreme Court struck down poll taxes in Harper v. State Board of Elections, 383 U.S. 663 (1966); various property ownership requirements in Kramer v. Union Free School District, 395 U.S. 621

(1969), Cipriano v. City of Houma, 395 U.S. 701 (1969), and Phoenix v. Kolodziejski, 399 U.S. 204 (1970); and durational residency requirements in Dunn v. Blumstein, 405 U.S. 330 (1972).

41. San Antonio School District v. Rodriguez, 411 U.S. 1 (1973).

42. Id. at 29–40.

43. Id. at 44.

44. 446 U.S. 55 (1980).

45. Id. at 65 (plurality opinion).

46. Id. at 76 (plurality opinion) (quoting Minor v. Happersett, 88 U.S. 162, 178 (1875)).

47. Id. at 77 (plurality opinion).

48. Karcher v. Daggett, 462 U.S. 725, 740 (1983).

49. 347 U.S. 483 (1954).

50. 384 U.S. 641 (1966).

51. 400 U.S. 112 (1970).

52. Petition for Certiorari i, Bush v. Palm Beach County Canvassing Board.

53. Id. at 20–21.

54. Id. at 21.

55. Id. at 23.

56. United States v. Hays, 515 U.S. 737, 742–743 (1995).

57. Id. at 475.

58. Fla. Stat. § 101.5614(5) (2000).

59. Fla. Stat. § 10102.168(8) (2000).

60. Ind. Code Ann. § 3–12–1–9.5(c),(d) (2000).

61. They also sought an adjustment of the vote total in heavily Republican Nassau County to exclude some votes in an adjusted total.

62. Unpublished decision. The transcript can be found at http://election2000.stanford.edu, a website that provides a massive archive of briefs, motions, orders, and opinions relating to the litigation generated by the ballot wars in Florida. Special thanks to Paul Lomio and Erika Wayne, the extraordinary librarians at the Stanford Law Library who are responsible for the site.

63. Fla. Stat. § 102.168(3)(c) (2000).

64. Gore v. Harris, 772 So. 2d 1243, 1253 (Fla. 2000).

65. Id. at 1254–1255.

66. Id. at 1262.

67. Bush v. Gore, 121 S. Ct. 512 (2000).

68. Id. at 512.

69. Bush v. Gore, 121 S. Ct. 526, 529 (2000).

70. Id. at 532.

71. Id. at 530.

72. Id.

73. Id. at 530–531.

74. Id. at 531.

75. Id. at 532.

76. Id. at 530.

77. Ill. Election Code, ch. 10, § 17–11.

78. Pullen v. Mulligan, 561 N.E.2d 585, 609 (Ill. Sup. Ct. 1990).

79. Scribner v. Sachs, 164 N.E.2d 481 (Ill. Sup. Ct. 1960).

80. Green v. Bjorseth, 350 N.E. 469, 481 (Ill. Sup. Ct. 1932).

81. Iseburg v. Martin, 127 N.E. 663 (Ill. Sup. Ct. 1920).

82. See Pamela S. Karlan, The Newest Equal Protection: Regressive Doctrine on a Changeable Court *in* The Vote: Bush, Gore and the Supreme Court (Cass R. Sunstein and Richard A. Epstein eds. 2001).

83. Planned Parenthood v. Casey, 505 U.S. 833, 867 (1992).

84. Id.

85. Id.

86. 85 146 U.S. 1 (1892).

87. See Karlan, *supra* note 81; Pamela S. Karlan, Nothing Personal: The Newest Equal Protection from *Shaw v. Reno* to *Bush v. Gore*, 79 North Carolina Law Review (2001).

6

THE E-COLLEGE IN
THE E-AGE

JACK N. RAKOVE

I think it is a waste of time to talk about changing the Electoral
College. I would predict that 200 years from now, we will still have
the Electoral College.

> **Former President Jimmy Carter, at the**
> **initial meeting of the National Commission**
> **on Federal Election Reform, held at the Carter**
> **Center, Atlanta, March 26, 2001[1]**

IN THE DAYS IMMEDIATELY PRECEDING THE PRESIDENTIAL
election of 2000, the recognition dawned that Americans might well
deliver a split verdict, granting a plurality in the popular vote to one
candidate and a majority in the electoral college to the other. Text-
books commonly report that the last time that happened was 1888,
when Benjamin Harrison trailed Grover Cleveland in the popular

vote but gained the presidency by a margin of sixty-five electors. In fact, a plausible case can be made that John F. Kennedy actually lost the popular vote to Richard M. Nixon in 1960,[2] and in 1976, a relatively small swing of votes in Ohio and Hawaii would have given Gerald Ford an electoral majority, although his opponent, Jimmy Carter, enjoyed a national plurality of well over a million votes. On the weekend before the 2000 election, the prospects for a split decision seemed exceptionally promising. Although George W. Bush maintained a slight edge in virtually every national poll, state-based surveys indicated that Al Gore could still carry the electoral vote, especially if the three largest "battleground" states of Pennsylvania, Michigan, and Florida all broke his way.

The most likely scenario for a split decision was thus a popular plurality for Bush and an electoral victory for Gore. A week before the election, the *New York Daily News* quoted unnamed Bush aides warning that should this result obtain, the Bush campaign would "fight" the outcome by organizing "a massive talk-radio operation" designed to convince the requisite number of Gore electors to "ratify the popular verdict" by casting their votes for Bush.[3] As it turned out, the voters produced a different scenario. By the morning of November 8, it was evident that it was Al Gore who was destined to enjoy a popular plurality, yet still lose the election if George Bush retained his narrow margin in Florida and thus carried the state's twenty-five electors.

For a few days after November 7, the split decision aspect of the election attracted a modicum of public attention. In Congress, Senator Dick Durbin and Representative Ray Lahood (both of Illinois) offered a constitutional amendment to replace the electoral college with a direct popular vote, Senator-elect Hillary Rodham Clinton quickly endorsed the same idea, and a few op-eds also tackled the subject. But the doings in Florida, the endless parade of lawyers and spinners, the daily turns of fortune down to the U.S. Supreme Court's climactic decision of December 12, even the existentially hypnotic quality of C-Span telecasts of the vote recount, all made for better political theater. Even had Congress immediately held hearings on the Durbin-Lahood amendment, the tedious business of considering a constitutional amendment with little prospect for adoption could hardly compete for public attention with the tumult in Florida.

Common sense suggests that there is little point in discussing the electoral college. If the country is in the mood for electoral reform, it would better devote its energies to feasible projects, such as the improvement of voting systems, than to undertaking a futile effort to amend the Constitution. Simple political arithmetic indicates that any such amendment would be easily blocked by a coalition of the least populous states, which have a strong incentive to preserve the advantage they derive from the constitutional formula that gives each state the same number of electors as its total representation in both houses of Congress. If we can assume that the obvious alternative to the electoral college would be to elect the president by popular vote in a single national electorate in which every citizen's vote would count exactly the same, why would the representatives, legislators, and voters in the smaller states ever consent to a change that would presumably reduce their own influence in the name of the abstract principle of one person, one vote? Under the new allocation of electors following the census of 2000, twelve states will still cast three or four electoral votes, only one state short of the number needed to block ratification of any amendment. Or again, seventeen states will cast five electoral votes or fewer, and two times seventeen is the number of senators required to prevent Congress even from proposing amendments. Given this arithmetic, it is hardly surprising that not a peep was heard about reform of the electoral college after the new Congress convened in January 2001.

Yet if there was ever an election that exposed what a puzzling anachronism the electoral college is, it was the election of 2000. The disparity between the popular vote and the electoral result identified only the most conspicuous problem. Consider, for example, the way in which the extraordinarily close division within the Florida electorate (or that of five other states where only a whisker separated the two candidates) illustrated the arbitrary character of the winner-take-all rule that nearly all of the states have used since the early nineteenth century. If the Florida returns revealed anything, it was that the state's 6 million voters were divided into two perfectly equal blocs, separated only by a statistically insignificant margin of a few hundred (or a few thousand, depending on how many were counted) votes. Yet under the prevailing fiction of the winner-take-all rule, the state would finally vote as one integral unit, and the narrow margin that would decide the outcome in Florida would also decide the outcome in the nation at large.

Or again, consider the questions raised by the belated efforts of the Republican-dominated Florida legislature to appoint its own slate of electors. There is no question that, prior to November 7, the legislature could have reserved the appointment of electors to itself. But could it also reassert that authority after election day, to assure that the slate reported to Congress was chosen in a manner consistent with its own understanding of the state's election law? How could the legislature's willingness to assert that authority after November 7 be reconciled with the constitutional authority of Congress to designate the time when electors in all the states had to be appointed?

A different puzzle also surrounded the eligibility of Richard Cheney to receive the twenty-five electoral votes from Texas. The Constitution requires electors to cast one of their two votes for a candidate from a state other than their own. When Governor George W. Bush of Texas announced that Cheney, then an inhabitant of the same state, would be his running mate, Cheney promptly registered to vote in his native Wyoming, presumably restoring his status as an inhabitant of that state, and thereby allowing the Texas electors to vote for both Republican candidates. But if Cheney never really returned to Wyoming to take up residence—something the campaign made it rather difficult to do—

had he in fact satisfied the constitutional requirement in good faith? After cursory review, two federal courts in Texas agreed that he had, but anyone taking the constitutional requirement seriously could wonder whether the judges had simply swept the question under the rug.

One last problem was revealed when the electors actually cast their ballots on December 18. If diehard Democrats still hoped that three conscience-stricken Republican electors might spontaneously cast their votes for Al Gore, their faith in miracles was misplaced. Instead, a lone Democratic elector from the District of Columbia cast a blank ballot, in protest against the denial of basic rights of self-government to the nation's capital. She thereby added her name to the intrepid handful of "faithless electors" who, over the past two centuries, have not voted as legally required or morally bound. But suppose a few Republican electors, feeling guilty that the popular vote winner was being denied the presidency, had cast a conscience vote for Al Gore, would their "faithless" act have been regarded as constitutionally legitimate? Would Congress have any authority to challenge their votes?

In all of these ways, then, the election of 2000 exposed a variety of problems with the electoral college. The most important, of course, was to demonstrate that a split result between the popular and electoral votes was not a merely speculative possibility of concern only to a handful of oddball academics. In analyzing this outcome, it also became evident that Bush's margin of electoral victory depended on his carrying a larger proportion of the least populous states. Bush carried thirty states with 271 electoral votes, Gore twenty (plus the District of Columbia) with 267. Bush averaged nine electoral votes per state carried; Gore thirteen and change. Bush's margin of victory in the electoral college thus rested on the eighteen additional electoral votes he gained simply for carrying more states.

Should we be troubled enough by this result to give serious consideration either to replacing the entire electoral college with a national popular vote or to requiring electors to be chosen by districts or allocated in proportion to a candidate's share of a state's vote? Or should we treat the election of 2000 as a strange aberration that should not tempt us to revise or scrap a system that has worked reasonably well in most elections? The strongest arguments in favor of reform are that the existing system permits the loser in the popular vote to carry the election and that it violates the fundamental democratic principle of one person, one vote by making votes in small states more valuable than votes in more populous states. But the arguments for retaining the electoral college are no less serious. For one thing, the doctrine of unintended consequences suggests that we cannot safely predict the results of replacing a familiar set of rules and practices with an untested system. More important, defenders of the electoral college argue that a state-based system of presidential elections is an essential element of our Constitution's larger federal design. By requiring candidates to campaign on a state-by-state basis, it encourages the parties to pay attention to issues of provincial concern and to attempt to form broad national coalitions rather than seek to capture the presidency by pursuing a strong regionalist strategy. Were it not for the electoral college, its defenders argue, candidates would ignore whole states and entire stretches of the country, bypassing rural constituencies and focusing their efforts on the mass of voters concentrated in the metropolitan centers of the two coasts and the industrial Midwest. The small and predominantly rural states, having relatively few voters, would be particular losers; candidates would focus all their attention on the large urbanized states.[4]

The persistence of these arguments since November 7 is somewhat surprising. For in fact, although the national electorate was closely divided, whole swaths of the country, comprising large and small states alike, essentially sat the campaign out because there was never any doubt in whose column their electoral votes would fall. Voters in the three most populous states (California, Texas, and New York) could watch the Olympics and every round of the baseball playoffs and never see a commercial devoted to the presidential campaign; the same would be true of virtually all of the western and ex-Confederate states that make up the big Republican L that swoops down the Rockies and Great Plains and then turns right across the cotton belt until it hits the Atlantic. Far from diffusing active campaigning across the country, the logic of the electoral college effectively concentrates political activity and media expenditures only in those states that remain competitive. Thanks to the wonder of daily tracking polls, there is no mystery as to which states are "in play" and which "safe." Even in a national electorate as closely divided as was the case in 2000, the "battleground" states constituted only a small fraction of the fifty-one constitutional constituencies.

Once one understands the factors that place some states "in play" while most others are not, the flaws in the federalism defense of the electoral college against the countervailing challenge of the democratic principle of one person, one vote will become evident. But the illogic of the electoral system is also tied to the winner-take-all rule that has been the general practice since the early nineteenth century. That rule owes much more to expedient political calculations than to any constitutional rationale for treating states as integral units; it was far more a product of the political innovations that accompanied the creation of the first political parties in the 1790s than of the original design of the presidency in 1787. The rapidity with which these innovations occurred reveals a deeper irony in the history of presidential election. Today it is a commonplace to dismiss the Framers' scheme as an anachronism rooted in the world of gentry politics they inhabited. From a distance of two centuries, the idea that a group of provincial notables, called electors, might actually select a president seems like a quaint tribute to the limits of their imagination and their doubts about democracy. In fact, the original conception of 1787 was verging on obsolescence as early as 1796, and had certainly become an anachronism by 1800.

Two centuries later the system put in place between 1787 and 1800 remains intact, and even though the millennial election of

2000 exposed its real flaws, its reform or replacement is difficult to conceive. Yet the daunting political arithmetic that militates against constitutional amendment should not be enough to stifle critical thinking about the illogic of the electoral college, an institution whose defects the election of 2000 sorely exposed.

CREATING THE E-COLLEGE:
A DEFAULT DESIGN

Conventional wisdom about the electoral college begins with an important misconception. The reason for its adoption, we often hear, is that the Framers of the Constitution did not trust the people at large with the appointment of so critical an official. If left to their own devices, what was to stop them from following the first demagogue to come cantering along? History was full of tales of other republics which had done just that; why should Americans be free of the same passions and temptations?

The Framers were not great democrats, but fears of presidential demagoguery do not explain why they invented the electoral college. We have to start instead by asking why they found the task of constituting a national republican executive so daunting.[5]

The first problem was a lack of useful or applicable examples. Monarchy was still the dominant form of executive power in the eighteenth century, and Americans, as self-conscious republicans, were hardly about to restore kingship. (The idea that there was serious discussion of giving George Washington a crown is another myth.) Nor did the primitive form of cabinet government that was just emerging in Britain offer an attractive alternative. Before the Revolution, many Americans had seen these ministers as the real source of the sinister measures that the British government attempted to impose on the colonies. Moreover, Britain had not yet developed the mature form of parliamentary government that now characterizes its constitution. The choice of prime minister still depended significantly on the pleasure of the king, and in practice, Parliament proved highly susceptible to management by the crown. Control of Parliament depended on negotiations among aristocratic grandees who commanded their own factions in the Commons; elections rarely affected the composition of the government, the electorate was small and easily influenced, and popular political parties simply did not exist.

Many Americans also retained deep prejudices against the idea of a politically independent executive. Under most of the original state constitutions, governors were typically elected by the legislatures for a term of a single year. "Stripped of most of those badges of domination called prerogatives," as John Adams put it, they were generally seen as exercising power that was merely executive. That is, they were supposed to carry out someone else's (the legislature's) decisions, not act independently in their own right. In only two states, New York and Massachusetts, did the people elect the governors, and it is noteworthy that the two most potent governors of the Revolutionary era, George Clinton and John Hancock, emerged in those states. But states were relatively small constituencies, and it was a fair question whether a system of popular election could be transferred from the state to the national level of politics.

Given these uncertainties, it is not surprising that the presidency emerged from the Federal Convention of 1787 only after what James Madison called "tedious and reiterated discussions." Madison himself went to Philadelphia confessing that he had "scarcely ventured to form my own opinion either of the manner in which it ought to be constituted or of the authorities with which it ought to be cloathed." Other delegates, notably Alexander Hamilton, had more advanced ideas. But after agreeing to vest the executive power in a single individual, the Framers quickly discovered that there was no consensus about how the president should be elected, how long he should serve, and whether he should be eligible for re-election or subject to removal by impeachment, a strange procedure which had occasionally been used in England to little effect.

Fully seven weeks passed before the presidency became a subject of serious debate. When the Framers finally took it up on July 16—immediately after the "great compromise" giving each state equal weight in the Senate—the extent of their uncertainty became evident. Over the next ten days, they cycled through all three of the possible modes of election—by Congress, the people, or electors—before winding up where they had started, with an executive to be chosen by the national legislature for a single term of seven years. What is striking about this debate is that it revolved around the relative *disadvantages* of each mode of election, and few delegates displayed great enthusiasm for any particular choice on its merits.

The problem with popular election was not, as our conventional wisdom holds, that the Framers feared democracy succumbing to demagoguery. Two other problems were paramount. First, if the president was elected simply by the people, with each qualified citizen casting one vote, the southern states would be at a serious and lasting disadvantage because so high a proportion of their population consisted of African-American slaves who would never vote. In a single national constituency, comprising voters only, the slaveholding population of the plantation states would gain no extra boost for owning property in people.

Second, and more important, the Framers genuinely doubted whether the citizens of a decentralized, provincial polity like the United States could ever make an effective or decisive choice, without engaging in an ongoing round of elections. There would be too few "national characters" with reputations distinguished enough to attract anything like a popular majority. State voters would opt for favorite sons.

An election by Congress would solve these problems but create others just as troubling. No one could be more knowledgeable of "national characters" than Congress, but allowing it to make the choice would raise basic separation of powers problems. Reacting against the perceived weakness of the governors in the states, most of the Framers hoped to make the national executive as independent of congressional control as possible. If elected by Congress, it would become necessary to give the president a lengthy term of office (so that he would have time to grow in office) or render him ineligible for reelection (so that he would not toady to Congress). But here other objections emerged. An extended term smacked of monarchy, whereas restricting the president to a single term would deprive him of the incentive to perform ably in the hope of securing a second term.

The idea of electors first emerged as an alternative to these two more obvious modes. For a moment in July, it became almost a panacea and briefly gained the support of the Convention, in the form of a proposal to have the state legislatures elect twenty-five electors who would gather in one place to make the selection. But almost immediately, it was objected that these electors would not "be men of the 1st nor even of the 2d grade in the States." The Convention thus returned to the idea of congressional election for a single term of seven years.

There was no genuine consensus behind this judgment, however, and when the Convention returned to the subject in late August, it found itself evenly divided on the "abstract question" of election either by Congress or special electors. At that point, the matter passed to the so-called Committee on Postponed Parts. Its report of September 4 proposed the critical change. Each state would receive as many electors as it had members of both houses of Congress. They would gather in the separate states, vote once—with each elector casting two ballots, one for someone from another state—and submit their ballots to Congress. If no candidate received a majority of the votes cast, the decision would fall to the Senate.

This report had several advantages and one great problem. First, it embraced the same political compromise that the Convention had already accepted in apportioning representation in Congress. The large states would have the edge in promoting candidates, but the small states would benefit whenever the electors failed to produce a majority, which some delegates thought would be the usual result. The South would count its slaves for purposes of electing a president as well as the House of Representatives. Second, even if the electors failed to produce a majority when no incumbent was running, the existence of the electoral college would liberate a sitting president from toadying to Congress, because in his case, the electors would have a sufficient basis for determining whether he should be returned to office or turned out. Third, by restricting the electors to meeting only once, on the same day, in the separate states, it avoided the risk that this unknown and potentially obscure group of citizens would be subject to improper influence and "cabal."

But because the same committee that endorsed the electoral college also proposed major changes in the *powers* of the presidency, it created a difficult problem that the Convention needed three days to solve, and even then only in a nearly accidental way. Previously the power to appoint major officials and to make treaties had been given to the Senate. Now it was placed in the president, acting with the advice and consent of the Senate. If the Senate could choose a president when the electors did not render a majority, however, the independence the Convention wanted to give the executive would be compromised. Yet because the political compromise embodied in the proposal envisioned giving the small states the advantage in the second round of an election, and the Senate was the one institution where states voted equally, it was difficult to imagine how any other arrangement would work.

After three days of debate, filled with charges that the electoral college would never really elect and the president would thus be the captive of an "aristocratic" Senate, the Convention accepted the committee's proposal. But almost immediately, two delegates stumbled on a solution. Hugh Williamson of North Carolina first moved that the eventual choice be made by the members of both houses, voting by states, and Roger Sherman of Connecticut then modified this proposal to substitute the House of Representatives, also voting by states. Sherman's solution had the dual advantage of preserving the political compromise between small and large states while "lessening the aristocratic influence of the Senate." With nary a word of further debate, the proposal was adopted.

No one reading Madison's notes of these debates could conclude that the Framers knew how the electoral college would work, much less believed that it would work well. Its principal merit was to avoid the greater disadvantages that weighed against the other modes of election. The Framers had manifestly not answered the objection that had cut against the idea of electors back in July. They imposed no qualifications for electors, and in fact left all the decisions over their appointment to the state legislatures. The fact that electors had to meet on a single day, cast their ballots, and then disperse, hardly suggests that the Convention placed any great confidence in their deliberative abilities. If it had, it could have allowed the electors to meet as one faculty, at one campus, there to vote, deliberate, and vote again until a president was chosen. The electoral college could have been constructed like that other famous body, the college of cardinals of the Church of Rome, who kept balloting until a pope was chosen. But to eighteenth-century American Protestants, any example set by that Church was not worth emulating.

In effect, most of the Framers probably regarded the electoral college as the equivalent of a nominating caucus or primary. Its great virtues were to replicate the political compromises over representation, to lay a foundation for the independence of incumbent presidents, and to avoid the uncertainties of popular election. Whether the Framers would have accepted the idea of popular election had they believed that the people could indeed make an effective choice cannot be determined. Perhaps George Washington would be the only truly "national character" Americans would ever know. Once he retired from the initial presidency that everyone expected him to occupy, the competition would never rise above the level of favorite sons. That was the principal reason why the Constitution required electors to cast two votes, one for an inhabitant of a state other than their own. Under such a rule, as Madison observed, "the second best man in this case would probably be the first, in fact." Every elector would pick a favorite son with his first vote, but the second might actually be awarded for merit.

As a device for accommodating the claims of large, small, and slaveholding states, the electoral system thus made some sense. But how well did this accommodation anticipate the real interests that would come into play once elections actually took place? The clearest winners in this case were the southern slaveholding states. For them, the three-fifths clause was now doubly generous, allowing them to count slaves in the allocation of both representatives and electors. Slavery was clearly an interest that the southern states would wish to protect indefinitely, and getting this double boost in political clout was therefore a substantial achievement.

But was it equally important to accommodate the small states as well, not only by giving each state an equal vote whenever the electors failed to make an appointment, but also by giving each state two electoral votes to represent its senators? Why should small states be favored in the allocation of electoral votes when they had already gained the key point in the composition of the Senate? The size of a state was certainly a legitimate interest when, as at the Convention, one had to decide whether representatives and presidential electors should be apportioned by population or simply allocated to all states equally. But once the rule of voting was settled, one way or another, would anyone—either citizens or representatives—ever again vote on the basis of the size of his state's population? Did the conflict between large and small states that dominated the politics of the Convention have anything to do with the real political decisions Americans would take thereafter?

The most important feature of the electoral college, however, went virtually unnoticed. This was the simple fact that the Constitution allowed the state legislatures to decide how electors were to be chosen. In vesting this power in the legislatures, there is no indication that the Framers thought that the state legislatures were peculiarly well qualified to make the choice themselves. In two places in *The Federalist*, for example, Alexander Hamilton casually assumed that the electors would in fact be chosen by the people, with the legislatures doing nothing more than framing the appropriate acts to govern the requisite elections.

The Constitution had given the states similar power to set rules for "the Times, Places and Manner of holding Elections for Senators and Representatives," but these regulations were subject to alteration by Congress "at any time." In the case of the presidency, however, the states could do whatever they wanted, free from congressional review. In effect, the Constitution left all the real decisions about the nature and function of the electoral college to be determined by the states. Congress could set "the time" (not necessarily a day) when electors were to be chosen, and the particular day on which they would have to cast their own ballots, but everything else that really mattered was left open to political experimentation. Nothing better indicates how little progress the Framers had finally made in imagining or anticipating the political dimensions of the presidency. All they had really accomplished was to come up with a formula for allocating electoral votes among the states and a procedure for selecting the president when the electors predictably failed to do so. On the fundamental question of deciding exactly whom the electors were supposed to represent, the Framers finally had no wisdom to impart. Preoccupied by other concerns, they punted.

EARLY ADAPTATIONS

As long as George Washington reigned as president, it did not matter how electors were chosen. The result was foreordained, and the states were free to establish any system they wished. By 1796, three modes of choosing electors were operating: popular election of individual electors by districts, popular election of a statewide slate, and appointment by the state legislature.[6]

Far more important, however, was the organization of what scholars call "the first party system" pitting the Federalist supporters of the administration against its Democratic-Republican critics, led by Madison and Jefferson. By 1795, it was clear that Washington's retirement would be followed by an intense competition to capture the presidency that would pit Vice President John Adams against Jefferson. But this competition was complicated by the machinations of Alexander Hamilton, the Federalist *eminence grise* and no admirer of Adams. Hamilton hatched a scheme to use the constitutional rule requiring presidential electors to cast two ballots to displace Adams and make Thomas Pinckney of South Carolina the Federalist standard-bearer. Under the original Constitution, electors did not distinguish between presidential and vice presidential candidates; if the electoral college reached a verdict, the candidate receiving the greatest number of votes, provided that it was "a majority of the whole number of electors appointed," would become president, and the runner-up became vice president. If enough Federalist electors could be persuaded to throw away Adams votes, Hamilton calculated, Pinckney might actually sneak in as president.

In fact, Hamilton miscalculated badly. Smelling a rat, eighteen Federalist electors in Adams's home region of New England threw away their second votes to John Jay, enabling Jefferson to slip into second place and become vice president with sixty-eight votes to Adams's winning seventy-one. But the election was even closer than that, or so Jefferson's supporters quickly realized. Adams carried the election only because he managed to pluck one vote each from the Democratic-Republican heartland states of Virginia and North Carolina, where electors were chosen by districts. Had those two states voted as states, Jefferson would have won, and Adams would have become our only three-term vice president.

This first contested presidential election revealed two profound truths about the electoral system. One was that the Framers of the

Constitution had been completely wrong to think that a post-Washington contest would not present the electorate with a clear choice of national candidates rather than provincial favorite sons. Even though Washington had delayed announcing his retirement in the hope of aiding Adams, the Democratic-Republicans were still ready to campaign when the announcement came. Had a popular vote been held in 1796, the citizenry would have been able to make an informed and decisive choice between two prominent candidates.

But the deeper revelation lay in the arithmetic of electoral votes. In a tight election, as we have just been reminded, every vote does count. The price of defeat was those two tantalizing votes lost in Virginia and North Carolina. Had those states chosen a different procedure—election by the assembly or a statewide general ticket—the result would have been reversed.

When the rematch between Adams and Jefferson loomed in 1800, then, political arithmetic required asking not only where the electoral votes necessary for victory were to be found, but which rule of choosing electors promised the greatest reward. The Democratic-Republicans struck first. As early as September 1799, Charles Pinckney of South Carolina reminded Madison "that Mr Adams carried his Election by One Vote from Virginia & North Carolina." The lesson was clear: Madison had to persuade the state legislature to replace its existing mode of selecting electors by district with appointment by the assembly. "The Constitution of the United States fully warrants it," Pinckney added, "& remember that Every thing Depends upon it."[7] In fact, the Virginia assembly opted for a different solution, implementing a statewide winner-take-all popular election of electors. In response, the Massachusetts congressional delegation, dominated by Federalists, urged their state legislature to answer in kind. Massachusetts had previously chosen its electors by districts, but just as pockets of Federalist strength could be found in Virginia, so were there areas of the Bay State where support for Jefferson ran high. Rather than trust the voters at large, the Massachusetts assembly played it safe and adopted (in effect) Pinckney's rule, keeping the appointment of electors in its own hands.

The most interesting variation on this story was played out in New York. In March 1800, a Federalist-dominated legislature rejected a Republican proposal to replace legislative election with a district scheme, confident that their party would retain control of the assembly in the spring elections and thus secure all the state's electors. But the skill with which that great political entrepreneur, Aaron Burr, organized New York City at the spring elections gave the Republicans control of the legislature that would cast the state's electoral votes in the fall.

This dramatic reversal in political fortune inspired a desperate Hamilton to urge Governor John Jay to reconvene the sitting legislature to adopt, in effect, the opposition proposal to choose electors by district, thereby salvaging a few Federalist votes. Like Pinckney, Hamilton argued from political necessity and constitutional permissibility. He did not mean to suggest "that any thing ought to be done which integrity will forbid—but merely that the scruples of delicacy and propriety, as relative to a common course of things, ought to yield to the extraordinary nature of the crisis. They ought not to hinder the taking of a *legal* and *constitutional* step, to prevent an *Atheist* in Religion and a *Fanatic* in politics from getting possession of the helm of the State." Given the willingness of the other party to summon "all the resources which *Vice* can give," the Federalist party could ill afford to abide by "the ordinary forms of delicacy and decorum." Jay, a man of greater honor, was unmoved. At the bottom of Hamilton's letter he docketed his response: "Proposing a measure for party purposes wh. I think it wd. not become me to adopt."[8]

Few if any of his contemporaries were as scrupulous. For in politics, as elsewhere in life, necessity is also the mother of invention. In fact, going into the election of 1800, no fewer than six states altered their rules for appointing electors. They did so, too, amid an election campaign that was conducted as a battle of constitutional principle, with each side arguing that a victory for its opponents would gravely wound the Constitution. Jeffersonians accused Federalists of favoring a presidency so strong as to verge on monarchy, while Federalists treated their opponents' states' rights principles as a blueprint for restoring the Articles of Confederation. Yet in exploiting the possibilities created by the Framers' decision to leave the rules for appointing electors to the discretion of the states, both sides were equally opportunistic. When it came to electoral arithmetic, the only constitutional value that mattered was carrying an entire state's electors when you were confident of being in the majority or trying to salvage a district or two when you were not. The necessity of victory was the only constitutional argument that counted.

In the end, of course, the final key to victory in 1800 proved stranger than anyone had imagined. The real story of that election, we usually read, is that the victorious Jefferson-Burr slate was too well coordinated for its own good. Republican electors should have thrown a few votes away from Burr, assuring that Jefferson would become president and Burr vice president. Instead, both men finished in a tie, each with a majority of the whole number of electors, throwing the election into a lame duck House of Representatives where the defeated Federalists could prevent Jefferson's election. The Federalists, in effect, had the option of attempting to elevate Burr, someone with whom they thought they could deal, and relegating the dangerously principled Jefferson to the vice presidency. It was a close call, but Hamilton, on mature thought, exerted the necessary influence to permit Jefferson's election on the thirty-six ballot. Burr's revenge came a few years later.

This was the dramatic part of the 1800–1801 election, but emphasizing the Jefferson-Burr-Hamilton triangle will distract us from the deeper lesson. The preparations for 1800 ultimately had greater significance than its strange outcome, for these preparations revealed that there was one optimal solution to the electoral puzzle—winner-take-all, statewide popular voting—and this solution had virtually nothing to do with the Framers' concerns of 1787. Wherever one party believed it would enjoy a commanding majority of the popular vote and was in a position to write the appropriate law, it had every incentive to impose a winner-take-all rule. It would do so, however, not because all the constituencies of the state were in fact thinking alike, but rather because the minority party might be strong enough to pluck a few votes here and there if electors were chosen by district. For example, it was the fact that Virginia Federalists under the leadership of John Marshall, the future chief justice, had made gains in the 1798 legislative elections that gave Jeffersonians all the more reason to take the lessons of 1796 to heart. The notion that an entire state, especially a large populous one, would be completely unified in its political views and preferences was thus a fiction.

Once some states had moved decisively to this rule, other states had a natural incentive to follow suit. In most states, one party or the other would enjoy the clear advantage and calculate its gains accordingly. Even where the parties were evenly balanced, the hope and expectation of victory would probably incline partisan leaders to prefer the greater gain of total victory to the more prudent course of accepting a division of stakes. The notion that a state voting by districts would somehow lose influence relative to other states voting winner-take-all would provide an additional incentive for making the switch. The winner-take-all rule was thus the equilibrium (as economists or political scientists would now say) that the electoral college system was destined to attain. It would take another quarter century for all the states to fall into line, but then again, after 1800 the Republican lock on the presidency and the steady decline of the Federalists reduced the urgency of electoral manipulation. (Recall that James Monroe was reelected in 1820 with only a single elector casting a vote away on principle.) By 1828, South Carolina was the only state where electors were chosen by the assembly. Everywhere else winner-take-all, popular voting prevailed.

FALLACIES WORTH EXPOSING

There is, then, a nice irony in the fact that the election of 2000 commemorated the bicentennial of the election of 1800. For although it went unnoticed at the time, the wrangling in Florida masked one of the fundamental questions about the operation of the electoral college. Throughout the recount, it was painfully evident that 1) Florida was for all intents and purposes evenly divided between Gore and Bush partisans; 2) whatever margin either candidate finally gained would be equivocal in the face of all of the questions raised about chads, butterfly ballots in Palm Beach County, misinformed voters in Jacksonville, postmarked absentee votes, and the like; and 3) all of the state's twenty-five electoral votes would nevertheless go to one candidate or the other. A truly Solomonic solution to this mess would have been to divide the electors between the candidates, giving the final odd vote to whichever candidate had the less dubious claim to a popular plurality. No other decision could have represented more accurately the real preferences of Florida voters or better exposed the fiction on which the electoral college rests: that states really are integral units whose interest in being counted as one community outweigh the split preferences of their citizens. Florida's voters (and voters in every other state) cared far more about seeing their candidate victorious than in seeing their state united. Or to put the point another way, voters want to see their state's electoral votes cast as a unit only when they know those votes will go to the candidate they favor.

What should be at issue here, however, is not the propriety of the winner-take-all rule itself, but rather the fundamental idea that the states, as such, are the appropriate units for conducting presidential elections. Defenders of the electoral college repeatedly cite two principal reasons why states should indeed play that role. First, the existence of fifty provincial contests encourages the contenders to develop strategies that will appeal to different constituencies across the nation. If, by contrast, presidents were selected by an at-large popular vote, campaigning would be tailored to the most populous areas, and entire areas of the country, including the less-populated states, would be neglected. Second, retaining a state-based system of presidential elections is said to be conducive to federalism. As former Solicitor General Charles Fried observed shortly after the election, "The Electoral College is one of the political safeguards of federalism: those structural features of our constitutional system— like the allocation of two senators to each state, whatever its size— that of their own force and without court intervention assure that the states count as distinct political entities, not merely administrative units of one central government."[9]

These are serious arguments, but they are vulnerable to equally serious criticisms. Start with the rule for apportioning electors among the states according to their representation in both houses of Congress. The effect of that rule is to give added weight to the least populous states, which get to double or triple their electoral votes in relation to their population. In a close election like the last one, this reward for the simple fact of statehood may be consequential, even decisive. (Of the seventeen states casting five or fewer electoral votes in 2000, Bush carried eleven, giving him a net advantage of ten electoral votes.) In terms of its impact on the electoral college, a vote in a small state is worth far more than one in a large state. This disparity may have been justifiable in light of the original constitutional design, but it cannot be reconciled with the modern democratic principle of one person, one vote. Why should a citizen's vote cast for a slate of three electors in Wyoming count far more than a vote cast for a similar slate in California?

A satisfactory answer to that question would have to depend on the arguments to be made for maintaining an essential role for the states as such in the election of the president. If states have such a role, then the injury done to the one person, one vote principle might be tolerable. If one could argue, however, that the arguments based on federalism considerations are flawed or even fallacious, then the illogic and injustice of the current system should be evident.

After the election just past, it is difficult to see how the existence of fifty separate constituencies actually works to force candidates to compete actively throughout the country, catering their appeals to the political demographics of each decentralized polity in the Union. The reality seems to be otherwise. Active campaigning in 2000 was confined to the "battleground" states where the outcome was uncertain. In terms of receiving active interest and attention from the major candidates, entire states and regions basically sat the election out until November 7, because both sides knew from the outset which way their voters would go. This lack of attention was not a function of size. The three most populous states—California, Texas, and New York—were largely uncontested, even though the candidates did drop in to each occasionally (mostly to raise money); but so were many of the smallest states. Bush had no incentive to campaign in the Mountain West or the old Confederacy, nor did Gore have any reason to try to turn out the Democratic vote in the Black Belt that appears so clearly on maps of county-by-county voting. Voters in Idaho and California could feel similarly unloved and neglected simply because the outcome in those states was virtually a given from the start.

What the election conclusively demonstrated, then, is that the existence of the electoral college system per se is no guarantee that campaigns will be highly decentralized or truly national in scope. Those who wondered why prescription drugs for seniors had become such a hot issue now know why: Both sides knew that Florida, with its large numbers of elderly voters, would be extremely close, and that the outcome of the election might finally come down to that state, with its bumper crop of retirees. Candidates pick the states where they will invest time and media buys for simple reasons: Is that state competitive, and will it prove essential to an electoral victory? Where the results are foreordained, there is no reason to waste time and money that will not alter the outcome.

But what is it that makes some states competitive and others reliable building blocks of one party's electoral foundation? The real determinants, again, have nothing to do with statehood as such, nothing to do, that is, with the idea that the states, as distinct communities or jurisdictions, are the necessary elements of a presidential election, or that the presidency as an institution exists to foster the interests of states. States become competitive because of the distribution of different types of voters within their arbitrary boundaries. It is the mix of citizens, defined in terms of political preferences and affiliations that have little to do with residence within a particular state, and almost nothing to do with its size, that determines which states are in play, which safe. These preferences are not evenly distributed across states, of course. Demography, geography, history, religion, and ethnicity all affect how citizens think and vote, and the strength of each of these factors obviously varies from one state to another. But the crucial point is that each of these factors is ultimately an attribute of citizens—that is, individual voters—and not states as such.

To illustrate this point, consider some of the many affinities that cut across state lines. If gun control operates as a "wedge issue," working-class hunting enthusiasts in the "venison belt" of Michigan and Pennsylvania may have more in common with their fellow sportsmen in Idaho and Montana than with their fellow state residents in Detroit and Pittsburgh, who might prefer candidates who want to take Uzis and AK–47s off the streets. African-American voters feel the same loyalty to the Democratic Party wherever they live, in Harlem or the South Side of Chicago or Compton or the old Black Belt counties of Alabama and Mississippi. The same generalization holds true for any of a number of variables that are the real determinants of how we vote. Soy bean farmers on the Iowa bank of the Mississippi River have the same interests as soy bean farmers on the Illinois side, although Illinois now casts twenty-one electoral votes to Iowa's seven. Residence in a state, although not irrelevant to which issues matter to us, will always be secondary to the issues, concerns, and values that shape our political loyalties.

If this is right, then key arguments against a direct popular election of the president are misplaced. The oft-repeated argument that smaller states would drop off the candidates' and parties' radar screens seems particularly open to question. Under the current system, again, there is no incentive to pay attention to voters who live in states that are safe for one side or the other. Under a system in which everyone's vote counted equally, regardless of the accident of residence, candidates would actually have a strong incentive to develop strategies to improve turnout in their base constituencies as well as in more hotly contested locales. A vote in Delaware might no longer count more than one in Pennsylvania, as it currently does, but it would not count less, and in a closely fought election like the past one, turnout everywhere would matter.

Nor can it be argued that the large states as such would dominate the results, imposing their desires on the residents of Alaska, Idaho, and Rhode Island. The same logic applies. Voters in the most populous states do not have different kinds of preferences than voters in small states; they do not vote as blocs on the basis of the size of their states but rather in response to the same mix of attachments and concerns. Texas is a large state, and so is New York; so what? Moreover, the past election suggests that the more populous states tend to be more divided than many of their smaller counterparts, precisely because the diversity of their populations gives candidates and parties greater incentive to form and reform coalitions by appealing to groups, notably suburban voters, who can swing either way. If large states with concentrated populations would nevertheless receive more attention than the sparsely populated mountain states, it would in any case be for reasons akin to Willy Sutton's for robbing banks: That is where the voters are.

There remains the argument that a state-based system on presidential elections is a safeguard of federalism because, as Professor Fried says, it assures that states "count as distinct political entities, not merely administrative units of one central government." In the wake of the past election, that seems like a mistaken judgment.

Given what we now know about the vagaries of balloting in different states and counties, the idea of treating the states simply as administrative units for conducting national elections should seem more attractive, not less. How do the Republic and the Union benefit when an election can turn on a flawed ballot design in a single county in a single state? But again, a more fundamental criticism of this defense of the electoral college requires reflection on the place of the states in the federal system.

Federalism is not primarily about the role that states play in the electoral system, although that is certainly one ingredient in its definition. Rather, federalism is essentially concerned with the division of powers and duties between two levels of government. That division begins with, and is preserved by, the text of the Constitution, which delegates certain powers to the national government, prohibits and implicitly reserves others to the states, and sets up mechanisms for determining which government will gain the upper hand when these responsibilities overlap. In constitutional terms, the defense of federalism owes almost nothing to the presidency but depends instead on the other two branches of the national government as well as the course of ordinary politics.

Historically the task of policing the boundaries of the federal system has fallen to the Supreme Court, a duty the current Court seems especially happy to accept. But federalism also depends on the composition of Congress. Whether the national government is going to act vigorously, exercising or "usurping" powers otherwise executed by the states, requires fashioning durable congressional majorities to enact the requisite legislation. Historically, that has required a lot of heavy lifting, but on certain occasions, in the 1860s, the 1930s, and the 1960s, for example, that work has been accomplished, often to be followed by periods of retrenchment, like the one we are living in now. Franklin Roosevelt's first reelection in 1936 and Ronald Reagan's victory in 1980 might be cited as instances where a presidential election had a significant impact on the structure of federalism. But even in those celebrated cases, the shifts in national policy ultimately depended on a particular administration's political capacity to persuade Congress to enact the appropriate legislation. The only authority presidents enjoy to impinge upon the authority of the states comes from their duty to "faithfully execute" the laws that Congress passes. Presidential candidates can and do campaign on the basis of whether they support stronger or weaker exercise of national or state power, but that is hardly the same thing as saying that their selection in a state-based electoral college system is essential to that end. They would presumably take the same positions if we had a national popular vote.

SOLUTIONS?

If these arguments are valid, then the case against the electoral college, on the merits, is a powerful one. Electors have never really fulfilled the deliberative function that apologists erroneously ascribe to the intentions of the Framers of the Constitution. Even to say that the Framers had coherent intentions as to how the electoral college would operate stretches the historical truth. Contrary to their expectations, it is possible that an at-large national election would have produced a decisive result as early as the first contested election of 1796. In its actual operations, the electoral system was quickly captured and manipulated by partisan interests bent on maximizing gains through a winner-take-all rule that belies the actual diversity of the polity. If states really were unitary polities, with a common interest shared and recognized by all citizens, no such rule would be necessary. The allocation of electoral votes among the states, although explicable in terms of the politics of 1787, now transgresses against our contemporary democratic standard of one person, one vote. Nor are the arguments about the federalizing benefits of the electoral system persuasive. Far from encouraging truly national campaigning, the recognition that most states are safe for one candidate or the other can produce exactly the focus on a limited number of competitive states that marked the 2000 election. Nor does a state-based system of electing presidents have any material effect on the division of power between national and state governments that is the essential attribute of federalism. And as we now know, it is indeed possible in a closely divided electorate to produce a split decision in which one candidate gains a popular plurality and the other, fortified by the arbitrary boost that some states get by the rule of allocating senators, carries the electoral college, and thus the election.

If we were to attempt to reform or abolish the electoral college, what would we replace it with? Three alternatives immediately present themselves. One is to replace the winner-take-all rule with the system used in Maine and Nebraska, which choose two electors statewide and the remainder within the existing congressional districts. (In practice, however, this has never produced a result different from what would have obtained under a winner-take-all regime.) A second would be to cast each state's electoral votes in proportion to the actual distribution of the statewide popular vote. These two reforms could be adopted either by a constitutional amendment, or (in theory) by the voluntary legislative action of some or all of the states. The third and most radical alternative would be a system of direct popular election by a single national electorate. That reform requires constitutional amendment, and its adoption would be complicated not only by the obvious reduction it entails in the electoral weight of the numerous less populous states but also by considerations of how large a plurality would be required for the election of a president, or whether a system of runoffs or preferential voting should be required to produce a president who can finally claim the support of a majority of the electorate.

At first glance, the idea of instituting a district system for appointing electors seems to offer the most attractive and practical reform. Because it would not require altering the existing formula for apportioning electors among the states, it might assuage the predictable objections of the small states and therefore be more amenable to approval through the formal mechanism of constitutional amendment. By breaking states down into individual constituencies, it would increase the likelihood that the awarding of electoral votes within any state would more closely resemble the distribution of the popular vote.

On closer examination, however, this proposal is subject to challenge on several counts. First, it would only reinforce the strong incentives that already exist within our political system to gerrymander congressional districts in the interest of securing partisan advantage. The boundaries that separate states may be arbitrary, but at least they are not subject to political manipulation. But electoral districts within the states would be redrawn with every census and would be susceptible to the same calculated construction that regularly marks congressional redistricting. Second, there is no principled logic that makes residence in a particular district the key determinant of our preferences for presidential candidates. Again, we need to ask whether or in what ways our individual votes for president are contingent on residence in the jurisdictions we know as states or congressional districts. The same considerations that suggest that residence within a particular state has little bearing on how individuals vote also apply to the salience of residence within a particular electoral district. That is, when we vote for president, are we thinking primarily of the benefits that one candidate or the other will bring to the particular jurisdiction we inhabit (whether state or local), or do we act on the basis of the particular interests and preferences we possess as individual citizens? If the latter provide the real determinants of our political behavior—as this essay clearly supposes they do—then the idea of increasing the number of constituencies that would participate as such in presidential elections has no advantage. In a sense, a district scheme would compound, not resolve, the fundamental problem that a state-based system of presidential elections already creates. It would multiply the number of arbitrarily defined jurisdictions candidates would need to carry, yet most of these districts would likely be no more competitive than most states proved to be in the 2000 election.

The problem of multiplying jurisdictions would not exist, of course, if each state's electoral votes were cast in proportion to a candidate's share of the statewide vote. Such a reform would have the advantage of eliminating the fiction that each state is an integral unit with a valid interest of its own in the outcome of a presidential election. Such a system would run the risk that a closely fought election between the two major party candidates with a strong third-party challenger might prevent any candidate from winning a majority of the electors, thereby throwing the election into the House of Representatives. It might also give third-party candidates a stronger incentive to run in more populous states. (The larger the number of electors a state possesses, the smaller a fraction of the popular vote one would need to gain an elector; a candidate could pick up an elector in California with less than 2 percent of the statewide vote, whereas in neighboring Nevada, with its five electoral votes, he would presumably need 20 percent.)

Both of these schemes of electoral college reform could be accomplished, in whole or in part, either by constitutional amendment or by the voluntary legislative action of individual states. Again, because neither change would reduce the advantage the less populous states enjoy under the current constitutional rule for apportioning electors, their predictable objections to the reform or replacement of the electoral college might be obviated. But a constitutional amendment would not in fact be required; the states are already free, should they so wish, to institute either change legislatively. In fact, there is no constitutional reason why the states could not experiment with a mixed electoral regime in which some states maintained the current system, others adopted the Maine-Nebraska variant of districts, and still others apportioned electors by the statewide vote.

But why should the states even consider, much less pursue and finally favor, either of these reforms of the electoral college? Some of the various newspaper stories about the potential split vote that appeared shortly before the election of 2000 intimated that such a result would produce wholesale demands for reform. But the election has come and gone, George W. Bush has taken office, and there is no sign of a public clamor for constitutional change. Even if there were, it is difficult to imagine why the states would want to pursue either a district model of appointing electors or proportional allocation on the basis of statewide results, merely because the election of 2000 demonstrated that one can win the national popular vote and still lose the election. State legislatures, as such, have no natural incentive to respond to this lesson by voluntarily altering their existing rules. As the behavior of the Florida legislature after November 7 so clearly demonstrated, the state legislatures are as likely to act on the basis of partisan calculations as are presidential candidates or the popular constituencies they represent. In states where one party dominates the legislature and is confident that its presidential candidate will regularly carry the statewide electorate, what incentive would exist to move to a system that would enable the minority party to pick up some electoral votes? Or suppose a different scenario in which one party usually controls the legislature but its presidential candidates rarely carry the state, might it not then make sense to adopt one of the first two reforms, knowing that one can still salvage some electoral votes for one's own side while weakening the opposition in a state it needs more?

Much has changed in the structure of national politics since the states first started manipulating the rules for choosing electors two centuries ago, but one constant remains: the capacity of political leaders to calculate how alterations in the procedures for elections will affect their partisan interests and loyalties. But if this hardball observation generally holds true, what reason is there to think that the more radical form of electoral college reform—the adoption of a constitutional amendment replacing the state-based system of electors with a single national electorate—would stand any better chance (or any chance) of success?

One would have to be a terrible naif to suggest that such an amendment would easily pass Congress or be ratified by thirty-eight states, but a case for this more radical proposal could be made on at least these grounds. Unlike the other two reforms, which could also be accomplished by formal constitutional amendment but would more likely proceed at the legislative discretion of the states, this proposal absolutely requires constitutional amendment. Two potential (although admittedly problematic) political advantages could flow from this daunting requirement. First, it would permit and hopefully encourage a focused national debate in a way that the other proposals, relying more on the discretion of individual states, would not. Second, in such a debate, the essential inequity—one could say injustice—that lies at the heart of the electoral college could receive the attention it deserves.

At bottom, the debate over retention of the electoral college can and should be reduced to the conflict between the modern democratic norm of one person, one vote on the one hand, and the ostensible defense of the existing system grounded on principles of federalism on the other. As I have attempted to show, the federalism defense of the electoral college, although superficially plausible, ultimately rests on a fundamental misconception about the basis on which individuals actually vote as well as the stake that states, as states, have in presidential elections. Once the fallacy inherent in this conception of the role of states is exposed, then the injustice the current system does to the fundamental democratic value of equality becomes evident. Today, there is simply no longer any principled justification for the idea that votes cast in some states deserve greater weight than votes in others. Nor is there any compelling rationale that explains why voters in the least populous states somehow deserve a disproportionate weight because their interests would otherwise be trampled upon by citizens of the big states. Different clusters of voters across the nation share similar political attitudes and preferences independently of whether they live in large or small states. The establishment of a single national electorate would admittedly reduce the extra influence that citizens of the small states exert, but it would only do so in the name of a fundamental principle that each of us would espouse if we individually did not know whether the accident of our residence would situate us in a small or large state. To the post-Florida cry that every vote should be counted, the elimination of the inequitable disparities imposed by the electoral college would endorse the further principle that every vote should count equally across the entire nation, and not merely within individual states.

NOTES

1. In response to my testimony making many of the arguments developed in this essay. For the transcript, see http://www.reformelections.org/data/transcripts.

2. In Alabama, six of the Democratic Party's slate of eleven electors were not pledged to vote for the national candidate, Kennedy, and eventually cast their ballots for Senator Harry Byrd. If the popular votes for the entire slate are apportioned between pledged and unpledged electors, and the share assigned to the latter subtracted from Kennedy's reported popular vote, Nixon's national popular deficit of 118,574 votes becomes a plurality of 60,132. But this begs the question of how well the electors' votes corresponded to those of a popular electorate voting for a statewide slate. For a more detailed discussion, see Brian J. Gaines, "Popular Myths about Popular Vote-Electoral College Splits," *PS: Political Science and Politics* 34 (2001): 71–75.

3. Michael Kramer, "Bush Set to Fight an Electoral College Loss," *New York Daily News*, November 1, 2000, p. 6.

4. For representative statements of this view, see Robert M. Hardaway, *The Electoral College and the Constitution: The Case for Preserving Federalism* (Westport, Conn.: Praeger, 1994); and Judith Best, *The Case Against Direct Election of the President: A Defense of the Electoral College* (Ithaca, N.Y.: Cornell University Press, 1975).

5. The following analysis tracks the argument in Jack N. Rakove, *Original Meanings: Politics and Ideas in the Making of the Constitution* (New York: Alfred A. Knopf, 1996), 244–287.

6. For the early operations of the electoral system, see Tadahisa Kuroda, *The Origins of the Twelfth Amendment: The Electoral College in the Early Republic, 1787–1804* (Westport, Conn.: Greenwood Press, 1994); Richard P. McCormick, *The Presidential Game: The Origins of American Presidential Politics* (New York: Oxford University Press, 1982), 52–57.

7. Pinckney to Madison, Sept. 30, 1799, in Robert Rutland et al., eds., *The Papers of James Madison* (Chicago and Charlottesville: University Press of Virginia, 1991), XVII: 272, reiterating his earlier (and unanswered) request to the same effect in a letter of May 16, 1799, ibid., 250–251.

8. Hamilton to Jay, May 7, 1800, in Harold C. Syrett, ed., *The Papers of Alexander Hamilton* (New York: Columbia University Press, 1961–1987), XXIV: 464–466, 467n.

9. Charles Fried, "How to Make the President Talk to the Local Pol," *New York Times*, November 11, 2000.

Afterword:
Can a Coin-Toss Election
Trigger a Constitutional
Earthquake?

STEPHEN HOLMES

Electoral politics looks considerably more impressive when observed from a filmy distance than when examined under a microscope. American democracy's inherent disorders and defects, it turns out, extend beyond abysmally low turnout, candidates manufactured by advertising agencies, and campaign financing shenanigans. The 2000 presidential election, in particular, revealed that a virtual draw in a winner-take-all contest assigns ultimate decision-making power not only to untypical swing voters (an outcome that is undemocratic enough) but also to unavoidable inaccuracies in the tabulation of ballots. Even if the hand recounts in Florida had been conducted more scrupulously and thoroughly than they were, the difference in votes between the two candidates would have remained statistically meaningless, that is to say, would have been less than the margin of error. Where the electorate is evenly divided, the identity of the U.S. president, who happens to hold the fate of the world in his hands, can be settled only by the flip of a coin.

Imaginative attempts have been made, in this volume as elsewhere, to attribute some deep meaning to this underlying fortuity. Partisans on both sides have treated the intense polarization of the post-election circus, culminating in *Bush v. Gore*, as if it mirrored the state of the polity more accurately than the mind-numbingly bland campaign that preceded it. And the post-election rekindling of the same partisan passions that, a year before, had inflamed the struggle over impeachment, where law was manifestly subordinated to politics, gives some plausibility to this search for a deeper level of significance. Did not partisan politicians, unable to prevail at the ballot box, once again resort to highly malleable law, wielding it as a weapon to rout political foes?

The most incendiary, and not entirely implausible, way to elevate the post-election contest into a portentous showdown between rival worldviews has been to interpret it as a reprise of the battle for and against black enfranchisement. No one can plausibly deny that a poor black man is less likely than a rich white one to receive a fair trial in the United States. Before Florida 2000, however, most Americans imagined that the battle to extend the franchise to African-Americans was a thing of the past, largely resolved by the passage of the Voting Rights Act of 1965. But the nearly forgotten struggle against racial restrictions on the suffrage resurfaced rudely in the 2000 election, and not only in the legally questionable scrubbing of "possible felons" from voter lists. Although only 11 percent of Florida voters are black, 54 percent of the spoiled ballots were cast by blacks.

Democrats make much of such statistics. They do so because the tendency of Republicans to glamorize private initiative and denigrate government is not as immaculately race-neutral as it initially seems. In practice, the Republican predilection for purchasing private prosperity at the price of public squalor implies not so much an across-the-board as a *selective* defunding of public institutions. In poor black counties with a small tax base, antiquated voting machinery effectively dilutes the power of voters to influence the electoral outcome. In the aftermath to the 2000 election, the exasperation of African-Americans at minor episodes of disenfranchisement was quickened by sarcastic Republican comments, uttered with a social Darwinist edge, to the effect that voters themselves are responsible if they fail to follow written instructions. In affluent white counties, superior machinery and more professional poll watchers alerted voters who did not follow instructions to correct their mistakes on the spot. This suggests that, rhetoric aside, partisan Republicans are fully aware that the exercise of individual rights, such as the right to vote, depends critically on public expenditures. The reason they deny this publicly may not be intellectual incoherence and ignorance of political theory, therefore. Rather, they may simply hope to benefit from public expenditures themselves while starving the public institutions that give reality to the rights of others, including black Americans, who overwhelmingly tend to vote for the opposite party. Their strategy, if this analysis has any merit, is fairly simple: to fortify the castle of the strong, it helps to enfeeble the siege equipment of the weak.

That diverse levels of spending on voting technology, which must be kept in good repair and up-to-date by public expenditures, may have a significant discriminatory effect, is one of the unexpected lessons of election 2000. Thus, in optical-scanner counties, only 1 percent of the ballots registered no presidential selection, whereas 4 percent of the ballots in punch-card counties registered no choice. Such a differential strongly suggests that the rate of ballot invalidation can be reduced by public investment in better equipment. Contrariwise, an existing asymmetry that broadly favors Republicans can be consolidated, intentionally or inadvertently, by "reducing spending to balance the budget." Exclusively local funding of vote-tabulating machinery turns out to promote the unequal distribution of American citizenship itself.

Skepticism about Republican motives, fueled by such observations, has been reinforced by the curious and still inadequately theorized satisfaction that Republicans seem to feel at having won the White House without securing a popular plurality. Their repeated claim that the United States is "a Republic" and not "a Democracy," often articulated in this context, implies that our old-fashioned institutions, such as the electoral college, serve as "bulwarks" against "raw populism." But what does such logic imply about old-fashioned and therefore vote-diluting equipment in the poor black counties of Florida?

Conceivably, after the routine electoral contest had turned into an astonishing stalemate, some panel of "elder statesmen" could have appeared on the scene and formulated a procedure for resolving the conflict that would have appeared fair to both sides. Instead, both parties mobilized former secretaries of state—Warren Christopher for the Democrats, James ("Consigliere") Baker for the Republicans, lawyers both—to take the lead in presenting the respective cases for and against further recounts. Absent nonpartisan intervention, the post-election contest quickly degenerated into a mutual filing and flinging of charges and countercharges, rival camps vilifying each other as unpatriotic liars, with virtually no attempts being made at democratic deliberation. The outcome that had not been decided according to clear rules known in advance, it soon became clear, was going to be decided by crafty maneuvering within and around the rules, which turned out to be remarkably vague and elastic, as rules usually are. More to the point, the winner was destined to be the party with the best back-channel connections to powerful institutions in a position to bend the rules to reach a univocal solution.

The most important of these institutions, needless to say, was the U.S. Supreme Court. The problem with its clamorous intervention was not that it crossed a sacred line or entered into the political thicket. What made it so bitterly controversial was that the majority's decision violated the fundamental legal principle that an arbiter cannot have a stake in the outcome. The fact that *Bush v. Gore* has a much weaker basis in jurisprudence than *Dred Scott v. Sandford* is deplorable but not exceptional. The scandal lies in an appearance of vulgar favoritism. The majority is very unlikely to have decided as it did if the parties had been reversed. This is not to deny that the majority, despite disclaimers about an "unsought responsibility," *also* desired to look decisive, to play an eye-catching role in a once-in-a-lifetime American drama. That is to say, the justices who voted to consider the case were also intoxicated by self-importance, which is obviously not the same as turning themselves into pliant tools of the litigants they happen to like.

But at the very least, they also created the appearance of deciding the case on extralegal grounds. In the end, the majority's holding seems less ideological than political. On its face, the decision appears to have been driven by considerations of expediency, with ad hoc rationalizations very loosely attached. This apparent triumph of expediency over principle was symbolized most remarkably by Justice Antonin Scalia's sensational declaration (in his concurring opinion justifying the stay order of December 9) that the Court had to act in haste to ensure "public acceptance" of the Bush presidency, as if he imagined himself to be some sort of spin doctor, with an unparalleled grasp of the conditions of "democratic stability," able to engineer the attitudes of his countrymen from his chambers. Worst of all, the conservative faction was, or appeared to be, attempting to protect the interests of George W. Bush to consolidate and perpetuate the dominance of conservative thinking in the jurisprudence of the Court. (A President Gore might have rained more moderate liberals on Scalia's anti-liberal parade.) Apparently unembarrassed at being perceived as black-robed operatives in James Baker's run-out-the-clock campaign, the conservative majority took ample advantage of the special status of the Supreme Court, a body unique in our polity because subject to no higher authority empowered to correct its trespasses. The culmination of the justices' unaccountable conceit came in the famous disclaimer: "Our consideration is limited to the present circumstances." Once they had poured candidate

Gore down the drainpipe, they comforted us with assurances that no extra babies were in the bath water.

It is now said that the opportunism of the conservative majority was made plain by its willingness to abandon, in this unique case, its deep commitment to states' rights and its unswerving hostility to judicial activism and equal protection.[1] To elevate their man to the White House, critics assert, they were willing to traduce their own judicial philosophy. And there is a lot to be said for this claim. But we should not overestimate the role of steady adherence to principle in the current majority's thinking.

True, conservatives have often found it useful to defend states' rights as a means of defending the rights of certain social groups, most notably the rights of southern whites against the rights of southern blacks. The traditional association of states' rights rhetoric with arrangements designed to keep blacks down is well known. For its part, the current majority has consistently sided with the strong against the weak, smiling, say, on corporations while frowning on the disabled. And to put their preferences into effect, they have not hesitated to invoke states' rights. They have done so, for instance, to favor gun owners and disfavor the victims of discrimination.[2] As if to confirm liberal suspicions, the conservatives on the Court regularly defer to state courts in death penalty cases. This probably has as much to do with their support of the death penalty as with any piety toward residual state sovereignty, however. The proof is that the same conservative majority, well before *Bush v. Gore*, did not hesitate to override states' rights if the social groups it favors could be helped by so doing.

An instrumental attitude toward states' rights among American conservatives is not of recent vintage. Federal fugitive slave laws are often mentioned as the great precedent in this context. In the famous case *Lochner v. New York* (1905), the Court similarly expressed its fondness for employers by denying the right of state legislatures to experiment with the regulation of labor contracts in favor of workers. More recently, conservatives' championing of federal tort reform reveals their willingness to trample lesser rights (namely, the rights of states) to defend greater rights (the rights of business). A cynic might even say that the principal purpose of "the rule of law," according to American conservative thought, is to help rich people keep their money. To this higher norm—which is not necessarily immoral as a matter of policy—they hold unswervingly, exhibiting little or no opportunistic shifting back and forth. Their selective and sporadic tenderness for states' rights, by contrast, suggests that the latter is only a means, not an end. Whatever slogans they toss around, America's judicial conservatives do not view themselves as citizens of separate states but rather as members of an exclusive and obviously nationwide, not merely local, club.

This is one of the keys to *Bush v. Gore.* Whatever its other merits and demerits, it drove dramatically home, for the first time, the conservative majority's fundamentally instrumental attitude toward states' rights. But the members of the current majority have often preferred political opportunism to ideological consistency. As a result, *Bush v. Gore,* however weakly reasoned, does not represent a radical rupture with their previous approach to states' rights.

If the Florida Supreme Court was correct in its claim that, "These statutes established by the legislature govern our decisions today," there would have been no federal question and no grounds for Supreme Court intervention to save Bush. Thus, the three far-right members of the Court were driven to invoke Article II of the federal Constitution, which by their reading vests plenary authority over the conduct of presidential elections in the state legislatures. What is especially interesting about their Article II claim is less its weakness as a matter of law than its extraordinary coincidence with the disinformation campaign orchestrated by the Republican camp. Justices Rehnquist, Scalia, and Thomas know perfectly well that "the rule of law" leaves considerable latitude for judicial discretion and prudence (one example: the majority vote in

Bush v. Gore). But they apparently found it useful to bury this basic truth for propagandistic ends. According to them, the Florida Supreme Court violated Article II, § 1, cl. 2 of the federal Constitution by rewriting—rather than merely interpreting or making coherent—the Florida election code, without any "reasonable" grounds. This charge, on its face, reinforced strongly the Bush campaign's charge that Democrats were trying to change the rules for electing the president halfway through the game. (Because the rules of the game, as conventionally understood, produced no winner, both sides were naturally attempting to massage and interpret the rules to their own advantage.)

To claim that the Florida Supreme Court's interpretation of Florida law was flagrant and unreasonable, of course, required the U.S. Supreme Court to set itself up as the final arbiter of the meaning of Florida law, something the three most conservative justices would most certainly have refused to do had a Democratic candidate been the likely beneficiary. In the public relations battle, the Bush team invoked Article II to suggest that the Constitution had assigned decisive discretionary authority, activated when an election produced no clear winner, to the Republican-dominated Florida state legislature. But Article II stipulates that "Each State shall appoint, in such Manner as the Legislature thereof may direct, a Number of Electors," and it empowers Congress to fix the time when such electors must be appointed (which ever since 1845 has been the Tuesday following the first Monday in November). It does not imply that partisan majorities in state legislatures may, after the fact, rewrite the rules for selecting electors that they had set down beforehand.

The Florida legislature has given Florida courts the power to interpret Florida statutes. The Florida Supreme Court could therefore reasonably claim to be basing its decision to continue the hand recounts on the clear intention of the Florida legislature, which had also stipulated that "no vote shall be declared invalid or void if there is a clear indication of the intent of the voter as determined by the canvassing board." The Florida Supreme Court also assumed that that state's paramount interest in case of an electoral deadlock was correctly assessing the discernible intent of the voters and thereby identifying the rightful winner. If the Florida Supreme Court's claim to be acting on the commands of the Florida legislature were allowed to stand, of course, the Supreme Court's grounds for intervention in the case would have been considerably weakened.

The rules that the Florida state legislature had established *before* November 7 can be summarized as follows. In a presidential election, (1) all legally valid votes must be counted; (2) a legally valid vote is one in which the clear intent of the voter can be discerned, whether or not instructions were strictly followed; (3) if the outcome of the election is contested, recounts to determine the rightful winner shall be conducted; (4) courts shall play an important role in handling disputes arising from such recounts; (5) circuit court decisions are subject to appellate review; and (6) when faced with conflicting statutes and issues not explicitly covered by statute, courts have the power of "statutory construction," that is, the authority to identify solutions and methods of reconciliation compatible with fundamental state interests. That the Florida Supreme Court violated Article II of the federal Constitution by flagrantly ignoring the will of the Florida legislature—as set down in the foregoing six points—is not even remotely plausible. A much more powerful case can be made that the Supreme Court itself violated Article II by wantonly overriding the explicit will of the Florida legislature that, in close elections, recounts will be held to ensure that all legally valid votes are counted.

To bolster their claim that the electoral dispute in Florida raised a justiciable federal question, a majority of five justices appended an equal protection argument to their Article II claim. "Having once granted the right to vote on equal terms, the State may not, by later arbitrary and disparate treatment, value one person's vote over another." This second argument is now widely viewed as extremely tenuous, even by those who cheered the results of *Bush v. Gore*. What is worse, by heaping one argument on top of the other, the majority seemed to be replicating the strategy of Bush campaign operatives, namely to spew forth as many miscellaneous arguments as possible, in the hope that at least some would strike the target.

However preposterous as constitutional law, the majority's opportunistic invocation of the Equal Protection Clause of the Fourteenth Amendment was not as inconsistent with their previous approach as is sometimes alleged. The conservatives on the Court have long been willing to embrace equal protection in much the same way that they have supported states' rights, that is, instrumentally, on a case-by-case basis, whenever they could thereby defend the interests of groups they favor (as in cases involving reverse discrimination). If white Americans seek a remedy, the conservative majority is much more likely to see the relevance of the Equal Protection Clause than if black Americans seek a remedy. Thus, the way they invoked equal protection in *Bush v. Gore* may be blameworthy and unprincipled, but it is not especially innovative or unprecedented.

What is galling, instead, is the recklessness with which the majority implicitly declared unconstitutional important provisions in the Florida election code itself (and, in fact, cast doubt on settled electoral practice throughout the country). It declared the intent standard that the legislature had established for conducting recounts to be impermissibly vague, because allowing excessive variation from one county to the next in methods of recounting. Rather than merely invalidating an ostensibly aberrant decision of the Florida Supreme Court, the conservative majority's equal protection argument strikes directly at the Florida legislature. That is to say, it assigns the Equal Protection Clause of the Fourteenth Amendment precedence over Article II, which denies that a state legislature's power to regulate presidential elections as it sees fit may be judicially circumscribed. Their desperate search for a federal question that could be endorsed by at least five justices drew them into this trap, from which they tried ludicrously to extricate themselves by saying good-bye to *stare decisis*, peremptorily stating that their decision had no value as a precedent.

The comic quality of this line of argument should be plain. Conservatives who have been adamant about the importance of devolving power away from the federal government and back to localities suddenly discover that local decision making engenders variety instead of uniformity. That was apparently a revelation. Differently designed ballots are counted by different technologies and recounted by different officials in different counties. To declare such settled practice to be unconstitutional, however, is to flirt with electoral nihilism. What makes the argument unsavory rather than merely comic is the way it implicitly denigrates the noblest legacy of the Supreme Court, namely the invocation of equal protection to intervene in state elections on the side of black Americans. The Equal Protection Clause of the Fourteenth Amendment was written to protect former slaves and their descendants from discrimination and to guarantee them rights of citizenship equal to the rights of white Americans. *Bush v. Gore* does not merely turn this tradition on its head, it does so with nose-thumbing contempt, refusing to offer any remedy to the real inequities in the American system of voting. This contempt was most clearly visible in the last-minute suggestion by Justices Kennedy and O'Connor that a recount could have been conducted if the Florida Supreme Court had had time to set a fixed statewide standard disallowing any variation in the way voter intent was established. The lack of time to do so, of course, was at least partly due to the Supreme Court's own prior failure to notify the Florida Supreme Court that uniform standards would be a decisive issue.

Finally, some defenders of *Bush v. Gore* present it as an act of "statesmanship," even implying that the conservative majority willingly sacrificed some of its own prestige to save the country from political turmoil and perhaps even a train wreck of unforeseeable proportions. The country was staring into an abyss, we learn, and the Court saved us all from a looming constitutional crisis. Unfortunately, such a claim assumes that the Supreme Court is competent to make empirical predictions about the course of political events. Because it possesses no such competence, the "train wreck" argument looks like just another sophistical rationalization of a self-serving partisan gambit.

The evident feebleness of the jurisprudential basis for *Bush v. Gore* has tempted partisan Democrats into making all sorts of predictions of their own, most of them echoing Justice Stevens's claim that, "Preventing the recount from being completed will inevitably cast a cloud on the legitimacy of the election" and Justice Breyer's suggestion that the decision was "a self-inflicted wound—a wound that may harm not just the Court, but the Nation." This bungled decision will come back to haunt the right, critics have repeatedly alleged. Not only will the federal courts be flooded by lawsuits whenever there is a close election, but the Bush presidency itself will be illegitimate and tainted. The Supreme Court is even said to have thrown away in an instant the social prestige it had painstakingly accumulated over decades. And, finally, the public's faith in the rule of law, as something distinct from partisan political maneuvering, has supposedly been shattered.

This is all a great exaggeration, however, especially since no one takes *Bush v. Gore* seriously as constitutional law. And what exactly does it mean for the Court's credibility to be destroyed? Will Congress and the states now begin defying the Court at will? That hardly seems likely. To understand why so many distinguished legal academics were nevertheless aghast and dismayed by *Bush v. Gore*, we need to focus on *the Dworkin illusion* from which many of them suffer. By "the Dworkin illusion" I mean the association of judicial review with socially progressive causes, as avowed most prominently in the writings of the legal philosopher, Ronald Dworkin. This unjustifiable pairing attains a superficial plausibility from the common tendency to misinterpret the historical anomaly of the Warren Court as a typical case that best illustrates the purpose and function of judicial review. Legal academics with a liberal bent were appalled by *Bush v. Gore* because, until now, they have stubbornly refused to recognize, despite mountains of historical evidence, that the judiciary is almost always a status quo power. By behaving true to form in such a high-profile case, the Supreme Court may finally have released liberals from their outdated fantasy that judicial review was created to protect the weak against the strong.

The legal academy's subjective perception of a constitutional upheaval is not shared by the wider public. Why not? One explanation is economic prosperity and political indifference. The country is doing too well economically to discover a constitutional crisis in electoral disarray. Another explanation is that the legitimacy of the Supreme Court (like that of the Federal Reserve) depends as much on opacity as on impartiality. The reasoning of the Court, whether sound or unsound, is too cryptic to have much of an impact on ordinary citizens. A third possibility is that most Americans harbor no liberal illusions about the Court that could be shattered theatrically by *Bush v. Gore*. But this is not the whole story.

Most politically conscious Americans understand quite well that the rules of the game, laid down before the 2000 election, produced no clear winner. An additional function of voting, alongside the filling of public offices, is to allow the electorate, at regular intervals, to paint its self-portrait. In 2000, the American electorate disclosed itself, to itself, as divided down the middle. In this case, although some decision obviously had to be made, neither candidate could possibly have enjoyed greater democratic legitimacy than the other. That would have been true even if the hand recounts had been conducted in the most orderly and exhaustive manner possible. Neither Bush nor Gore, in sum, could plausibly assert superior legal pedigree. The clock was ticking, and a patently tie vote somehow had to be alchemized into a victory and a defeat. A coin toss would have done perfectly well to decide between the two contenders because the next president, in any case, was going to accede to office by accident.

The fact that the presidency was awarded by flipping a *loaded* coin was not necessarily lost on public perception. Most Americans presumably recognize that the conservatives on the Court are partisan Republicans besting partisan Democrats, not moral heroes salvaging morality from dishonorable liberals. But the unprincipled opportunism and self-serving bias of the Court was not viewed as the basis for a "legitimacy crisis" because the Gore team, for its part, had failed to offer any procedurally neutral method, fair to both sides, for choosing a winner. Because they did not promptly propose a procedure that, ex ante, would leave the eventual winner unknown, they looked like they were fishing for votes rather than standing up for the disenfranchised. After proposing manual recounts according to the loosest possible standards in heavily Democratic counties—not to mention floating the idea of a special election in Palm Beach county—the Gore camp was unable to protest credibly against loaded dice. And anyway, the real reason Gore failed to prevail in the election was the defectively designed ballot in Palm Beach. That was not the fruit of some vast right-wing conspiracy, however, but a sheer accident, the equivalent of the faulty horseshoe that led to the loss of a kingdom.

Although the Republicans won and the Democrats lost, the losers did not resort to defiance or a refusal to cooperate. Thus, "the system worked." This too helps to explain why the public does not feel that the United States is undergoing a constitutional crisis. Ordinary Americans apparently believe that achieving a vital purpose is more important than cleaving meticulously to formal procedures, especially when both sides in a conflict raise equally plausible arguments about "what the rule of law requires." They were therefore by and large satisfied that the process ended with closure. The outcome may have been bad luck for Gore, but it was not a constitutional cataclysm for the country. An additional reason for acquiescence in a Bush presidency is that Democrats know they will have a chance for a comeback in the next elections. African-Americans feel less forgiving precisely because they feel that their turn will never come.

If a crisis of legitimacy is in the cards, this has less to do with the way Bush became president than with the way he began to behave after he took office. That he is a feeble figure unable to articulate American interests with any force has nothing to do with the way the electoral deadlock was finally resolved. After John Kennedy squeaked to victory in 1960, he appointed several prominent Republicans to key posts in his cabinet, in effect establishing a coalition government as an acknowledgment that the electorate was basically evenly divided. Bush did nothing of the sort. Instead of splitting the difference with Democrats, he pursued one-party rule on the basis of a tie vote. His legitimacy problems have been exacerbated by the manifest conflict between his ideological message, emphasizing individual responsibility, and his own life history, where social promotion plainly played a prominent role. Because his family always protected him from suffering the worst consequences of his irresponsible behavior, he is personally not in a good position to invoke "moral hazard" as a reason to defund programs offering some modest security to the poor. For *Bush* to state publicly that safety nets kill gumption is an invitation to laughter. That he is willing to say such things is deeply discrediting, perhaps even delegitimating, but this has nothing at all to do with the turmoil of election 2000 or *Bush v. Gore.*

Finally, what can we say about proposals to abolish the electoral college, a vestige of the past that cannot easily be justified today in a way most citizens could accept or even understand? The critical role of this eighteenth-century relic in determining the outcome of the election was somewhat overshadowed by the intervention of the Supreme Court. And awareness that sparsely populated states are unlikely to accept the curtailment of their unjust privileges has by now put a damper on the idea of abolishing it. But historians have nevertheless been busy reminding us that the electoral college is a typical case of special-interest constitutionalism, designed to favor slave-holding states. The disappearance of slave-holding states has not made the origins of the institution seem politically irrelevant because Bush won the electoral vote by prevailing in the sagebrush country, while Gore's victory in the ethnically mixed melting pot along the coasts gave him a popular plurality but not a majority in the electoral college.

The tainted origins of the electoral college are not especially relevant to the current value (or lack of value) of the institution. The proof is that the disproportional Senate is now barely controlled by the Democrats while the proportional House remains narrowly in Republican hands. In other words, those who propose to abolish the electoral college have an unjustifiable confidence in their ability to predict the political consequences of a change in constitutional rules. The electoral college is unlikely to be abolished, given the vested interests of sparsely populated states. But that is not necessarily a harm to one party or the other. Revisions in the structural provisions of a constitution very often have unintended consequences. Out of respect for our own weak grasp of social causality, we should hesitate to make such changes unless the reasons are overwhelming.

Finally, is election 2000 really unfinished, as the title of this book itself suggests? This is far from obvious. For one thing, it was a statistically extraordinary event that is very unlikely to repeat itself. Moreover, *Bush v. Gore* seems finally to have persuaded liberals to shed their last illusions about the progressive potential of judicial review. Mission accomplished, case closed. Admittedly, political partisans may have good reasons for continuing to revisit those frenzied thirty-six days. But should we not all be wary of law school generals who cannot stop fighting the last war?

NOTES

1. Alan Dershowitz, *Supreme Injustice: How the High Court Hijacked Election 2000* (New York: Oxford University Press, 2001).

2. U.S. v. Lopez, 514 U.S. 549 (1995) and Printz v. United States, 521 U.S. 98 (1997); Seminole Tribe v. Florida, 517 U.S. 44 (1996).

INDEX

policy of equality during Reconstruction, 162
realignment and, 14
state legislatures choosing electors and, 215
U. S. Supreme Court's distrust of, 174–176
Congressional Black Caucus, 93
conservatives
political party coalitions and, 52–54
Republicans and, 59–62
Constitution. *See* U. S. Constitution
contest phase. *See* Florida Supreme Court, contest phase
Cooper, John Milton, Jr., xv
County Canvassing Boards
acceptance of late returns from, 111–112
Bush v. Palm Beach County Canvassing Board, 125–126, 180–181
defining errors in vote tabulation, 109–110
Florida Supreme Court rulings and, 132–133
structure of Florida's election code and, 108
county unit system, vs. equal protection, 166–167
cultural issues, politics and, 45–46

democracy
anti-democratic impulses, states on voter rights, 79–80
anti-democratic impulses, U. S. history of voter rights, 82
defects of U.S. system of, 235–236
deficiencies in ballot system as threat to, xv–xvi
right to vote and, 169–170
Democrats
anti-government rhetoric and, 33–35
black enfranchisement and, 236–237
breakdown of "New Deal coalition" causes realignment, 13–16
campaign 2000 weaknesses, 4
characteristics of, 47, 94–95
civil rights movements and, 15–16
comparing presidential platforms of 1896 with 2000, 40–42
election of 1888 and, 7–8
ideology of, 31–32
liberals and, 59
losing white vote in South due to black supporters, 20–21
loss of influence following election of 1896, 42–44

point of view on election 2000 results, xiii
policy/ideological differences with Republicans, 27–30, 55–59
populism and, 22–25
state comparisons of 1896 and 2000 elections, 9–12
voting groups within, 60–62
Democrats, coalitions, 48–55
liberals vs. conservatives, 54–55
occupational groups, 50–51
overview of, 48–50
race and social issues, 52–54
union membership, 51
demographics, Gore vs. Bush supporters, 24, 26
de Tocqueville, Alexis, 159
disenfranchisement. *See also* African-Americans; black voters
election 2000 controversy over, 76
of felons, 85–88
Giles v. Harris and, 162–163
Reconstruction and, 161–162
Dixiecrat revolt, 15
Dukakis, Michael, 13
Durbin, Dick, 202–203
Dworkin illusion, 246–247

economic issues
Bush vs. Gore on, 63–64
election of 1876 and, 19–20
predicting election results based on, 23
Republican vs. Democrat ideology, 32–34, 42
economic liberalism-conservatism, 47, 56
eight box system, 89
election disputes. *See* post-election disputes
election of 1800, 151, 219–220
election of 1876
Congressional handling of, 151
Democratic influence after, 42–44
economic divisions at time of, 19–20
partisanship in decisions of, 7
U. S. Supreme Court's role in, 7, 160
election of 1888, 7–8, 201–202
election of 1896, 40–41
election of 1968, 13–14
electoral college, 208–215
advantages over other election modes, 213–214
anachronism of winner-take-all rule, 207–208

ABOUT THE CONTRIBUTORS

HENRY E. BRADY is Professor of Political Science and Public Policy and Director of the Survey Research Center at the University of California, Berkeley. He has also taught at MIT, Harvard, and the University of Chicago. He has written about elections and political participation in the United States, Canada, Eastern Europe, and the former Soviet Union. He is coauthor of *Voice and Equality: Civic Voluntarism in American Politics* (Harvard University Press, 1995) and *Letting the People Decide: The Dynamics of a Canadian Election* (Stanford University Press, 1992). In November 2000 he served pro bono as an expert witness in citizen suits in Palm Beach County, Florida, regarding the "butterfly ballot."

JOHN MILTON COOPER, JR., is E. Gordon Fox Professor of American Institutions at the University of Wisconsin-Madison. His books include *The Warrior and the Priest: Woodrow Wilson and Theodore Roosevelt* (1983) and *Breaking the Heart of the World: Woodrow Wilson and the Fight for the League of Nations* (2001). He is a member of the Center for National Policy and the Council on Foreign Relations and Chief Historian for the television biography of Woodrow Wilson to be broadcast for the *American Experience*.

STEPHEN HOLMES is Professor of Law at New York University Law School. From 1985 to 1997 he was Professor of Politics and Law at the University of Chicago, and from 1997 to 2000 he was Professor of Politics at Princeton. His fields of specialization include democratic theory, the history of liberalism, constitutional and legal change after communism, the Russian legal system, and comparative constitutional law. He is editor-in-chief of the *East European Constitutional Review* and co-author (with Cass Sunstein) of *The Cost of Rights: Why Liberty Depends on Taxes* (1999).

ALEXANDER KEYSSAR is the Matthew G. Stirling, Jr. Professor of History and Social Policy, John F. Kennedy School of Government, Harvard University. He is the author of *The Right to Vote: The Contested History of Democracy in the United States* (2000), which was a finalist for the Pulitzer Prize in History, and *Out of Work: The First Century of Unemployment in Massachusetts* (1986). His political writings have appeared in *The New York Times, Nation, The New Republic,* and other journals.

PAMELA S. KARLAN is the Kenneth and Harle Montgomery Professor of Public Interest Law at Stanford Law School. She is the author of many influential books and articles on legal regulation of elections, including *The Law of Democracy: Legal Structure of the Political Process* (2d ed. 2001). In addition, both as assistant counsel for the NAACP Legal Defense and Educational Fund and since she entered teaching, she has done a substantial amount of litigation involving the Equal Protection Clause and voting rights, including many cases before the U.S. Supreme Court.

LARRY D. KRAMER is the Samuel Tilden Professor of Law at New York University Law School. His primary teaching and research interests are in the areas of constitutional law and constitutional history, with a special focus on the role of political parties. He clerked at the U.S. Supreme Court for Justice William J. Brennan in 1985–1986 and consults regularly in litigation before the Court.

JACK N. RAKOVE is the Coe Professor of History and American Studies, and Professor of Political Science, at Stanford University. He is the author, among other books, of *Original Meanings: Politics and Ideas in the Making of the Constitution* (1996), which received the Pulitzer Prize in History, and *James Madison and the Creation of the American Republic* (2001). He writes frequently on the historical origins of contemporary constitutional and political issues for *The New York Times, Los Angeles Times, Chicago Tribune, Boston Globe,* and *Washington Post.*